DISCARD

THE
SOLAR HOUSE

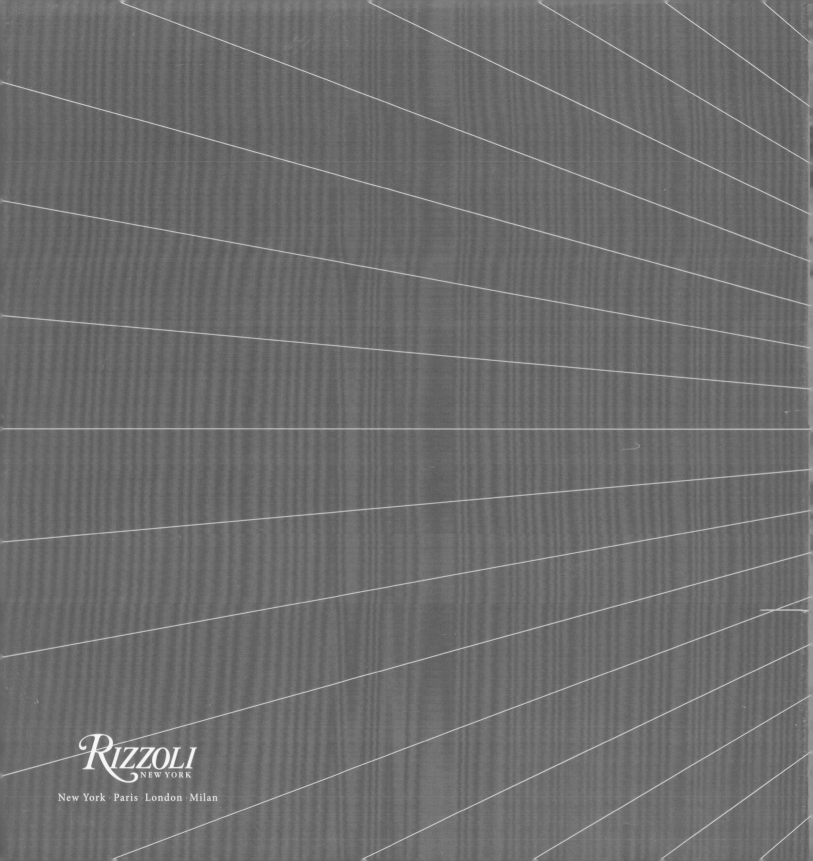

RIZZOLI
NEW YORK

New York · Paris · London · Milan

PIONEERING
SUSTAINABLE
DESIGN

THE
SOLAR

Anthony Denzer

HOUSE

First published in the United States of America
in 2013 by
Rizzoli International Publications, Inc.
300 Park Avenue South
New York, NY 10010
www.rizzoliusa.com

ISBN: 978-0-8478-4005-2
LCCN: 2012954852

Designed by Naomi Mizusaki, Supermarket

Distributed to the U.S. trade by Random House,
New York

Printed and bound in China

2013 2014 2015 2016 2017 / 10 9 8 7 6 5 4 3 2 1

✳ CONTENTS ✳

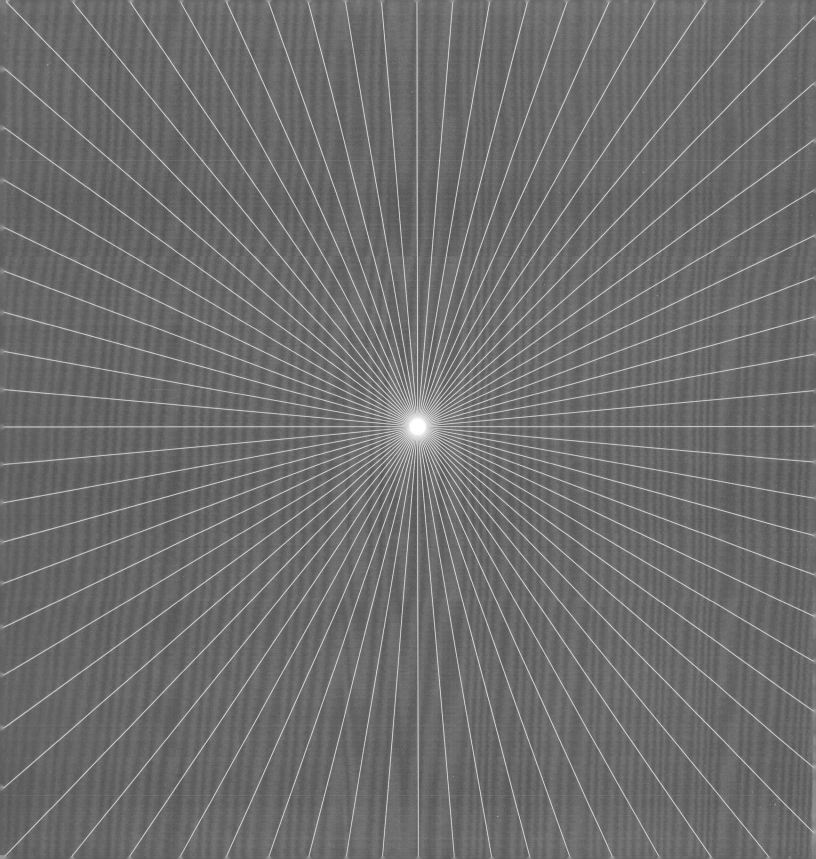

✳ PREFACE ✳

However obvious it may appear, on the slightest reflection, that the history of architecture should cover the whole of the technological art of creating habitable environments, the fact remains that [it] still deals almost exclusively with the external forms of habitable volumes as revealed by the structures that enclose them.

—Reyner Banham (1969)[1]

A stereotypical example: The Ark, by the New Alchemy
Institute, Spry Point, Prince Edward Island, 1976.
Author's collection

From familiar accounts of architectural history, one gets the impression that passive solar design is not something that occupied the minds of "great" architects. Could it be that this reflects as much on the historians as it does on the architects?

—David Pearlmutter (2007)[2]

The label "solar house" typically conjures an image, I think, from the 1970s: an eccentrically shaped structure with an oversized sloped glass wall and diagonal cedar siding. Perhaps an earth berm. A Volkswagen van nearby. And this image is not false; after 1973, the solar house became both a mass cultural movement and an authentic architectural style rooted in technological developments and, to some degree, the aesthetics of the counterculture. But this image is incomplete, as it obscures the extensive and rich history of experimental solar houses *before* the 1970s, which has been overlooked by both architects and historians. Given the contemporary interest in solar houses and the green building movement in general, this is a stunning oversight. The aim of this book is to reconstruct and interpret that history.

This book probes the character of solar architecture as it developed, including technical and aesthetic issues. The larger question *How should a solar house perform?* was accompanied by *How should a solar house look?* This discussion is particularly relevant now. In fact, many architects and builders today struggle with challenges for which there is an extensive but unknown knowledge base and intellectual discourse dating back to the 1930s. I begin in the 1930s because the solar house is a distinctly modern concept. Surely it is fascinating to study the sun-responsive features of some ancient and premodern vernacular buildings, and it is not incorrect to observe that "our building history is a history of solar architecture," as Richard G. Stein has written.[3] Still, the phrase "solar house," first used in 1940, specifically describes a building that uses solar energy for space heating in a deliberate critical and creative manner. The protagonists in this history consciously worked against the tide of mainstream building practices that increasingly relied on mechanical heating and cooling. Many were prescient; they knew coal and oil to be finite resources and they knew buildings should not be dependent on them. The history, then, includes a pronounced ethical dimension.

Early solar architects and engineers assembled all the elements of a robust social movement. They generally did not experiment in isolation but formed a well-connected community

THE DEVELOPMENT OF THE SLAB APARTMENT BLOCK

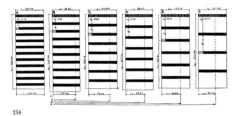

255

256

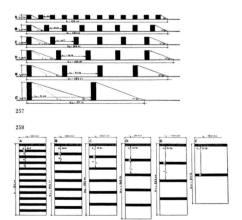

257

258

Bauhaus solar diagrams, c. 1930. Sigfried Giedion, *Walter Gropius: Work and Teamwork* (New York: Reinhold, 1954)

with a common agenda, a shared experimental approach, and significant publicity. Indeed, *Life* magazine and *Reader's Digest* promoted the solar house in the late 1940s, as did institutions such as the Museum of Modern Art. More than 1,000 people attended a 1955 symposium. At various times, the solar house occupied a significant position in the architectural discourse and the culture at large. To some extent it is possible to speak of a solar house movement which began in the 1930s and remains active today.

If you browse the literature from the solar house movement in the twentieth century—a literature which is vast but scattered and often obscure—you will find an ancient quotation which has been used repeatedly to suggest the eternal wisdom of solar heating:

> In houses with a south aspect, the sun's rays penetrate into the porticoes in winter, but in summer the path of the sun is right over our heads and above the roof, so that there is shade. If, then, this is the best arrangement, we should build the south side loftier to get the winter sun and the north side lower to keep out the cold winds.
>
> —Socrates (c. 400 BCE)[4]

Indeed, historical justifications appeared consistently, from architects and engineers, from the 1930s through the 2000s. The passage quoted from Socrates above was highlighted and discussed in the major professional journal for architects as early as 1947. The inventors of the heliodon noted that Francis Bacon had discussed the design of rooms shady for summer and warm for winter more than three hundred years earlier (in *Of Building*). In 1955, a seminal report stated: "Man's interest in harnessing the sun's rays exceeds the period of recorded history," and in *Progressive Architecture* an MIT engineer exclaimed: "We are more than 2000 years behind the times!"[5]

Of course the relationship between architecture and the sun is ancient and enduring, and of course the logic for solar heating in premodern buildings was compelling. But these appeals to tradition seem curious in the age of mechanical heating and cooling. Why would solar practitioners invoke history so consistently? The specific design connections were tenuous at best; nobody seriously studied or mimicked ancient or vernacular "solar architecture," and truthfully there would have been little value in doing so. A common theme found in these appeals is a desire to reassure the public. An example from 1980: "There is nothing mysterious about passive design. Today's passive homes use contemporary versions of ancient principle . . ."[6] Perhaps the simplest explanation is best: cultures often look to the past during periods of great change and anxiety.

If the twentieth-century solar house differs by definition from premodern solar architecture, it also occupies a different historical space than a strain of sun-responsive architecture in the 1920s and '30s, which accommodated sunlight for reasons of health and hygiene (heliotherapy) rather than space heating and energy savings. This genre, which may be known as *heliothera-peutic architecture*, encompasses early-twentieth-century sanatorium architecture, canonical sun-responsive dwellings by architects like Richard Neutra, Maxwell Fry, and Le Corbusier, and curiosities such as Villa Girasole ("the sunflower"), which rotated on a turntable. Planning methods by Walter Gropius and his German contemporaries, which Catherine Bauer called "Heliotropic Housing," also belong in this category. At the third congress of CIAM in Brussels in 1930, Gropius presented a diagram (probably by Bauhaus students) which showed how housing blocks should be spaced to avoid self-shading using a low winter sun angle. This diagram is sometimes misinterpreted as an early demonstration of passive solar heating, but the goal was to provide illumination and therapeutic sunlight, not to save energy.[7] Heliotherapeutic architecture is immensely interesting and deserves more study, but is not explored here because these buildings did not specifically seek to provide solar heat for the purposes of saving energy.

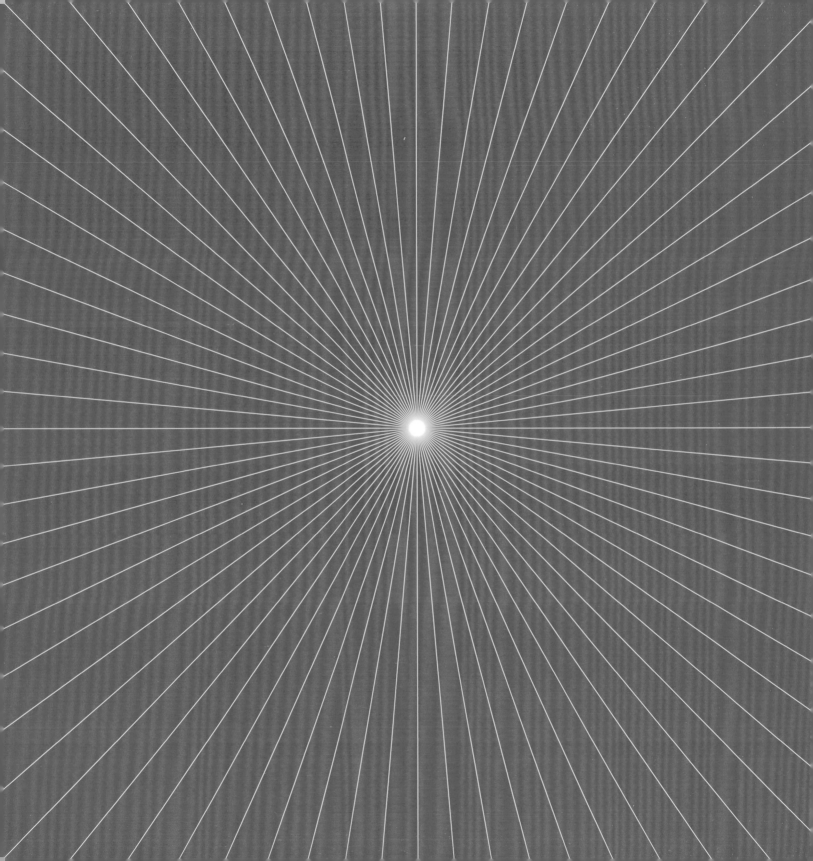

CHAPTER 1

FRED KECK: THE FIRST SOLAR ARCHITECT

The solar designer opens up ways of living for American families where they can search deeply within themselves for what a house should mean as a place to reach greater intellectual and spiritual fulfillment. This is designing in one of the great American traditions, the tradition of Thoreau.

—Keck client Hugh Duncan[1]

Howard Sloan House I by Fred and William Keck, Glenview, Illinois, 1940. Photograph by Hedrich-Blessing. Chicago History Museum, Hedrich-Blessing photograph collection

In 1940, Chicago architect George Fred Keck built a house for his friend Howard Sloan, which changed the course of twentieth-century architecture. The Sloan House launched a movement that would culminate in the 1970s, when Keck would be recognized as the "father" of the passive solar house (with credit to his brother William[2]). Long before the oil crisis or the green building movement, Keck developed a palette of relatively simple architectural strategies which saved his clients as much as 40 percent on their heating bills. Even today, anybody building a passive solar house would be well served to study Keck's approach.

The story of the solar house begins here, in part because Sloan called it a "solar house," coining the term. Sloan, a real-estate developer and master of public relations, would quickly become Keck's most important champion—the solar house's first patron. He persuaded writer Al Chase to use the "solar house" label in a *Chicago Tribune* headline in late 1940.[3] What defined a "solar house"? Chase explained to *Tribune* readers:

> The Solar House is over 100 feet long, with all rooms on one floor. The building faces south and practically all of the south elevation is plate glass. There are only a few windows on the north. The big living room, dining room, kitchen, study, and three bedrooms all face south.
>
> The eave line projection is worked out so that the summer sun high in the heavens, doesn't enter the house, but the winter sun, nearer the horizon, does. Thus solar heat is taken advantage of to an unusual degree.[4]

Sloan opened the house to the public in the Chicago suburb of Glenview: "In an effort to keep out the merely curious, I charged a dime admission. We had as many as 1,700 on a single day, and around 5,000 visitors [in four months]."[5] Keck recalled:

> The house proved popular and Mr. Sloan sold many like it. The house was most salable during the coldest winter weather, because as happens in the Chicago area, most sub-zero weather is sunshiny with frigid northwest winds and on such days the "solar house" was an agreeable and a pleasant place to be.[6]

Beyond marketing and public appeal, the Sloan House legitimately earned canonical status due to its technical innovations and architectural refinements. By 1940, Keck had already experimented for years after his "discovery" of solar heat at the 1933 House of Tomorrow (see chapter 2). As architecture, the Sloan House was Keck's "first comprehensive solar design"[7] because it aggregated earlier lessons about glass placement, shading geometry, orientation, and a linear organization of space. It established a pattern for solar houses going forward. The "uplifted" roof (covering a screened porch) represented a unique and expressive form; the house seemed to dynamically reach for the sun, especially as photographed by Hedrich-Blessing. It is tempting

to suspect that Keck sought to create an iconic image for Sloan's publicity campaign, and he never repeated this type of roof.

The Sloan House also represented a quantum leap in technical sophistication, because William Keck attempted to calculate how much solar heat gain would be realized. No precedent for such calculations is known, either by an architect or an engineer.[8] These are handwritten computations to compare daily losses and gains, dated December 1940, after the Sloan House was completed. Therefore they should be regarded as a validation exercise rather than a design procedure. The goal seems to have been to predict Sloan's savings for the winter and later check the prediction against the actual energy use. As he developed these computations, William found it difficult to locate good data, only finding values for radiation falling on a horizontal surface. (He did not attempt a geometric conversion to account for the vertical windows.[9]) He found that the house would collect about twice as much heat as it would lose from 10 a.m. to 2 p.m. on a sunny day, and wrote "overload" in the margin.[10] In the end, after looking at a full twenty-four-hour period and accounting for cloudy days, William estimated that Sloan would save about 20 percent on his heating bills. How did it perform? The *Chicago Tribune* reported Sloan's observations from a day in December 1940:

> At 6 a. m. it was 11 below at the Glenview airport. At 8:30 he set his thermostat at 55 and left the house. He came back at 2 p.m. The temperature on his north porch was 1 below zero. He found the furnace cold but the temperature in the house was 73. The furnace heat went on at 3:30 p.m., after having retired in favor of the sun for nearly 7 hours.[11]

After the winter, Sloan examined his heating bills and figured he had saved 20 percent compared to a typical house.[12]

Howard Sloan seized the moment. He purchased twenty acres in Glenview, just blocks from his "model" house and in 1941 planned a development called Meadowbrook Village. He then decided to conduct an experiment of his own to see how modern solar houses would sell compared to homes of familiar styles. One street would consist of Keck's designs and an adjacent street would be populated with "colonial, Cape Cod, French, and other conventional types of architecture." (Sloan included the traditional styles, at least in part, to ensure he would receive FHA mortgage insurance. Keck did not design the conventional houses.) "Never has a developer gathered more precise data on the public reaction to the modern house," *Architectural Forum* opined.[13] Remarkably, Sloan found, the solar houses "sold faster than we could build them."[14]

In some Meadowbrook homes in 1941, Keck introduced "ventilating louvers" to provide fresh air below the fixed panes of glass. This simple device consisted of fixed wooden louvers, an insect screen, and a wood panel door on the inside.[15] Similar vents were used traditionally in the southeast and produced by manufacturers in the 1930s for garages and attics.[16] Keck's

House at Howard Sloan's Meadowbrook subdivision by Fred and William Keck, Glenview, Illinois, 1941. Photograph by Hedrich-Blessing. Chicago History Museum, Hedrich-Blessing photograph collection

House at Redwood Village Cooperative by Paul Schweikher, Glenview, Illinois, 1942. Photograph by Hedrich-Blessing. Chicago History Museum, Hedrich-Blessing photograph collection

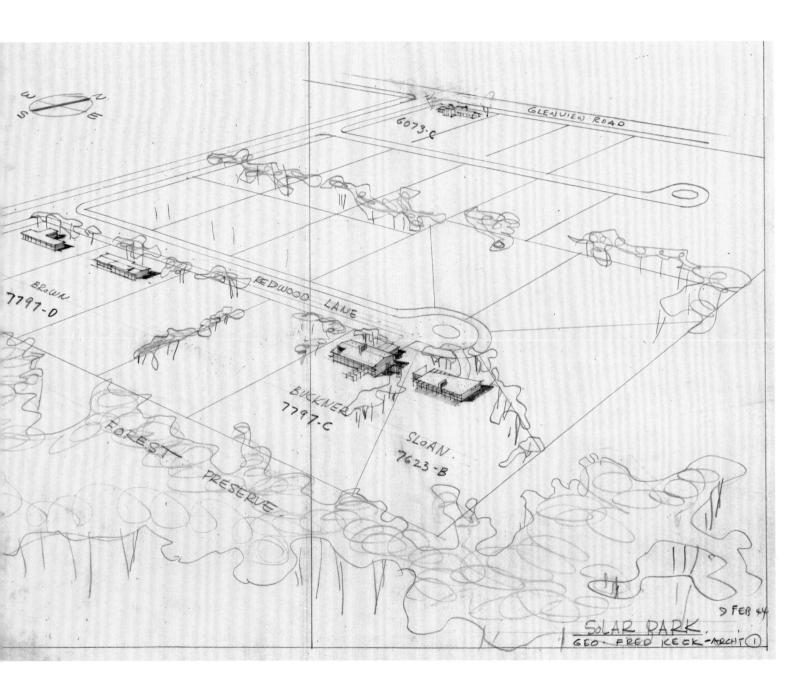

N W S E

GLENVIEW ROAD

6073-C

BROWN
7797-D

REDWOOD LANE

BUCKNER
7797-C

SLOAN
7623-B

FOREST PRESERVE

9 FEB 44

SOLAR PARK.
GEO. FRED KECK - ARCH'T 1

associate Paul Schweikher, with William Fyfe, used ventilating louvers earlier, in their 1940 Herbert Lewis House.[17] Keck believed traditional windows needed to perform too many contradictory functions: first, they required insect screens which in turn interfered with a clear view; and second, they could not be left open for security reasons when the homeowners were away, or at night, thus limiting their effectiveness for ventilation. This desire to dissect a window's functions is reminiscent of Le Corbusier's 1929 declaration: *la fênetre est faite pour éclairer, non pour ventiler* (the window is for light, not for ventilation), which Keck certainly knew. Schweikher, who shared office space with Keck for a time, recalled: "We were almost obsessed with the idea of separating the view from the circulation of air."[18]

Schweikher's Redwood Village Cooperative also indicated his dynamic interchange with Keck. This project may have predated Meadowbrook as the first modern solar neighborhood. Schweikher worked with the North Shore Cooperative Society, a group of ten families, beginning in 1939 (before the "solar house" had its name). The members purchased land in Glenview and envisioned a community of fourteen homes and a common house, but they did not specifically request solar heating. Schweikher probably designed the Redwood Village houses in 1941, and seven houses were built in 1942 adjacent to Meadowbrook Village.[19] Schweikher's architecture blended Keck's influence with his own interest in Japanese architecture and Frank Lloyd Wright's work. Stanley Tigerman must have thought of this project when he wrote: "Paul Schweikher was evolving post-prairie school permutations."[20] Much later Schweikher provocatively responded to a question about Kenneth Frampton's concept of Critical Regionalism and its relationship to the solar house:

> I don't see regionalism as a philosophy. I see regionalism as something imposed on you, that you yield to. You say, 'It's damn cold here; I've got to build a warm building.'[21]

Schweikher's deep pragmatism was surely shared by Keck. In this sense, some early motivations for the solar house were rooted in common sense rather than ideological or stylistic commitment.

Buoyed by the success at Meadowbrook Village, Keck and Sloan developed a twenty-four-house, all-modern subdivision that he called "Solar Park" (Glenview, Illinois, 1942–44)—"the first completely sun-oriented residential community in the modern United States."[22] Sloan even named one street "Solar Lane," which remains in Glenview today. Within a typical suburban plan, Keck provided variety and site-specificity by mirroring, rotating, or shifting common groupings. The living spaces always faced south, but they could be located at the east, west, or center of the linear plan. At Solar Park, Keck designed a second house for Howard Sloan, an experiment in restraint and simplicity, pointing toward the concerns he would pursue in the following years. Sloan II had no grand gestures, perhaps because the realtor did not expect to use it as a showpiece. Indeed, with a single-level flat roof and simple footprint, the building attained a rather modest appearance. Keck also treated the south overhang in a new way:

Drawing of "Solar Park" development for Howard Sloan by Fred Keck, 1944. Wisconsin Historical Society

Howard Sloan House II by Fred and William Keck,
Glenview, Illinois, 1942. Photograph by Hedrich-
Blessing. Chicago History Museum, Hedrich-Blessing
photograph collection

rather than being a structural extension of the roof, the shade was expressed as an attachment, with an extremely thin fascia profile and widely spaced wood posts.

For Sloan II, Keck continued to employ new environmental technologies. He used "triple Thermopane," a Libbey-Owens-Ford product consisting of three layers of insulated glass. For the first time the ventilating louvers appeared above and below some glass sections. And most significantly, Keck used a radiant floor heating system employing hollow clay tiles and hot air. Sloan II's hollow floor was described as "unique" in a trade publication, but Keck liked to explain that the method had ancient origins, and, as Robert Boyce noted, the Kecks were aware of such a system at the Liverpool Cathedral (1904).[23] More immediately, Schweikher and Fyfe used this heating method in their 1942 Lewis House. (Schweikher later credited Fyfe, a Taliesin apprentice from 1932 to 1934, for both the hollow floor and the ventilating louvers, but Fyfe did not use either method in his own work.[24] In any case, Keck popularized these techniques but did not invent them.) While Keck had built several water-type radiant floors, the hot-air method was prompted by the scarcity of copper and iron during wartime.[25]

Keck soon became recognized as an expert in hollow floor systems and in 1943 he began to develop the method in collaboration with engineers for the Clay Products Association. They developed a few major conclusions. For comfort the floor temperature should not exceed 85°F; this would produce air temperatures of 67°–70°. They also acknowledged the problem of heat loss to the ground, which should be addressed by "light weight insulation below and around the floor."[26] Keck generally understood slab heat loss to be a complex problem due to the many variables of soil composition, temperature, and moisture, and he remarked: "the heating guide makes certain recommendations which are way on the conservative side, in my opinion. It will have to remain [undecided] until adequate engineering data is found."[27] His own houses of the mid-1940s were not insulated beneath the floor. The "adequate engineering data" he sought began to appear a few years later.[28] Additionally, Keck and his team described the hollow tile floor as "essentially massive" and recognized the phenomenon of lag time and the need for "anticipatory" controls.[29] In general, the brothers did not attempt to design for solar heat storage and did not try to calculate lag time. William later recalled: "We have only tried to take care of momentary conditions as they exist, taking advantage of a natural phenomenon."[30] The hollow floor system was marketed as "RadianTile" and its commercial success appears to have been limited. Keck and the Clay Products Association patented the technology in 1944 and 1947.[31]

When Sloan II was complete it saved about 40 percent in heating costs compared to the utility company's expectations for a house of that size. Sloan, in a lengthy testimonial in the architectural magazine *Pencil Points*, adopted his familiar role as enthusiastic promoter: "Our home is heated by a 115,000-pound radiator, made of 55,000 pounds of hollow tile over which was poured an estimated 60,000 pounds of concrete. Hot air flows through the tile, warming the floor, producing the finest heat we have ever enjoyed."[32] Keck and Sloan did not work together after 1942 due to a dispute about Keck's compensation. In total, Sloan built thirty-one solar

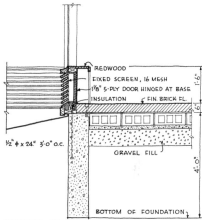

SECTION AT FOUNDATION AND LOUVRE

Top: Herbert Lewis House by Paul Schweikher and William Fyfe, Park Ridge, Illinois, 1942. Drawing in *Architectural Record* (March 1941)

Above: RadianTile system. Wisconsin Historical Society

Opposite: Herbert Lewis House by Paul Schweikher and William Fyfe, Park Ridge, Illinois, 1942. Photograph by Hedrich-Blessing. Chicago History Museum, Hedrich-Blessing photograph collection

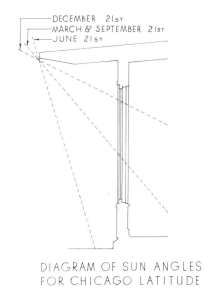

DIAGRAM OF SUN ANGLES
FOR CHICAGO LATITUDE

Solar angles for the Duncan House. Wisconsin Historical Society

Opposite: Hugh Duncan House by Fred and William Keck, Flossmoor, Illinois, 1941. Wisconsin Historical Society

houses designed by Keck, though neither Meadowbrook Village nor Solar Park were completed as planned.[33]

In Keck's house for sociologist Hugh Duncan (Flossmoor, Illinois, 1941), he introduced another technique: vertical shades, or "wing walls," that projected four to seven feet outside the south-facing glass. He called the vertical wood members "adjustable vanes." Clearly this device was meant to provide more shading on late summer afternoons. Keck probably found his earlier houses overheating at those times, and here we find him again engaged in an iterative investigation of new methods of climate control. Keck said the amount of glass—50 percent of the wall area—"was arrived at arbitrarily."[34] Just a few years later, he used proportions ranging from 27 to 35 percent.[35]

The Duncan project earned a special significance because here Keck finally persuaded Libbey-Owens-Ford to sponsor a performance test. (He had corresponded with the glass company throughout the late 1930s, and they seriously considered a purpose-built "test house" for a time.) The Illinois Institute of Technology (IIT) agreed to conduct the study, although the investigators—mechanical engineering professor James C. Peebles and graduate student William C. Knopf, Jr.—had no such experience (and no subsequent involvement in solar heating). "The primary objective," Peebles and Knopf said, "was to measure, if possible, the contribution of solar auxiliary heating to the comfort of the occupants and its effect upon the cost of fuel."[36] Knopf made comprehensive observations between October 1941 and October 1942. Keck must have eagerly anticipated the results. His own estimates at this time indicated that a radiant floor will "cut fuel costs about one quarter, and solar heat . . . will reduce the fuel bill another fifteen percent."[37] The stakes were recognized to be high. "If the results are satisfactory," Peebles said, "it opens up an enormous field for a new type of dwelling house construction."[38]

The test was plagued by problems: large cracks around the doors and windows due to bad lumber and poor caulking, Duncan's "sedentary habits" as a writer that required a 73°F interior temperature, and his propensity to "go outside to stretch and leave the door wide open." Additionally the structure frequently overheated because the automatic controls for the radiant floor did not account for solar lag. Peebles and Knopf reported: "The owners offset this heat gain by opening windows." Moreover, Knopf reflected openly on his inability to reconcile the theoretical methods of calculating gains and losses with his empirical results. The variables, he found, were too uncertain. He could not estimate infiltration or losses through the floor, he did not know the boiler's efficiency, and he did not develop insolation values. (The radiant floor was very inefficient, with a bottom temperature of 110°F and surface of 88°.) One additional noteworthy detail from the study: On a summer day the outdoor temperature peaked at 100°F at 3:00 p.m. The peak indoor temperature was recorded two hours later at 98°, although "the sun did not reach the floor at any time."[39] Clearly the Duncan House needed more effective methods of cooling, and by now this had become a recurring theme in the solar house movement.

In the end, Peebles and Knopf concluded: "No definite quantitative measurements can be derived from the test." But they acknowledged that the extra south window area probably created more gains than losses, and Knopf argued: "We . . . feel strongly . . . that if the house had had the proper heating system and heating controls, that if the house had been properly caulked, that if we could have kept the house at the normal low temperature, and that if the complete design of the floor had been changed to embody a smaller volume, that the over-all operating picture would be an extremely rosy one."[40] Keck convinced Libbey-Owens-Ford to issue a positive press release.[41] (A highly detailed summary of the Peebles and Knopf report was published in *Architectural Forum* by editor Henry N. Wright.[42]) Keck believed the test "confirmed" the value of his design methods.[43]

By 1942, Keck had introduced all the environmental techniques that he would ever use. Now that he had defined the essential elements of the solar house, experimentation ceased and the work involved technical and aesthetic refinements. For "Green's Ready-Built Homes" (1942–46), Keck tackled the timely problem of prefabrication while including his signature solar house features including the hollow-tile floor. Developer Ed Green marketed them as the Green

Hugh Duncan House by Fred and William Keck, Flossmoor, Illinois, 1941. Photograph by Hedrich-Blessing. Chicago History Museum, Hedrich-Blessing photograph collection

Opposite: Hugh Duncan House by Fred and William Keck, Flossmoor, Illinois, 1941. Photograph by Hedrich-Blessing. Chicago History Museum, Hedrich-Blessing photograph collection

Green's Ready-Built Homes, 1945. Drawing in
Architectural Forum (July 1945)

Opposite: Fred Keck and Ed Green with Green's
Ready-Built Home model, 1945. Photograph by Hedrich-
Blessing. Chicago History Museum, Hedrich-Blessing
photograph collection

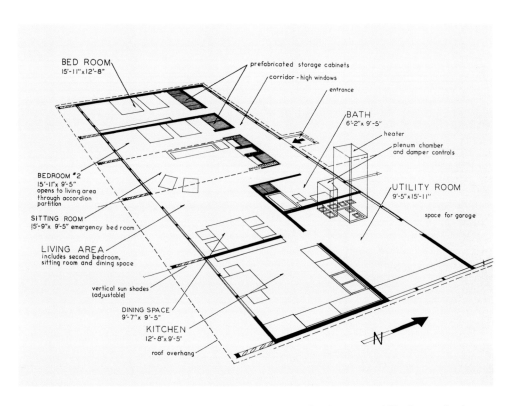

Solar Homes. Aesthetically, the demands of factory production caused Keck to submit to a
higher level of simplicity and clarity. In this project, Keck for the first time fully resolved the
ideas and impulses that had been building for a decade. Every expressive element reflected a
clear environmental purpose, while the whole possessed a visual strength on par with the
major monuments of modern architecture.

The solar house and the prefabricated house were potentially discordant concepts due to the
issue of orientation—prefabricated houses were usually meant to be oriented in any direction, but
solar houses needed to face south. Keck developed a method to accommodate fourteen different
models and four lot-types. The garage and service wing could be attached perpendicularly at a variety of points, creating L- and T-shaped plans. A lot with a north street-front was "easiest"; the other
three types required fences or hedges to create privacy between the glass wall and the neighbors or
the street. Most significantly, the project revealed a fundamental planning issue that frequently con-
fronts solar designers: lots facing north or south were required to be at least 100 feet wide.[44]

Again Keck offered valuable services to his clients based on his inclination to gather and
understand environmental data. For example, in November 1945 Green asked about winter

fuel costs for the model home. Keck subsequently sent Green a simple table of degree-days by month, with the percentage breakdown for each month. (September had .28 percent of the degree-days; October had 5.09 percent; November had 11.85 percent; and so on.) He then told Green: "It will enable you to estimate fairly accurately from a few fuel bills you now have, the total outlay for the season."[45] While these numbers would have been readily available to all architects, and reasonably easy to understand, it seems clear that the Kecks were almost unique in providing and interpreting such information. He estimated that fuel bills would be cut by one-third.

Within the prefabricated housing movement, Keck was among the very few to achieve some real success—after the model home was completed in April 1945 in Rockford, Illinois, "over a hundred" were built.[46] It would be fascinating to position the Green house in relation to Gropius and Wachsmann's 1942 Packaged House, for example, but Keck's project is inexplicably over-looked in recent studies.[47] Green's operation ultimately folded due to financial problems stemming from materials shortages and problems with labor unions. The effort lasted at least two years after the model home, and sales franchises existed in at least five states.

The Ready-Built Homes received a great deal of attention from the press, including a ten-page feature in *House Beautiful* written by Elizabeth Gordon.[48] Followers included a 1946 prefabricated solar house by the Wickes Corporation.[49] This project, designed by New Jersey architect Oren Thomas, reduced the Keck-style solar house to its minimal essence in terms of expression. A two-bedroom prototype was built in Camden, New Jersey, in August 1946, and the small houses intended to sell for $5,000 to $5,400. The buyer's contract stipulated: "Wickes will control orientation of all houses so that all glass walls will face within 11 degrees of south or north."[50]

More generally, a kind of Keck-inspired vernacular emerged. In the Chicago area, several architects (besides Schweikher) used Keck's strategies for admitting solar gain and providing shading, plus his general aesthetic sensibility, but without experimentation. Taliesin-trained William Deknatel blended Keck and Frank Lloyd Wright influences since as early as 1937 with the lavish and sun-responsive Kohler residence, which exerted "considerable influence on subsequent solar houses."[51] At Howard Sloan's Meadowbrook Village, Arthur Purdy designed a solar house for Robert Sidney Dickens which became a staple in Libbey-Owens-Ford publicity. After Henry P. Glass was "greatly influenced" by Keck's lectures at the New Bauhaus (later the Illinois Institute of Technology), he built a solar house for himself (Northfield, Illinois, 1948) which featured an entire south wall of Thermopane, with deep overhangs and ventilating louvers below the glass.[52] And in the Boston area, the Solaray Corporation launched a "solar subdivision" in 1947, where architect Nathaniel Saltonstall extended the Keck influence by vigorously sculpting the architectural form for dynamic solid-void and push-pull effects. Several basic plan-types were available, and at least sixteen homes were built.[53]

Wickes Prefabricated Houses, Camden, New Jersey, 1946. Photograph by Gottscho-Schleisner. Library of Congress

Opposite: Green's Ready-Built model home, Rockford, Illinois, 1945. Photograph by Hedrich-Blessing. Chicago History Museum, Hedrich-Blessing photograph collection

After the war, Keck continued to pursue the lean aesthetic of the Ready-Built Homes in custom-built private houses. Keck worked on over 100 house projects between 1945 and 1950, as Robert Boyce noted, most of them variations on the same theme.[54] For a 1946 house in Northfield, Illinois, builder Sidney Davies rejected Keck's early schemes and continually asked him to make the house smaller and simpler.[55] Every grace note seems to have been eliminated, even the intermediate wing walls. As a result, the project appears to have been produced on an assembly line (though it was not prefabricated and not perfectly repetitive). Never before had Keck submitted to such reticence of expression—it is not possible to "read" the facade in terms of interior space. For one critic, the spare appearance and repetitive plan of this type produced an "esthetic brutality."[56] More positively, the Davies House represented a clear, essential statement of the need for sun, shade, and ventilation.

At about this time, Keck offered a provocative remark about his aesthetic approach: "So far, the experimental forms have only scratched the surface, and within the next decade or two, enough changes and inventions will be developed to give us entirely new forms."[57] Robert Bruce Tague later characterized Keck's method as "just form following function without too much aes-

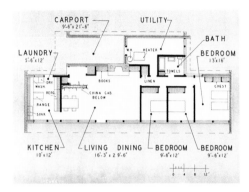

Above: Sidney Davies House by Fred and William Keck, Northfield, Illinois, 1946. *Practical Builder* (November 1949)

Right: Sidney Davies House by Fred and William Keck, Northfield, Illinois, 1946. Photograph by William Keck. Wisconsin Historical Society

thetic commitment or formalistic commitment to any particular final appearance," but this does not account for the refinements apparent in the Davies House, the Wrightian symbolism of its horizontality, and, perhaps, the influence of his crosstown acquaintance Mies van der Rohe.[58]

The Davies House fully exploited the ventilating louvers for both function and visual expression by running them all the way across the top and bottom of the "solar wall." Whereas earlier examples used the vents principally on the low side, it was later recognized that "high ventilating louvers are especially desirable in ground floor bedrooms because they are a safety factor, eliminate the need for closing the ventilating openings during most summer showers and can remain open when the family is away."[59] William Keck again calculated heat losses for the Davies House, and though the procedure had been refined since the Sloan House six years earlier it could not yet account for any losses beneath the hollow tile floor slab. For the first time here, Keck used brick cavity walls with insulation, and he included six inches of insulation in the ceiling, the greatest amount yet.[60]

After the Davies project, Keck's solar houses offered only minor variations on earlier themes and little technical exploration. One might criticize his conservatism, or praise his fidelity as he moved from prototype to type. Even in larger homes for more affluent clients, Keck continued to employ a Davies-style minimalist aesthetic of prefabrication but without the actual factory-made parts. Forest Crest, a twenty-six-house development (Glencoe, Illinois, 1952–53), demonstrated that Keck now worked from an established type for a new audience. Five different modular floor plans were created for developer Harold Friedman, but the spare style remained consistent. A minor variation on the ventilating louvers appeared: narrow, floor-to-ceiling units between full-height sheets of glass, a stylistic variation that did not significantly affect performance or character. The project's principal interest is in its larger social meaning.

"This will be the first attempt to use solar heat in a major residential project in the $28,000–$29,500 range," the *Chicago Tribune* reported. The solar house's appeal to a wealthier clientele at this time probably reflects a larger mood about energy use. Al Chase in the *Tribune* indicated something about the mood in 1952 when he foregrounded Forest Crest with the statement: "Sunlight [is] the only free fuel on the market today and the only one on which even Washington can't slap price ceilings or restrictions."[61] In this sense, the solar house embodied a history of scarcities as well as anxieties about the future.

After the projects for Sloan, Green, and Friedman, Keck could claim to be not only the first "solar architect" but also its most successful, both in terms of a critical contribution and sheer numbers. William Keck later claimed they built more than three hundred solar houses in total.[62] Indeed, it can be claimed that Keck was also the most commercially successful "solar architect" *ever*, including up to the present time. His true contribution—including the years *preceding* the first Sloan house, when he "discovered" solar heat and introduced numerous remarkable technical innovations—has never been well understood.

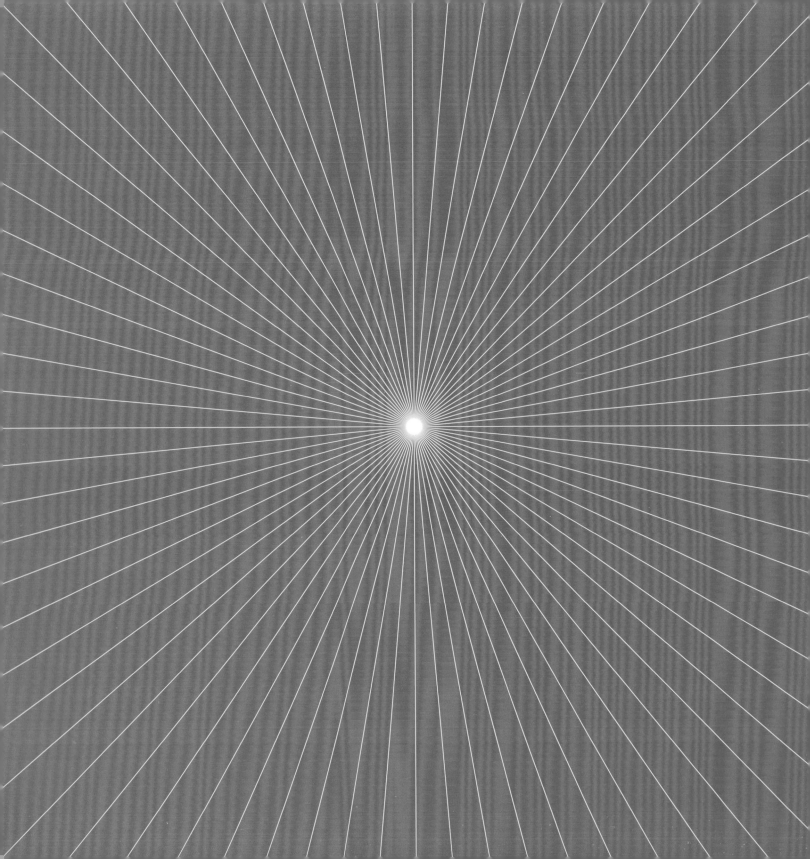

CHAPTER 2

THE SOLAR HOUSE AND THE GLASS HOUSE

Above all, these solar houses you are going to hear more about and see in ever increasing numbers are not at all "glass houses."

—*Chicago Tribune* (1948)[1]

Fred Keck, 1946. Photograph by Hedrich-Blessing. Chicago History Museum, Hedrich-Blessing photograph collection

Opposite: House of Tomorrow by Fred Keck at the Century of Progress Exposition, Chicago, 1933. Photograph by Hedrich-Blessing. Author's collection

To the extent that Keck's 1940 Sloan House constituted a breakthrough, it also represented the culmination of a period of vigorous and sensitive exploration. "After seven years," Ken Butti and John Perlin wrote, he "finally felt confident enough to expose the entire south side of a house to the sun."[2] That confidence was hard-earned, beginning with the 1933 all-glass "House of Tomorrow," where Keck said he "discovered" solar heating. The House of Tomorrow—Keck's most well-known project—has typically been interpreted, quite reasonably, as either: a pivotal instance in the evolution of glass-and-steel architecture; a futurist representation of machine-age domesticity; or more specifically a variant of Buckminster Fuller's Dymaxion House idea.[3] But it has not been analyzed as (loosely) the first solar house, or as the accidental instigator of an important and enduring movement. The House of Tomorrow looks quite different when viewed through the lens of environmental concerns. In particular, its meaning changes significantly when placed in the context of Keck's subsequent pursuits.

When Keck designed the House of Tomorrow for the Century of Progress Exposition in Chicago, he did not specifically intend to build a solar house—such a concept was unknown. Rather, he meant to create a futuristic provocation, and he followed a modernist tradition of using glass for polemical value (see Bruno Taut, Paul Scheerbart, and Ludwig Mies van der Rohe). He initially branded it "America's First Glass House."[4] Exposition visitors responded in droves. Eight hundred thousand people toured the house, even though there was a ten-cent admission fee while the other houses at the fair were free. At the time, Keck and his team did not mention solar heat at all. In fact, they promoted the house as having been "designed around an air-conditioning system,"[5] surely a wise marketing strategy for the summertime. The surprise benefit of solar heat was described later by the *Chicago Tribune*'s Al Chase: "This discovery was made one biting cold day when he found the workmen inside . . . working in their shirtsleeves and complaining of the heat. There was no artificial heat at that time in the building."[6] The "shirt-sleeves story" has become legendary. It appeared again in the *Tribune* and other newspapers in following years, and in *Reader's Digest* in 1944.[7] Then it lay dormant for decades. When Keck was invited to a momentous solar heating symposium at MIT in 1950 (to be discussed in chapter 6), he did not mention the shirtsleeves discovery to the distinguished audience. Instead, he said he had become "unconsciously aware" of solar heating as a child:

> My family lived in a house in Wisconsin, and my mother always had storm windows placed over the windows on the west, north, and east sides of the house. The south side never had sealing windows "because it did not need them." So our house had good ventilation and whatever sunlight was available in winter. Our living room was to the north, but we used the south rooms during winter months because they were pleasant and warmer. Later, as an architect, I remembered these facts, and took them into consideration when planning houses.[8]

Later the shirtsleeves story was resurrected and told dozens of times, mostly by William Keck. When receiving an award from the International Solar Energy Society (ISES), William told it this way:

> While the house was under construction in February, 1933 (before the heating plant was in operation, but with the house enclosed against the elements), my brother George Fred Keck visited the building on a sunny day with the temperature hovering between zero and 10° Fahrenheit. Upon entering the living room, he found carpenters and other workmen laboring in their shirt sleeves.[9]

The shirtsleeves story does not ring perfectly true. First, construction on the House of Tomorrow did not even begin until April 1933; it could not have been enclosed by glass until the middle of that month.[10] (One version, out of dozens, says the discovery occurred "during repairs"—the following winter?—but other versions say "during erection.") Second, the story did not appear until 1940 (first quotation above), when Keck was working with Sloan, at the very moment Sloan gave the solar house its name. At that time, perhaps, the new brand needed a memorable backstory.

A final reason to doubt the shirtsleeves story is that Keck showed serious interest in solar architecture (albeit in a rudimentary form) *a year before* the House of Tomorrow. In 1932, Keck and Paul Schweikher had completed solar studies of a hypothetical housing project for Chicago, using a makeshift heliodon.[11] Though the study showed clear affinities to earlier Bauhaus studies, it demonstrated a more sophisticated three-dimensional understanding of solar geometry, orientation, and building spacing. At this early stage the architects did not speak of "solar heat," but strongly implied it in seeking "to attain the utmost advantage of sunlight" and "mitigating the extremities."[12] The project was exhibited at the Museum of Modern Art and Century of Progress. In retrospect it represents an early move in Keck's larger effort to shape and promote an environmentally sensitive architecture by scientific validation.

Ultimately, though, the shirtsleeves story is probably true in an abstract sense, like any good myth. In fact, Keck most certainly discovered the potency of solar heat in 1933—*in the summer.* There is ample evidence that the House of Tomorrow overheated significantly, even with air-conditioning. William, who gave tours in the summer of 1933, later recalled that the house was "sweltering" when filled with visitors, despite the cooling system.[13] In early 1935, before the structure was moved by barge to Beverly Shores, Indiana (where it resides today), owners replaced the large panes of fixed glass with smaller operable windows set inside opaque wall panels. Still, the house regularly overheated in the 1970s, according to a resident, and inadequate air-conditioning "forced closure of the upper floors" in the early 2000s even though it was surrounded by mature trees.[14] A complete restoration is currently being planned, including a return to full fixed glazing. The structure will require a 10-ton air conditioner.

The Century of Progress Exposition proved to be so successful that organizers extended it into 1934. The House of Tomorrow remained open, with new interiors, and Keck planned a second all-glass structure, the Crystal House. In the exhibition's guide book, Keck did not mention solar heating as a goal. Once again, he emphasized "the house is designed around an air-conditioning system," but this time he offered a sweeping endorsement of cooling technology: "In the near future it is reasonable to suppose that all buildings in which people live and work will have such systems. Air conditioning units will be considered as necessary as central heating and bathrooms are today."[15] By 1940, Keck's language will change and become preoccupied with energy-saving topics, but while he built all-glass houses he exhibited a clear enthusiasm for the mechanical environment.

Keck routinely used the word "experimental" (or sometimes "laboratory house") for both the House of Tomorrow and the Crystal House. Initially he used these terms suggestively, to allude to the "experimental" nature of modern living. But at some point after experiencing the tremendous solar gain, Keck saw the houses as potential sites for actual scientific studies. He contacted the Libbey-Owens-Ford Glass Company: "I wanted Libby [sic] to keep this house open to see if the heat from the sun compensates for the additional fuel needed."[16] The glass company was interested, but the project did not materialize. From this point forward, he continued to use the word "experimental," but now in a literal sense. And for the next several years, Keck tried in sometimes stark and dramatic terms to persuade Libbey-Owens-Ford and others to sponsor scientific evaluations of his houses, finally succeeding in 1941 (as discussed earlier). All the while he continually tried to quantify his houses' performance, to fulfill their experimental promise.

In the Crystal House, Keck attempted to introduce an important environmental improvement: exterior venetian blinds. Keck associate Robert Bruce Tague discussed the rationale for exterior shading: "A blind, shade, or curtain on the inside of a window is inefficient inasmuch as the sun's rays when allowed to strike the glass, generate heat. This heat is then inside the house."[17] The blinds could not be installed outside, however, and consequently the Crystal House experienced significant overheating too. "We did the same thing as we did in the House of Tomorrow," William Keck recalled. "Everything was on the inside and we had the same problem . . . it got hotter than hell."[18]

Chicago housing project by Fred Keck and Paul Schweikher, unbuilt, 1933. Wisconsin Historical Society

Keck never designed another all-glass house after 1934—nothing even close. In the next two years, Keck planned five houses with restricted amounts of glass and exterior shading. It is immensely significant that the most urgent problem for Keck to address after his "discovery" of solar heat was control. He did not work to maximize gain. He did not work on storage, or lag time, or new materials. He worked on control, through a process of incremental testing and refinement that is fascinating to trace. When his iterative process matured, the solar house moved from prototype to type, both in terms of both technology and aesthetics.

Crystal House by Fred Keck at the Century of Progress Exposition, Chicago, 1934. Photograph by Hedrich-Blessing. Author's collection

His first houses after the fair employed the external venetian blinds that could not be realized at the Crystal House. Since no commercial product was available, he began to contact and work directly with manufacturers.[19] For the Bruning House, of 1935, Keck said the "summer sun load on equipment" was "greatly reduced" by the blinds.[20] And the 1938 Fricker House endured a summer with a maximum interior temperature of 78°F, with exterior blinds and no air conditioner.[21] Both houses, plus a few others in this period, had architectural "pockets" for the exterior blinds, which Keck articulated as exterior features. Still problems arose. In a 1939 house constructed in northern Wisconsin, Keck neglected to provide enough shading and the client complained of "roasting to death."[22]

For B. J. and Irma Cahn, who "wanted the house of the day after tomorrow,"[23] Keck refined his approach further by designing a deep structural projection to shade the glass, in addition to exterior blinds. And to demonstrate the overhang's performance, he created an architectural shading diagram which showed the solar angles at benchmark times and the amount of shading versus solar gain. Keck and Henry N. Wright both made diagrams such as these—probably the first ever—in about 1936.[24] They initiated an analytical and graphic convention that remains useful, and *de rigeur* for students, to the present day.

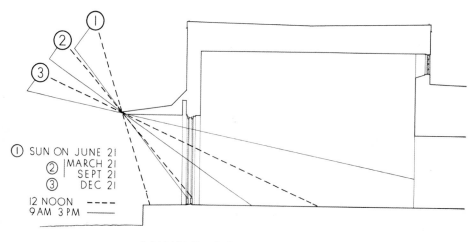

① SUN ON JUNE 21
② |MARCH 21
  | SEPT 21
③   DEC 21

12 NOON -----
9 AM 3 PM ———

LIVING ROOM SECTION SHOWING
ORIENTATION FOR SUNLIGHT

When Keck first employed the overhang as a shading device at the Cahn House, he built upon a powerful and immediate precedent: Frank Lloyd Wright's Robie House (Chicago, 1906–9). Both Fred and Bill lived three blocks away, starting in 1937 (and for the rest of their lives). Fred clearly admired the structure; he told a friend: "Many of Frank Lloyd Wright's houses, including the Robie house . . . could easily be called a Solar House,"[25] and he joined the campaign to save the building when it was threatened in the 1950s. It is not known how Wright determined the 66-degree shading angle at the Robie House—probably at that early date he relied on personal experience—but the design is generally believed to be "correct for proper shading."[26] Did Keck study Wright's solution in depth? It is tempting to speculate. His own solution for the Cahn House used a shading angle of 49 degrees; there would have been many logical reasons for Keck to provide more shading than Wright did thirty years earlier.

Keck's attention to the importance of shading would play a crucial role in the postwar popularization of the solar house movement. A 1944 booklet for consumers (to be discussed in chapter 4) included several illustrations of Keck projects and listed "Sun Control" as an essential feature of a solar house. Though Keck himself eventually abandoned exterior blinds, several companies manufactured such devices in the late 1940s ("Koolshade," for example), and popular and professional magazine articles informed homeowners of Keck's conclusion that interior curtains would not sufficiently control solar gain.[27] Another brochure for consumers, "Solar Orientation in Home Design" (1945), issued by the University of Illinois Small Homes Council, featured Keck's Bennett House (1943) on the cover, and its contents reflected many of Keck's findings up to this point.[28]

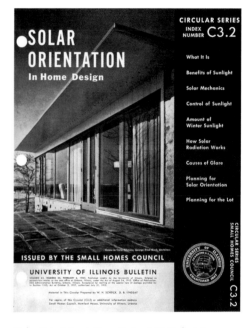

"Solar Orientation in Home Design," 1945, featuring Keck's Bennett House. Author's collection

Opposite: Bertram J. Cahn House shading angles by Fred Keck, c. 1936. Wisconsin Historical Society

A great deal of Fred Keck's achievement stemmed from his ability to bridge the "schism" between architecture and engineering and innovate simultaneously in both disciplines; and that schism would become an enduring theme in the history of the solar house. At the University of Illinois, Keck decisively chose the program in architectural engineering—a rare, specialized field aiming to integrate creative and technical work—rather than the Neoclassical-oriented architectural school.[29] He graduated in 1920 and called himself an architectural engineer throughout his career. He did not maintain a membership with the American Institute of Architects.

As he mastered solar geometry and shading, Keck also began to explore methods of natural ventilation and cooling, such as the water-cooled roof. At the Bruning House (Wilmette, Illinois, 1935–36), he designed a flat roof with interior downspouts, which would "carry a thin sheet of water in hot weather and further reduce load on cooling equipment."[30] The one-to-two-inch "roof pool" soon became a fairly standard feature in Keck's solar houses, and by 1946 he knew that this technique rejected up to 80 percent of the summer radiation falling on the roof.[31] When Keck explained this concept to the public, he was fond of saying the sun cools the house by evaporation, the same way it cools a swimmer in a wet bathing suit. He also

Keck project for *Ladies' Home Journal*, 1944. *Ladies' Home Journal* (July 1944)

noted that ancient Egyptians had used the same idea, with dampened wool on the roof. In winter, the water would be drained, and Keck asserted that snow collecting on a flat roof provided beneficial insulation.

With the water-cooled roof, Keck occupied a vanguard position practically alone. In 1935, the only similar experiment had occurred just a year earlier, when an irrigation engineer installed sprinklers atop a Washington, D.C., apartment building.[32] It is unclear if Keck was aware of this project. The Bruning House was apparently the first work of American architecture with a roof pool, and Keck's Johnson House of 1938 in Columbia, Missouri, was the first to have its roof pool specifically photographed and promoted. Pomerance and Breines of New York City are the only other architects known to have used a roof pool in the prewar period. By 1940, the concept aroused the interest of the American Society of Heating and Ventilation Engineers (ASHVE), the forerunner of the American Society of Heating, Refrigerating and Air-Conditioning Engineers (ASHRAE), which conducted a study and published data demonstrating the effectiveness of water-cooled roofs.[33] (Sprinklers were found to be better than pools.) The ASHVE guide included this data for many years. Again, the striking historical points are: Keck's prescience; his eagerness to pursue an engineering solution and give it refined architectural expression; and the fact that cooling was a primary concern in the earliest solar houses.

Keck's water-cooled roof reached its widest audience in 1944–45, when he designed a model house for the *Ladies' Home Journal*. When photographed from above, Keck's model was dominated by the roof pools, and consequently his project was labeled "Water on the Roof."[34] Then, the Museum of Modern Art (MoMA) displayed this project alongside designs by Philip Johnson, Frank Lloyd Wright, and others. Although the other projects did not claim solar heating, most had extensive glass and shading rooflines, leading one observer to conclude: "every one of the designs represents, with some variations, the principles of the 'solar house.'"[35] In MoMA's bulletin, Elizabeth Mock discussed Keck's project by explaining its solar geometry, shading, and insulated glass. She alluded to energy savings and praised the "long, narrow plan" for being the "logical end [of a] principle."[36]

In 1940, at the same time the Sloan House was introduced as a "solar house," *Coronet* magazine published a house Keck had designed especially for the publication. In a sense, the Coronet House distilled Keck's ideas and packaged them for consumers. Not surprisingly, it resembled the Sloan House, especially in its general organization and environmental features, but with a water-cooled roof. Keck wrote a lengthy article to accompany his watercolor rendering and the floor plan. You might call it a manifesto if it were not so pleasant. To a general audience, Keck explained how to read the rendering:

Water on the Roof

Note the wide eave line; its extent is calculated to shut out the hot summer sun and admit the warm winter sun, and also to protect the house from showers when the windows are open, making it unnecessary to get up at night to close the windows during a rainstorm. On the coldest winter day, when the sun is shining, enough of the sun's heat will enter the house to heat it comfortably, giving the interior the atmosphere of a spring day.[37]

Keck project for *Coronet* magazine, 1940. Watercolor by Fred Keck. *Coronet* (September 1940)

Keck understandably emphasized everyday activities and "atmosphere," and he notably avoided any discussion of energy savings or anything remotely technical in nature. The uniform eave line and varying sill heights meant that the living room (left side of watercolor) would receive much more solar heat than the bedrooms (right).

Keck also demonstrated the modern solar house could accommodate traditional "vernacular" elements that offered thermal benefits. The Coronet project (plus the Sloan House and many others) included a screened porch as a principal compositional element. Keck understood the screened porch to be an eminently sensible place to enjoy the summer's evening breezes, for those "who do not like to have visitations from mosquitoes and flies [and wish to] eat in comfort."[38] He also recommended sleeping there. Keck also accepted the value of the fireplace, even though he understood a fireplace generally created more heat losses than gains. He also may have valued wood as a fuel source for its low cost and future availability—there were no firewood shortages, or rations. Also there is little doubt that clients wanted fireplaces to accommodate traditional notions of comfort and domesticity. Additionally, Keck admired "old farm dwellings where the farmer, years ago, planted evergreens with the west and north of his group of buildings . . . Such a practice can still be in good tradition."[39] On the other hand, he argued forcefully against some other homebuilding conventions, particularly attics and basements.[40]

In a larger context, Keck's all-glass houses of 1933 and 1934 accelerated the general fascination with glass architecture, which began in the Victorian period, culminated in the 1940s and '50s, and continues today. Although Keck fully comprehended the basic problems of glass—overheating and nighttime heat loss—and abandoned the glass house after 1934, he did not exactly broadcast those conclusions. After all, the shirtsleeves story was cast as a positive, even formative, experience. It is not clear to what extent his peers in architecture would have recognized that Keck's solar house, as it developed, precisely contradicted the all-glass house designed irrespective of orientation. Today the contrast is clear and profound. How many architects in history have produced a definitive version of one type, and then so thoroughly developed its antithesis?

Yet the glass house proved to have a greater conceptual appeal than the solar house. Of course Philip Johnson's Glass House (1949) and Mies van der Rohe's Farnsworth House (1945–51) remain the seminal examples. The poor performance of these buildings—both summer

Farnsworth House by Ludwig Mies van der Rohe, Plano, Illinois, 1945–51. Anne Hornyak

overheating and winter heat loss—is widely known. A Johnson friend recalled: "his first oil bill was shocking. And oil was 11 cents a gallon when he built that house."[41] Likewise, Edith Farnsworth recalled her glass walls being covered in ice, and eventually litigated against Mies van der Rohe in part due to her discomfort and the house's high heating costs. Finally, Michael Benedikt has concluded that the two houses must be understood to "exemplify . . . [the] transcendence of ordinary human needs for thermal comfort," and he noted that both buildings "fail entirely as models for architecture in general, of course."[42] In effect the aesthetics of transparency trumped tangible issues of energy efficiency and comfort, and it is part of Keck's legacy that he failed to speak more forcefully against glass architecture in the 1930s and '40s.

At the time, critiques of all-glass architecture were rare but pointed. As early as 1930, Frank Lloyd Wright insisted: "Human houses should not be like boxes, blazing in the sun," an aesthetic critique of the International Style's lack of roof overhangs.[43] *House Beautiful* editor Elizabeth Gordon, a major supporter of the solar house concept, later extended Wright's argument:

> The much-touted all-glass cube of International Style architecture is perhaps the most unlivable type of home for man since he descended from the tree and entered a cave. You burn up in summer and freeze in the winter, because nothing must interfere with the "pure" form of their rectangles—no overhanging roofs to shade you from the sun.[44]

Though Gordon's position here served a larger reactionary political position, she effectively articulated the lessons of the House of Tomorrow and Crystal House to a wider audience in a manner that Keck never did himself. Historian James Marston Fitch called the fascination with glass architecture a "fetish" in 1960:

> Not only is the modern architect quite removed from any direct experience with climatic and geographic cause-and-effect; he is also quite persuaded that they "don't matter any more." Yet the poor performance of most modern buildings is impressive evidence to the contrary. Many recent buildings widely admired for their appearance actually function quite poorly . . . The fetish of glass walls has created further problems. The excessive light, heat and glare from poorly oriented glass places insuperable loads on the shading and cooling devices of the building.[45]

A pair of ironies underscore Keck's inability to stem the tide. First, Philip Johnson had visited the Century of Progress Exposition in 1933 and admired the House of Tomorrow. (One imagines he did not experience its overheating.) He also dropped in to visit the Keck office in 1936, but Fred was away.[46] Second, even Keck's most accomplished understudy, Ralph Rapson, eventually forgot the lessons he ought to have learned by working for Keck in the 1930s and succumbed to the illogical allure of the all-glass building. Rapson's 1974 weekend house in Amery, Wisconsin (the "Glass Cube"), was conspicuously unshaded, repeating the same fundamental mistake as the House of Tomorrow and Crystal House.

Just as Keck had developed the linear, directional, shaded, and ventilated solar house to correct the faults of the glass house, he also offered an alternative to the glass skyscraper. Beginning in 1950, Keck designed the Prairie Avenue Courts, a housing project which included a fourteen-story element. Could the typical Keck solar house be stacked vertically and horizontally? In terms of performance, the Kecks certainly knew that shared sidewalls and roofs/floors would reduce energy use. Projects such as the Davies house demonstrated an interest in repetition and in restricting the ability to look east and west; elsewhere he had built two-story solar houses showing the concept was stackable. Prairie Avenue Courts would be, in essence, a fourteen-story solar house. His project description said: "This unit is definitely a 'solar' type building."[47]

To organize the plan so that each unit had southern exposure, Keck needed to deviate from the public housing archetype—the highly efficient double-loaded corridor. In typical housing projects, half the residents were banished to a "thermal ghetto" on the north.[48] He persuaded Chicago Housing Authority (CHA) director Elizabeth Wood to accept a single-loaded corridor (with support from Mies van der Rohe).[49] Next, the design required projecting balconies on the south for shading, and for efficiency Keck and the CHA decided to make these balconies function as the corridors. An awkward condition resulted, with the all-glass living-room wall facing foot traffic. At the time a critic noted: "the bone of contention is whether the solar exposure . . . is worth the price of such full exposure to one's passing neighbors."[50] Prairie Avenue Courts was completed in 1958, and quickly the balconies proved to be a major issue for reasons other than privacy. According to Stanley Tigerman, who worked for Keck at the time: "For safety, to avoid people falling off or jumping off the balcony, [Keck] thought of putting on chain link fence to protect them. Well, of course, the inhabitants perceived it correctly—how else could you perceive it?—as if they were animals and this is a zoo and they were being penned in. It began the antagonism, which would cause all those projects to come down . . ."[51] The buildings were demolished in 2002.

Still, for all its faults, the Prairie Avenue housing project represented a positive alternative to the hermetically sealed glass skyscraper, which was being popularized at the same time. The dominant pattern, exemplified by Skidmore, Owings & Merrill's Lever House (1952) and the Seagram Building by Mies van der Rohe (1958), relied on mechanical methods of heating and cooling without concern for energy consumption. It was not until the 1973 energy crisis that all-glass skyscrapers were widely recognized to be "fantastically inefficient."[52] Even today, most histories of twentieth-century architecture celebrate these buildings without discussing the environmental problems. It was even forgotten that the earliest canonical example, Paxton's

Prairie Avenue Courts by Fred and William Keck, Chicago, 1950–51. Photograph by William Keck. Wisconsin Historical Society

Crystal Palace of 1849, experienced significant issues, particularly overheating.[53] In a fascinating reversal, the prototypical "green" office building in the early twenty-first century is remarkably similar in concept to Keck's public housing project: a narrow floor plate extended east-west, with opaque side walls, extensive shading on the south, and natural ventilation.

Today Keck's work is generally overlooked; his place in history does not seem to match his true importance. Robert Bruce Tague worked with Keck during this experimental period, and one historian recently asserted that Tague was "by all accounts the designer of the best houses produced by the Keck firm in the later 1930s and 1940s."[54] Although this claim is overstated, there is little doubt that Tague played an important role and later possessed a vivid perspective on the larger historical importance of the evolution from the glass house to the solar house. In an obscure exhibition catalog, Tague argued that Keck's work should be understood in the Chicago School tradition of William Jenney and Louis Sullivan because it successfully integrated "technical experimentation" and "aesthetic experimentation."[55] More provocatively for historiography, Tague served as Siegfried Giedion's "tour guide" when he visited Chicago in 1939. Keck's work at this time—both his glass houses and his embryonic unnamed solar houses—"failed to impress" the historian,[56] and Keck was never included in Giedion's *Space, Time and Architecture.*

Buford Pickens, who worked for Keck from 1930 to 1937 and later became an eminent architectural historian, maintained a friendship with Keck through the years. A witty 1977 letter to Keck offered this assessment, which finally seems quite prescient: "I predict that before the year 2000 the solar (green) house . . . will emerge as the historical prototype for the 21st century American home. The Crystal House will recede into oblivion as a transformer misplaced and the House of Tomorrow will be interpreted a shadeless hot box that led up to the true solar house."[57]

Imagine the alternative history that might have been pursued had Keck exerted a stronger influence. Suppose the House of Tomorrow had been well known to be a "shadeless hot box." Suppose architectural history had been less fascinated with Crystal Palaces and Crystal Houses. Suppose, instead, the textbooks had been filled with Sloan Houses and shaded high-rises, water-cooled roofs and radiant floors, expressive ventilation. The fundamental question—why the canon has consistently included glass houses but not (properly shaded) solar houses—can only be answered by allusion to Reyner Banham's great complaint that historians prefer to discuss "external forms" rather than "the whole of the technological art of creating habitable environments."

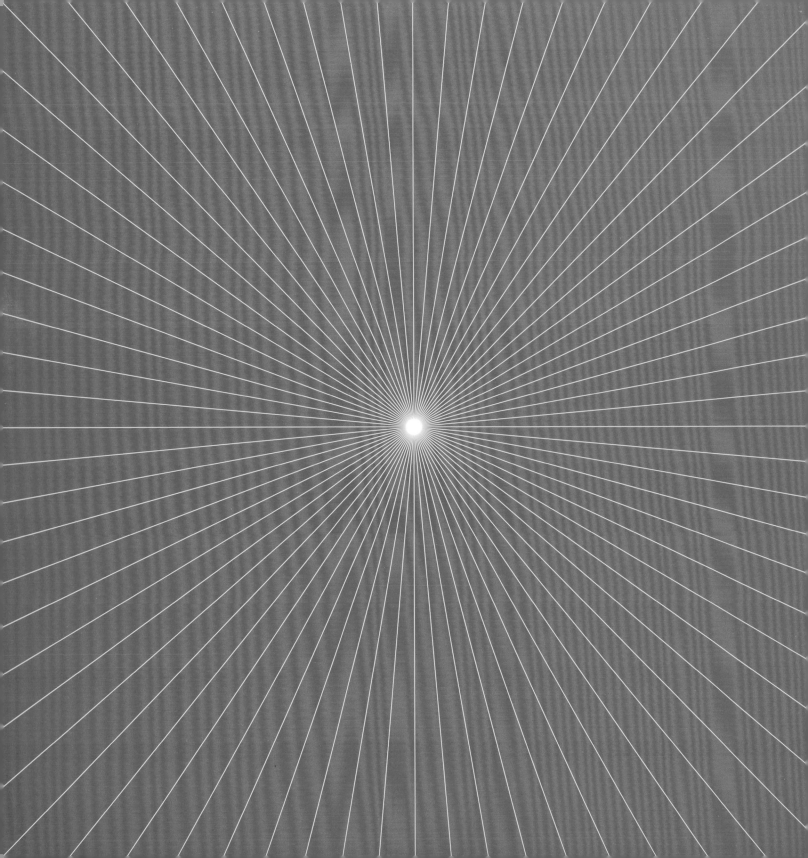

CHAPTER 3

FRANK LLOYD WRIGHT AND THE HEMICYCLE

Here, 30 years before the "energy crisis," was an instructive attempt to develop a "low-energy" architecture, deriving a lyrical form from the need to obtain maximum solar heat.

—John Sergeant (1984)[1]

Frank Lloyd Wright entered the solar house movement with his 1943–44 "Solar Hemicycle" for Herbert Jacobs, which remains a landmark structure and a signature project in Wright's oeuvre. Although this house is well-known and widely published, it has never been analyzed within the context of the emerging solar house movement, nor situated relative to other "hemicycles" that preceded and followed. Furthermore, it has not been discussed in terms of its specific aim, "savings of fuel."

Herbert and Katherine Jacobs did not initially ask for a solar house; it was Wright's idea. In fact, it was Wright's *second* idea for this site. He initially presented the Jacobses a fairly typical rectilinear scheme and did not give it a sun-related title. They found this first design to be "a palace" and rejected it.[2] At this point, inspiration struck and Wright decided the house should express the solar path. He remained coy with the clients, writing to them: "We are about ready to make you 'the goat' for a fresh enterprise in architecture. If you don't get what is on the boards some other fellow will. So 'watch out.' It's good. I think we have a real 'first' that you will like a lot."[3] Even though the clients did not specifically require solar heating, to their credit they rejected a weak scheme and forced Wright's imagination.

Whether Wright stood at the leading edge is a matter for debate. By this time, the solar house concept had achieved widespread currency in architectural practice, and its essential features were becoming well defined. "There are already, in the United States, several hundred 'solar' houses," *House Beautiful* announced in September 1943—just three years after Howard Sloan coined that term, and just before Wright conceived the hemicycle.[4] The number "several hundred" could only be justified by the loosest of definitions, but perhaps that is exactly the point: by a very generous interpretation, Wright had been creating solar houses for years (as Keck claimed for the Robie House). Now that a "movement" was gathering, Wright seemingly sought to occupy the forefront through a grand gesture. He was seventy-six years old at the time he designed the Solar Hemicycle. (In earlier drawings, the title is "Solar Hemicyclo," and later it became "Solar Hemicycle." "Hemicyclo" accurately reflects the term's Greek origins, according to Donald Kalec.[5])

In any case, Wright could justify his claim of a "fresh enterprise" due to the house's design—original in several respects. A semicircular house would respond to the sun in a way that (almost) no other solar house had before. To generate the Hemicycle's sophisticated geometry, Wright located a point which became the center of the garden, generated the arcs that became the front and back walls, and struck radius lines at 6-degree increments to organize structure and space. The centerline was oriented north-south. "Major elements were then proportioned by the grid" of radius lines, Thomas Heinz explained.[6] Though the sweeping roofline completed the full (180-degree) hemicycle, the floor spanned 120 degrees, and the south-facing glass wall was only 96 degrees—barely more than a quarter of the circle. The house would have functioned very poorly if it had been a true hemicycle with a 180-degree glass wall—think of the heat and glare problems that would be caused by 14-foot-tall glass sections facing directly east and west. Wright cleverly achieved the symbolic expression of a semicircle while mitigating the environmental hazards.

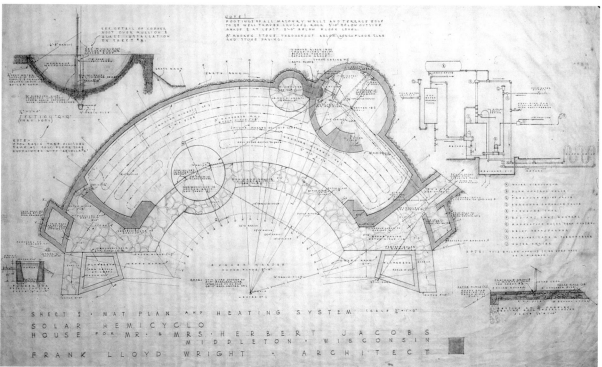

Previous pages: Jacobs "Solar Hemicycle" by Frank Lloyd Wright, Madison, Wisconsin, 1943–44. Photograph by author

Jacobs "Solar Hemicycle" by Frank Lloyd Wright, Madison, Wisconsin, 1943–44. Drawing by author

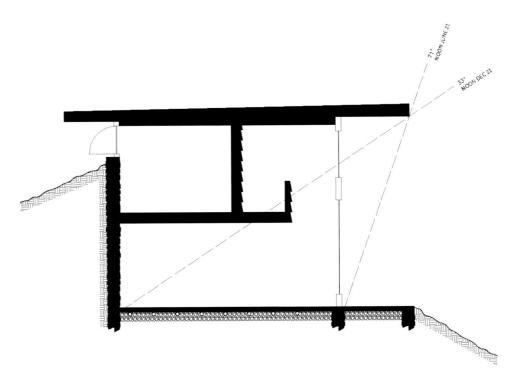

Wright, of course, designed the roof overhang with respect to the solar geometry. He told Jacobs: "With the big windows at the front, the low-lying winter sun would come way into the house and help to warm it, but the high summer sun would be cut off by the roof overhang."[7] Its two-dimensional shading angle was 66 degrees (the same as the Robie House), though the curvature created dynamic shading effects which are considerably more complex than suggested by a two-dimensional diagram. The solar altitude at summer noon is 70 degrees at this location. The heat was "stored" in the concrete floor slab and the rear stone wall. Wright did not use the term "thermal mass" but grasped the concept. The floor included a hot-water radiant heating system, beneath the concrete on an uninsulated gravel bed. The concrete was scored to articulate the 6-degree radius lines that shaped the plan, echoing the structure above and again expressing the notion of radiance.

Wright's design was meant to address another site-specific environmental condition besides the solar path: the prevailing winds. The Jacobs' site, a semirural location near the town of Middleton, Wisconsin (now encompassed by Madison), faced southwest directly into the winter winds. "How could the major glass area face the harshest winter weather?" Donald

Kalec asked.[8] Wright's solution was to create the circular "sunken garden" in front of the house, which would create "a ball of dead air" and force the winds up and over the roof. He told Jacobs he would be able to stand outside the glass and light his pipe in a strong wind. Jacobs later confirmed that the technique worked.[9]

Finally, Wright designed an earth berm up to a height of 12 feet against the entire sweep of the house's north face. Only a narrow band of clerestory windows serving the mezzanine bedrooms remained. This provided a very limited amount of north-facing building envelope, considerably buffering the interior space from the winter air. The "berm-type house," Wright said, was "good insulation—great protection from the elements . . . An actual economy and preservation of the landscape."[10] (The soil for the berm came from the foundations and sunken garden; it was a zero-sum operation, both poetic and pragmatic.) It would later become recognized as a landmark work in the history of earth-sheltered architecture. A 1970s handbook on the subject said Wright's "early plans . . . are very close to today's state-of-the-art designs."[11] Obviously this scheme would make perfect sense on a site where cold winds come from the north, as is typical in many cold climate locations.

Few buildings in all of architecture are so strongly oriented, mapped by geometry, and positioned within larger cosmological movements. The Jacobs Hemicycle became the first major contribution to the solar house movement to compose these effects in such a comprehensive and powerful manner. To stand in the living room is to experience the heavy sense of stone, soil, and horizontal compression at your back, but the lightness of glass, sky, and vertical expansion ahead. The sun comes from above, while the heat radiates from below. You measure your position against true south, and as the shadows move across the floor you follow the passing of time and changing seasons. At night you may close the curtains and start a fire; the cold side becomes the warm, and the warm side cold. The light side, dark; the dark, light.

The Solar Hemicycle is known as "Jacobs II" in Wright's oeuvre; Jacobs I (Madison, Wisconsin, 1936–37) is well-known as the first "Usonian" house and for its low cost of $5,500. It could not be called "solar"; its large east- and south-facing windows certainly created more losses than gains. Interestingly, the Jacobses did not move directly from the Usonian to the Hemicycle. In 1942, they moved to a "filthy" eighty-year-old farmhouse outside the city, in part to be self-sufficient in a time of economic scarcity. The poor thermal conditions at Jacobs I may have played a supporting role in their decision to leave; it was not insulated and the radiant floor system—Wright's first—proved inadequate.

Though the Jacobses had not initially envisioned a solar house for their second Wright commission, they responded positively to the idea and eventually used the (anticipated) solar heating as a central argument for its value. When Herbert Jacobs sought a construction loan in 1946, he wrote to the bankers:

The experimental design holds great possibilities for Wisconsin and the rest of the country in savings of fuel . . .

It goes without saying that it is desirable to build this house now, so that it may be studied and its good features adopted, before the major building boom hits the country.[12]

Although Jacobs had asked Wright (again) for a $5,000 house, the family needed to borrow $15,000 to finish the structure. They managed the construction themselves, with Katherine directing the masonry work and performing much herself. The process, which occurred between late 1946 and late 1948, is colorfully described and amply illustrated in the Jacobses' book *Building with Frank Lloyd Wright*.

The Jacobses' interest in a $5,000 house, their move to the country during the war, their rejection of Wright's first scheme for Jacobs II as too lavish, and the emphasis on "savings of fuel" all portray an ethic of frugality that is a relatively consistent theme among participants in the solar house movement (though there are exceptions). Keck and Keck also had a number of clients who urged modesty and simplicity, Duncan and Davies most notably. "Our interest in solar houses," William Keck later recalled, "was a response to the conditions brought about by The Depression of the early 1930's."[13] And Fred Keck said that the economy at that time had stimulated creativity because it encouraged builders to take risks: "In the thirties, they experimented because they weren't selling. I'm waiting for the next depression."[14] Likewise, solar architect Arthur Brown emphasized: "Those who went through the Great Depression will never forget it . . . [it was] a terrifying experience. I was out of work for many months and had little savings."[15] All of these examples point to the conclusion that the solar house was, in part, a product of the Great Depression.

How did the Jacobs Hemicycle perform? Accounts vary. "Usually by nine o'clock on a sunny [winter] morning, even in below-zero weather," the Jacobses wrote, "the heating system stopped, and did not resume until late afternoon . . . Of course the windows caused heavy heat loss at night. . ."[16] Katherine designed and fabricated a heavy curtain to address this problem. Still, the family would dress together in the bathroom, where they had installed a radiator, because the bedrooms were so cold by morning. When Bill Taylor acquired the house in 1982, he recalled: "I knew about the high heating bills—you had to pay almost $5,000 a year to be in a drafty and uncomfortable house."[17] By this time, wood rot had destroyed the window frames due to the regular problem of condensation on the single-pane glass. There may have been control problems and overheating as well. British architect John Sergeant recalled: "When I visited the house in the summer of 1969, the solar gain inside was excessive."[18] He suggested an external sunshade below the roof overhang and internal shutters.

In 1982, a University of Wisconsin professor and engineer asked his students to study the Jacobs Hemicycle and evaluate retrofit options which would improve its performance. They developed several conclusions: the single-pane glass should be replaced with insulated glass; the roof and foundation walls should be insulated; and, the floor slab should be insulated, with the hot water pipes placed in the slab rather than underneath it. These improvements, they concluded, would reduce the structure's heat loss by half.[19] The Jacobs Hemicycle was retrofitted in 1983 with strategies that the students had recommended, such as double-pane glazing, roof insulation, and a new radiant floor slab with insulation. Owner Bill Taylor said: "Basically, I had to redo the whole outer shell to solve the heating problem."[20] He also added air-conditioning.

Then, architect Donald Aitken (the Jacobses' son-in-law and a Taliesin Fellow) conducted a numerical performance analysis on the modified house and concluded that solar provided 53 percent of the total heat required: "quite a remarkable achievement for a direct-gain solar design with 26.8 percent unprotected glazing in the Wisconsin climate." (These numbers should include a major caveat: they were based on interior set-points of 63°F–64°F in the evenings and 60°F–61°F at other times.) Aitken concluded, dubiously, that the Solar Hemicycle represents "one of the best design solutions for passive solar architecture ever conceived."[21]

Aitken also claimed that, while the 1983 retrofits were meant to improve comfort, the original occupants had always been "comfortable and satisfied" in the structure:

> The Jacobses actually lived in the Solar Hemicycle the way people should expect to live in solar homes if they want to realize, in practice, the full economic and comfort potential of the benefits of such designs. They 'zoned' their daily activities according to the natural interior thermal zones of the house at different times of the day and in different seasons and weather conditions.[22]

The Jacobs family generally tolerated conditions that modern building standards would not permit. It was a different time. (Herb bicycled four miles to work, even in winter.) The house's third owners, Betty and John Moore, enjoy pointing out that the Jacobs family is often huddled by the fireplace in old photographs. In any case, the changes to the structure simply reflect that standards for comfort in America changed considerably through the later twentieth century. This fact often raises thorny issues for preservationists. Surely both Wright and Jacobs would have endorsed roof insulation and double glazing, though probably not air-conditioning.

Whatever its shortcomings, the Jacobs family found deep satisfaction with the structure; this is most poignantly demonstrated in the aforementioned *Building with Frank Lloyd Wright*. Herbert also wrote *Frank Lloyd Wright: America's Greatest Architect* and a touching essay entitled "A Light Look at Frank Lloyd Wright."[23] Long after the Hemicycle was complete, the Jacobs family maintained deep connections to Wright and his circle. Both daughters married Taliesin Fellows, and Susan became a graphic designer for Taliesin. Herb and Katherine drove to Taliesin West for Easter each year, even after Wright's death. They joined the Unitarian church in Madison "for architectural and spiritual reasons," and Katherine lectured at Taliesin as late as 1989.[24]

The Jacobs Hemicycle must be understood within the larger scope of Wright's practice of experimenting with environmental technologies, both modern and traditional, and his approach to comfort. For instance, although Wright claimed to have built the first large air-conditioned building (the Larkin Building of 1904), he did not rely on air-conditioning to cool his houses. In 1954 he wrote:

> Even in cold climates air conditioning has now caught on because the aim now is to maintain the degree of humidity for comfort within, no matter what is going on outside. I do not much believe in that. I think it far better to go *with* the natural climate than try to fix a special artificial climate of your own.[25]

For these reasons and others, Wright is increasingly understood, as Bob Koester has claimed, as "the first green architect of the modern Western experience."[26]

Wright remained somewhat active in the solar house movement. He served on the advisory board for the Association for Applied Solar Energy (AFASE) in the 1950s, and the 1955 World Symposium on Applied Solar Energy in Phoenix included a visit to Taliesin West. In 1959 (the year of his death), he was asked about the future of solar energy:

> My feeling about solar houses dates back to my early days of planning homes. I believed the sun a prime factor in a livable, properly oriented house, and utilized sunlight throughout the dwelling to the fullest extent. But to depend upon sun heat to substitute for the simple floor heating apparatus I used then and still use, I believe, would require more expenditure of space, construction, and apparatus than would be reasonable in a residence.
>
> To use the same apparatus for cooling in summer as used for heating in winter seems economical enough and demands no extra construction to provide a positive source of heat or cold. For this reason I have not been much interested in solar energy apparatus as the sole source of comfort in a building. Floor heat in the winter, the reverse in summer, seems economic-positive—if aided by proper placing.[27]

Wright's notion of not depending on an expensive apparatus for sun heat indicated his awareness of "active" solar collectors developed by engineers through the 1940s and '50s (see chapters 5 through 9). It is striking to note how vaguely Wright thought about economics com-

Bertram J. Cahn House by Fred Keck, c. 1936. Wisconsin
Historical Society

pared to these engineers. Yet Wright was probably more "correct" than the engineers despite
his imprecision, and paradoxically more successful by being unconstrained by data.

One proto-solar house preceded the Jacobs Hemicycle in its use of circular geometries: Fred
Keck's Cahn House of 1936–37 (Lake Forest, Illinois). This project—the "house of the day after
tomorrow"—was mentioned earlier because it prompted Keck to draw one of the first shading
diagrams. Its "crescent shaped" plan-geometry, "with the rooms following the path of the
sun,"[28] introduced the same concept that Wright developed in an inverse manner. Each scheme
"tracked" the sun, but Keck's structure presented its outer face to the south, whereas Wright of
course placed the inner ring facing the sun. In other words, both Keck and Wright found symbolic power in a circular shape but arrived at opposite forms.

The implicit disagreement—convex versus concave—is difficult to discuss in isolation
because Keck and Wright pursued so many other different strategies in these houses. For

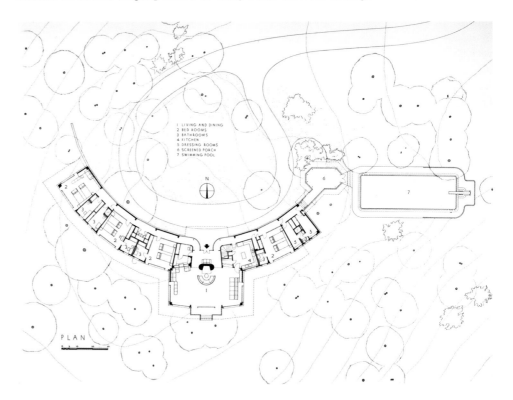

instance, the Cahn House sprawled horizontally on one level, while the Jacobs Hemicycle was stacked vertically. Keck did not use earth-berming or massive construction, except concrete floors (here covered in black rubber). Keck placed his hallways, as usual, to the north, while Wright's circulation path (more a balcony than a corridor) was located on the south, depriving the bedrooms of direct solar gain. The two houses also differed fundamentally in that Keck planned individual rooms, where Wright designed what is essentially a single volume of space. As a result, Keck's house would create warm and cold spaces, and possibly more ritual movement by the occupants or more auxiliary energy use. Between Keck and Wright, the divergent approaches cannot be explained by climate or site alone, because the conditions were quite similar. The houses were only about 100 miles apart; Madison has about 7,500 heating degree days, while Lake Forest (a Chicago suburb) has about 6,500 and more cloudiness.

Both projects interrupted the continuity of their long circular lines to divide space inside and relieve exterior monotony. Keck broke the "crescent shaped" form of the Cahn House with the living-dining room, which stepped forward to gather sunlight from three sides. Without this intervention, the south facade would have been a continuous planar curve of more than 180 feet. Instead, the plan created a strong hierarchy where the main public space is not treated simply as another wedge. Keck said he shaped the house in this manner "to afford a full view of the sunrise and sunset from the living room, and to give privacy to the bedrooms."[29] Wright also interrupted the outer arc of his plan with the cylindrical utility core, which protruded both into the earth and into the living room but did not exactly reach toward the sun. Without this feature, the curved stone wall would have stretched about 100 feet inside, and considerably longer at the earth berm. Both Keck's and Wright's formal counterpoints worked in the third dimension by rising above their respective sweeping rooflines.

Of course both projects featured the extensive use of glass and shading devices. Cahn's shading angle was 55 degrees compared to Jacobs's 66 degrees, meaning Keck provided more shade. This is not surprising for two reasons: Keck's convex shape created considerably more south-facing glass than Wright—about 1,800 square feet of double-plate glass for the Cahn House, compared to 672 square feet of single-pane glass for the Jacobs Hemicycle[30]; and as noted earlier, Keck was especially sensitive to overheating in 1936, more concerned with control than maximizing solar gains. The Cahn House, seemingly unconstrained by budget, included exterior blinds for additional shading and double-pane storm windows for use in winter. It was considerably better insulated than Wright's house, and included air-conditioning.

In the end there is no basis to judge whether the design for the Cahn House is "better" or "worse" than the Jacobs Hemicycle, but each represents an immensely interesting design response to a specific set of circumstances. Computer simulations could be performed, but the results would provoke more questions than answers due to the number of critical assumptions and unknown variables. Still, as an abstract design exercise, the underlying question remains compelling. Say you're designing a solar house, and for symbolic reasons you would like it to be shaped like a semicircle in plan—should it be convex or concave relative to the sun? Keck's

Curtis Meyer House by Frank Lloyd Wright,
Galesburg, Michigan, 1948–51. Michigan State
Historic Preservation Office

convex shape benefits by having a greater area of south-facing envelope, which allows for more glass and more direct gain (or, with a reduced amount of glass, the envelope still benefits by being heated). Both types of curvature create rooms or zones which may be relatively dark alternately in the morning and afternoon. Experientially, the concave shape of Wright creates a focal point in the landscape, while the convex shape promotes a scattering of views. Perhaps instead you should abandon the symbolism and pursue a linear plan. A pair of scholarly investigations posed this very question. One compared the concave glass wall to an equivalent straight glass wall and found positive results for the Hemicycle. When simulating a March day, the curve would admit more solar heat than the straight wall in the morning and afternoon and reduce the peak gains (overheating) at noon.[31] However another study of the geometry concluded that a straight window wall would admit 20 percent more solar heat on a seasonal basis than the hemicycle form, due to self-shading and angle-of-incidence effects.[32] Keck likely realized his form suffered the same limitations (in reverse). In the productive years that followed the Cahn House, he worked almost exclusively with rectilinear plans.

Keck and Wright both occasionally designed with arcs and semicircles later in their careers, but without the ethic of energy savings. Keck waited decades after the Cahn House before he returned to circular geometries, as seen in the gentle arc of the Payne House (Bucks County, Pennsylvania, 1959–61), where the convex glass area faced northwest, and the tightly curved Hirsh House (Highland Park, Illinois, 1960), where the all-glass inner ring pointed northeast.[33] In each case Keck privileged site-specific views when orienting the structure, rather than solar heating. He did not speak of them as solar houses, although he gave them floor-to-ceiling glass and deep overhangs as if they faced south. Indeed, both the Payne and Hirsh houses would make sense in Keck's oeuvre as late investigations, if they were properly oriented. Instead, they appear like weak compromises or misplaced prototypes.

Wright generated variants of the Hemicycle in several projects after Jacobs II. Two, in particular, merit some discussion. First, the Curtis Meyer House (Galesburg, Michigan, 1948–51), where he incorporated several refinements. Here he moved the center point further away from the structure and confined the house to less than a quarter-circle, creating a gentler arc.[34] He then used radius lines of 7.5 degrees to organize the geometry, rather than the 6-degree increments he had used for Jacobs II. This would create a straighter inner ring of glass and (in theory) more solar gains due to fewer self-shading and angle-of-incidence effects. Like Jacobs II, Wright organized the Meyer House on two levels but treated it like a continuous volume of space, with the bedrooms and balcony contained on a mezzanine set back from the two-story glass wall. Again Wright used a heavy cylindrical element to contain the stairs and some utility functions, but this time the drumlike piece anchored the curve at its end rather than residing along its length. By accenting the glass inner ring with the bubble-shaped dining room and

balcony above, and then extending that balcony to a point like a prow, Wright brought a sense of sculptural expressionism to the hemicycle genre. The wall construction, with custom-made concrete blocks, gave the building a more refined appearance than the Jacobs Hemicycle.

In Wright's house for Kenneth Laurent (Rockford, Illinois, 1948–52), he found a new theme by flattening the curve even further and reflecting it outside the building. The resulting figure, similar to a *vesica piscis* but narrower, gave shape to the exterior pool, planter, terrace, and retaining wall. Functionally the shallower arc, again, constituted a (theoretical) improvement, as it would face more directly south and include less problematic east- or west-facing glass. Laurent understood his house within the hemicycle genre: "The Jacobs House was really the first. But that was more on the theme of a circle, a tighter circle. This was more . . . shallow . . . It would take a pretty big circle to follow it out into the completion of a circle."[35] Wright did not inscribe radius lines into the design but instead used a square grid, and the anchoring formal elements became rectilinear figures.

Laurent was paraplegic and confined to a wheelchair, prompting Wright's first one-story hemicycle scheme. With the lower sweeping roofline, the house achieved a horizontal empha-

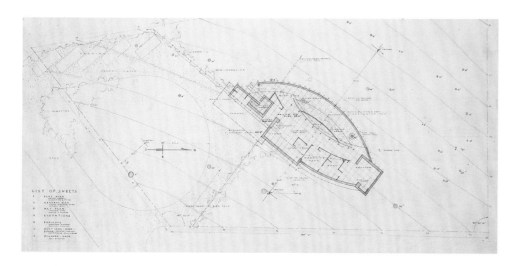

sis recalling Wright's early work and a pleasing modesty overall. Again, the bedrooms would not be located (in theory) to receive direct gain. Behind the glass Wright placed a generously proportioned "garden room," which also served as the corridor. "He was pretty pleased at the design," Laurent recalled, and the shallow-arc plan "became a prototype, or model, of a plan type first used here, and then applied in many variations in further plans for other clients," according to Bruce Brooks Pfeiffer.[36]

Both the Meyer and Laurent projects seem to be designed as solar houses, and may be understood so at first glance, but closer examination reveals that they were rotated to accommodate slopes and views on each site, like the late Keck projects mentioned above. The Meyer House was constructed with the glass wall facing north of east, and the Laurent House faced northwest. Neither was labeled as a solar house, and Laurent never mentioned solar heating in his original brief or other correspondence with the architect. Still, and most provocatively, when Wright published the Laurent project in *The Natural House*, he rotated the plan and omitted a north arrow to create the impression that the plan faced south. Wright may have conceived each scheme as a solar house and reluctantly compromised when he fully understood the site. This is especially plausible in the Laurent case, as he rejected the first location and told the client to find a better piece of land. Then he used publication drawings to idealize or "correct" his structures—a practice as old as architectural representation itself.

What does it mean that Wright's hemicycle-type designs after Jacobs II were not solar houses? According to this interpretation, Wright valued views more than heat and energy savings (a priority consistent with larger trends in architecture and falling postwar energy prices). And several other hemicycle-inspired designs by Wright were not designed for solar heating but, rather, they "demonstrate Wright's growing interest in a flowing architecture, free from the

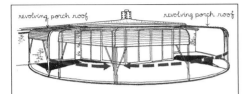

This sky shade does three jobs

1. *It prevents heat build-up indoors.* If you can keep the sun off the walls and windows during the hottest hours, you've taken the biggest step in keeping the house cool. A shading device, such as this movable awning, can also lessen the heat load of an air-conditioning system and cut its operating costs.

2. *It helps cut down heat-bounce from hard surfaces close to the house.* Here, the concrete terrace, continuing the concrete floor, is bound to soak up heat from the sun and retain it long after sunset. In cool weather this is an advantage, but on long hot days you want a fast cool-off period for comfortable sleep. Following the sun, this roof will create shade where you need it.

3. *It kills sky-glare.* On certain days, winter and summer, atmospheric conditions create a blinding white light that causes real eye discomfort. Sky-glare affects you indoors too. Many people pull their draperies on such days, but what is actually needed is a form of sky-shade. It can be made of canvas, plastic, wood, or, as in this case, corrugated aluminum.

Phyllis Ball and Patricia Paylore House by Arthur T. Brown, Tucson, Arizona, 1950. *House Beautiful* (October 1962)

Opposite: Phyllis Ball and Patricia Paylore House by Arthur T. Brown, Tucson, Arizona, 1950. Photograph by Maynard Parker. Maynard L. Parker collection, The Huntington Library

right angle."[37] These include houses for two of his sons—the David Wright House (Phoenix, Arizona, 1950–51) and the Robert Llewellyn House (Bethesda, Maryland, 1953)—and the Maude and Andrew Cooke House (Virginia Beach, 1953–60). Still, the corrective impulse, at least in Laurent's case, showed Wright communicating proper solar orientation to a wider audience. The Jacobs Hemicycle may appear to be Wright's only contribution to the solar house movement by virtue of its actual place in the world. But in the realm of ideas his contribution appears serious and sustained.

The hemicycle form could be subverted, as Arthur Brown demonstrated in an especially critical contribution to the genre. Brown was "Tucson's pioneer of solar design," to be discussed further in chapter 4. For the Ball-Paylore House (Tucson, 1950), he developed a novel shading strategy using circular "revolving porches." These were movable shades connected to the house which rolled on casters at the rim of the patio slab and a track in the eave line. The homeowners could shield the house from direct sun throughout the day or admit the sun when heating was needed. In essence, the house was conceived as a kinetic solar mechanism, compelling for its "lyrical" qualities.

Though the revolving porches constituted a hemicycle, the interior plan derived from a hexagon. Why a hexagon? The clients, Phyllis Ball and Patricia Paylore, "found the typical house for the average American family unsuitable for two independent adults who wanted to share a home."[38] Brown recalled: "It was the architect's first concern to see that the owners had rooms of equal importance and separated from the general living area. As the plan worked out, each person had access to the terrace and patio from her own room. If desired, each could even have a segment of the revolving porch."[39] In other words, Brown found the hexagonal plan to be non-hierarchical, and the revolving porches contributed to the feeling of equality by providing equal access to the sun (or the shade). After living in the house for thirty years, Paylore, a librarian, coedited the book *Desert Housing* and wrote an introduction entitled "From Cave to Cave."[40]

Brown noted that the Ball-Paylore shading system "does three jobs": preventing unwanted direct gain; shading the concrete terrace to prevent indirect gain; and protecting the interior from indirect glare.[41] Brown did not explicate the fourth job—to be retracted and allow solar heat when needed—but obviously he intended this functionality as well. He placed all-glass, south-facing walls behind the revolving porches, and he gave the living space brown concrete floors and masonry walls to the rear for thermal mass. Taken together, these "four jobs" demonstrate an environmental sensitivity that is usually not associated with 1950s architecture.

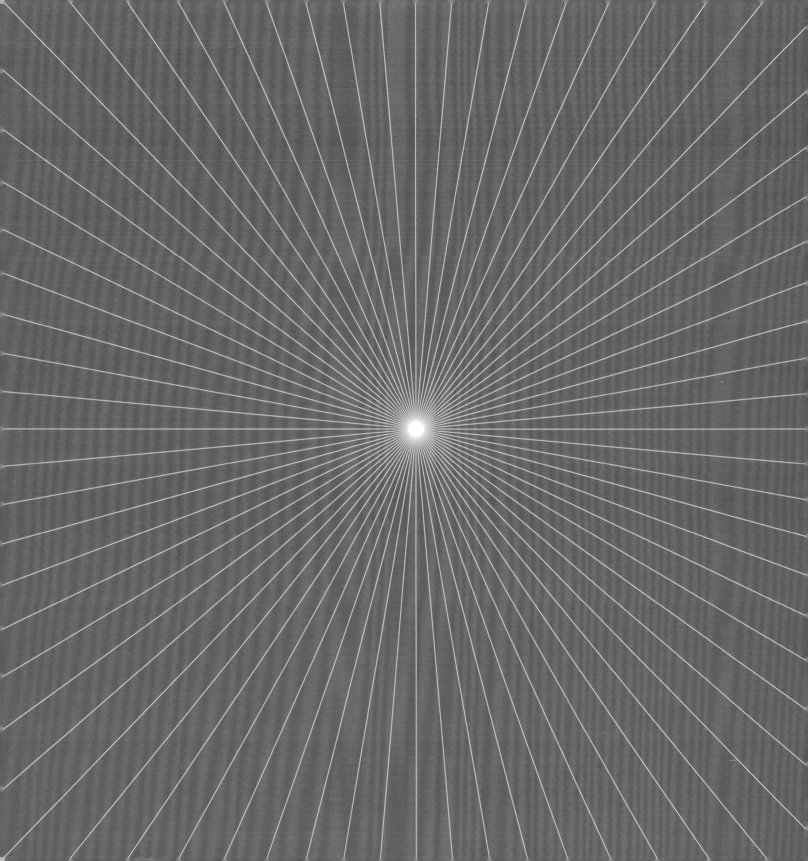

CHAPTER 4

ACRES OF GLASS: THE PROMOTIONAL EFFORT

No idea of the last 30 years has so fired the imagination of the American public as the one of letting Old Sol reduce the winter fuel bill.

—*House Beautiful* (1945)[1]

It was plain that a throng of Americans were interested in solar houses and presently would start building them across the land if they received even slight encouragement from any of the sources from which they sought guidance. It was also apparent that with such a trend flourishing, the company would sell acres more of glass.

—*Your Solar House* (1947)[2]

By the mid-1940s, the solar house concept clearly captured the imagination of the press and public. Even before the end of the war, some of America's most popular publications featured the new idea and sought to demystify the issues for the layperson. Substantial solar house features appeared in *Newsweek* (September 1943), *Reader's Digest* (January 1944), and *Parents* magazine, and the *New York Times* (April 1945). Additionally, the *Chicago Tribune*'s consistent efforts have been noted, and the role of *House Beautiful* and *Architectural Forum* are discussed below. And "motion-picture theaters from Maine to California brought the solar house alive to tens of millions in sight and sound and color."[3] But as the term solar house became more familiar, it was used indiscriminately to describe conventional houses with southern windows and overhangs. This lack of rigor probably helped the phenomenon grow, as it promoted inclusion. From a historical perspective, the imprecision indicates a movement in its infancy.

Why did the concept of a solar house—however poorly defined—resonate at this time? First, recall the "ethic of frugality" that was deeply engrained in people like Herbert Jacobs, raised during the Great Depression. To this powerful historical circumstance, add wartime energy shortages and rationing of coal and fuel oil. Much of everyday life in the early 1940s involved negotiations over one scarcity or another, and this mood of uncertainty shaped the political discourse as well. Harold Ickes, the longtime secretary of the interior, wrote an article entitled "We're Running Out of Oil!" in 1943.[4] In this setting, it is easy to understand how an energy-saving house would appeal to consumers.

A few key promoters stimulated the public appetite for solar houses, especially *House Beautiful* editor Elizabeth Gordon. She was considered "a missionary of taste to the American homemaker" and she used the magazine as "a propaganda and teaching tool" for more than twenty years.[5] No publication in America or elsewhere gave more positive attention to the solar

SOLAR HOUSES

an architectural lift in living

Just what is a Solar House?

Just what is a Solar house? Well, the answer is relatively simple. Fundamentally, it is a house designed to take advantage of Solar radiation as an auxiliary source of heat. By means of transparent glass walls on southern exposures, the radiant energy of the winter sun, when it swings low on southern horizons, is allowed to enter and warm homes. Overhanging roof constructions serve as visors to keep out the direct Solar rays during the summer months when entry of heat is not desired.

In the milder climates of our southern, southwestern and far western states, the trend to larger window areas, even to whole walls of glass, has been increasing as home owners sought to blend the outdoors with interiors for more enjoyable views and more abundant natural daylight within their houses.

With the development of an insulating windowpane, this trend to the open-plan type of dwelling became practical for all climates.

A Solar house can have most any kind of architectural design. Naturally, the principles of Solarization, with its many benefits which contribute to better living, can be achieved much more efficiently in the open-plan type of house, to a lesser degree in traditional types of architecture.

Solar housing has many advantages aside from sun utilization as a heating plus in cold climates, but before considering them, here are the three fundamental principles of such design: orientation, large windows and sun control.

Orientation
This means facing as many rooms to the south as possible to obtain the heating plus benefits of solar radiation in winter. Additionally, if the view possibilities are sufficiently inviting, plan window areas to the east, west or north to incorporate such scenes. If movable sash is used, orient floor plans and window areas with prevailing summer breezes if possible.

Large Windows
Large window areas are necessary to provide proper entry of solar radiant energy in winter months. Double-glass insulation should be used. From the standpoint of view possibilities, the surroundings should be studied with the idea of planning windows accordingly. Landscaping should be planned both for views and screening for privacy when conditions make it advisable.

Sun Control
This is achieved by the use of permanent or temporary roof over-hangs, visors or other means of controlling shadow areas on the windows so that sunlight can enter during cold weather and be shut out during warm weather. There are various elements involving sun control and it is suggested that Pages 12, 13, 14 and 15 be studied carefully. Architects should be consulted to assure proper engineering.

house. The September 1943 issue, for example, highlighted several projects, including Keck's Duncan House, in an eight-page feature and discussed the basic principles of solar geometry, orientation, and shading in simple terms. She even considered her own residence, by architect Julius Gregory, to be a solar house, although it included a great deal of north-facing glass for views of the Hudson River valley. She told readers she had "personally tested and found good" solar heating: "You'll probably want to use solar heat, as an auxiliary to the regular heating, in your own postwar home."[6] Her advocacy culminated in the magazine's famous "Climate Control Project" of 1949–52, a collaboration with the American Institute of Architects (AIA).

The Libbey-Owens-Ford glass company also mounted a serious and sustained campaign for the solar house. The company received "thousands of letters" in the early 1940s from curious consumers. "It was plain," the company recalled a few years later, "that a throng of Americans were interested in solar houses."[7] In 1944–45, the glass company developed a highly stylized and fairly comprehensive booklet, *Solar Houses: An Architectural Lift in Living*. It was the first standalone publication to attempt a definition of this new phenomenon:

> Just what is a Solar house? Well, the answer is relatively simple. Fundamentally, it is a house designed to take advantage of Solar radiation as an auxiliary source of heat.

> . . . here are the three fundamental principles of such design: orientation, large windows and sun control.[8]

The twenty-four-page booklet included a considerable amount of graphic information new to consumers, including a number of solar geometry diagrams provided by Keck and Keck. More than a dozen houses were pictured, with Keck's Duncan House presented as the center-piece example. Today the booklet may appear rudimentary in content, kitschy in style, and socially retrograde (with its emphasis on "solar housewives"). But it may also be understood as a well-intentioned public service, full of timeless good advice. For anyone seeking to understand the history of passive solar heating, the booklet is akin to a sonogram, picturing a vital energy in its formative stage.

Promoting the solar house served a powerful self-interest for Libbey-Owens-Ford—they would sell "acres more of glass." In a thorough conflation of public education and marketing, the booklet advertised an insulated double-glass unit called "Thermopane." Commercial motives aside, Thermopane legitimately constituted a major technological advance. Previously, with single-pane windows, large glass areas proved impractical in most regions because of heat losses at night. By reducing those losses, Thermopane made it feasible for homebuilders in cold climates to use more glass. Many projects advertised as solar houses, Elizabeth Gordon's included, were primarily houses-with-large-windows. They sincerely expressed enthusiasm for the technology of insulated glass, like Victorian houses celebrated the scroll saw or the

Libbey-Owens-Ford advertisement, 1955, featuring Albert Adelman House by Frank Lloyd Wright. *House Beautiful* (November 1955)

Opposite: Libbey-Owens-Ford publication, 1944. Author's collection

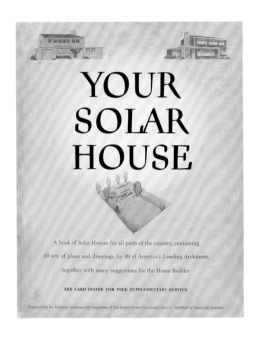

Above: *Your Solar House*, 1947. Author's collection

Right: South Dakota House by Harold Spitznagel for *Your Solar House*, 1947. Author's collection

Chrysler Building glorified stainless steel. Between 1930 and 1950, window glass production in the U.S. tripled.[9]

Despite the publicity, or because of it, the solar house did not have a consistent image; buyers did not know "what should a Solar House look like."[10] So Libbey-Owens-Ford launched an ambitious new program in 1945, *Your Solar House*, to commission a notable architect to build a solar house in each of the forty-eight states.[11] Some important figures agreed to participate, including Louis Kahn, Edward Durell Stone, Hugh Stubbins, and Pietro Belluschi. The glass company flattered the participants with high aspirations: "[It] will be the finest thing of its kind ever attempted in this country and could prove to be invaluable to the entire architectural profession for years to come."[12]

How would a diverse group of architects, most of whom had never designed a solar house before, respond? When the organizers selected and notified the architects in August 1945, they mistakenly assumed the concept of a solar house was already fully formed and well understood. Some architects seem to have asked for more direction, and the glass company soon distributed supplemental materials, including their booklet *Solar Houses: An Architectural Lift in Living*, to reinforce the basic principles. Still, the organizers offered no direction about issues of appearance, and they assured the architects: "we have no intention of tinkering with your designs."[13] Perhaps organizers at Libbey-Owens-Ford used the label "solar house" vaguely in order to stimulate variety. If the program sought to establish a new style, it did so with the lightest of touches.

The background process between *Your Solar House* organizers and architects included practically no "technical" information beyond the simple information about orientation and solar geometry in the booklet. A novice solar architect, as most of them were, would have no means for determining how much glass to use, for example, and no method for understanding how much heat would be gained. Issues such as thermal mass were (seemingly) unknown. Likewise, the "active" solar heating systems which existed were not of interest; the challenge did not imply a machine-age response. One transmittal from Libbey-Owens-Ford to the architects reflected the general character of the discussion. It noted the problem of "drapes [being] bunched at each side of the room, thereby covering so much glass area . . . Undoubtedly, you have given this much thought . . ."[14] (One imagines the amused reaction of a technically proficient architect like the Illinois delegate Fred Keck.)

As the process unfolded, the organizers abandoned their original plan to build the houses and decided to focus on creating a book of the forty-nine designs (the District of Columbia having been included). They also planned to sell construction blueprints to interested consumers. The plans were finished in mid-1946, and the book *Your Solar House* was published in fall 1947.

Your Solar House captured the broad diffusion of an idea just a few years after its inception. Most of the designs seemingly followed the "three fundamental principles" of proper orientation, large windows, and sun control. And most appear to have understood the fundamentals of overhang design to provide shading in summer but admit winter solar gain (although the presentation did not include sections or diagrams). But none explored more advanced issues of passive solar heating that should have interested a progressive architect in 1947.[15] None addressed, even in general terms, the primary underlying objective of saving energy by reducing mechanical heating and cooling needs. None discussed how they had arrived at the amount of glass area relative to the size of wall or volume of space behind it.

Clearly the participating architects possessed an impressionistic notion rather than a rigorous set of expectations. Many wanted to bring more daylight and openness to the house for aesthetic or curative reasons, not for heat. For example, Stonorov & Kahn omitted any shading on the east because "the percentage of ultra-violet rays (therapeutically beneficial) is greatest in the morning because of the clarity of the atmosphere and could be allowed to penetrate the house." Similarly, Harwell Hamilton Harris argued that "effects of . . . lightness and airiness . . . are principal reasons why a solar house differs from other houses in looks and feel." Here we find the influence of modern architects like Le Corbusier and Richard Neutra, who had explored the heliotherapeutic benefits of glass since the 1920s. Harris's design for Southern California, and a few others for warm climates, actually placed the major glass walls *facing north*. And (as professor and ASES Fellow John Reynolds enjoys telling) the Oregon house by Belluschi had as much glass to the north as the south. Some plans did not indicate orientation, so that readers could imagine the design in a variety of lot conditions, as was common in modern housing pattern books, even though it flouted the fundamental point.

Anyone attempting to use *Your Solar House* to evaluate the actual technical development of the solar house in 1947 would have come away with a dim view. A majority were not experimental in any sense. None of the architects at this time were able say anything remotely specific regarding building performance, either in terms of energy use or occupant comfort. Even Fred Keck avoided any technical discussion in the presentation of his Illinois house. Upon close inspection, Keck's house implied a depth of experience and creative thought that surpassed the others in the book. But, remarkably, his design was less experimental than the real houses he built for actual clients at the same time. For instance, when the 1946 Davies House was published in *Architectural Forum*, Keck made several technical diagrams to indicate how the building would perform, quite unlike the pictorial presentation in *Your Solar House*. Certainly this dichotomy reflected the project's conservative nature.

Perhaps, in the absence of technical innovation, *Your Solar House* architects might have contributed to the aesthetic development of the solar house, but here too the program failed to stimulate innovation. As a result of the solar house's vague definition, the architects submitted a wide variety of aesthetic responses. A few would have been considered progressive at the time, and these might have provided a model for future work by giving new expression to a new design problem. Many adopted traditional styles and simply added larger windows, and many more were simply uninteresting on any level. At least one participant, H. Ray Burks of Arkansas, took an explicitly anti-modernist position:

> Although startling scientific discoveries will have terrific impact on our way of living, it will take more energy than the split atom generates to change people's tastes and desires in the planning of their homes. Regardless of doctrines advanced by theorists, we will not strip our abodes down to the bare essentials of basic forms, and this refusal is by no means a sign of enslavement to the past.[16]

Readers were left to conclude that the solar house had an indeterminate relationship to modernity and lacked a clear architectural identity. It was a pattern book without a pattern. The general character of *Your Solar House* designs can be interpreted as a meek symbolic response to an ill-defined problem.

Your Solar House editors called it "a book of inspirations rather than of specific patterns."[17] The substantial introductory matter that was meant to address the "thousands of letters" the company had received from consumers. Questions ranging from practical ("Can I get a bank loan on a solar house?") to absurd ("Do you get sunburn in a solar house?") were answered. The volume remains a fascinating object due to its odd mix of architectural contributions, consumer education, and bald advertising. As Daniel Barber has noted, it was "clearly a product of the Libbey-Owens-Ford marketing department," while Adam Rome correctly observed that "the first major backer of the solar house was a manufacturer of insulated glass."[18] But what does this mean for the movement and for architecture in general? *Your Solar House* architects must have perceived an indirect obligation to promote the company's product, since an increased use of glass was embedded in the very definition of the solar house—a deep concordance between a marketing agenda and a creative principle. Architects of this era were quite familiar with the costs and benefits of commercially sponsored architectural competitions, which "proliferated" in the 1930s and '40s. Although these programs "clearly threatened" the architectural profession by offering free plans, Andrew Shanken has shown that the American Institute of Architects (AIA) "recognized the value of corporate competitions," particularly for "young, vigorous and ambitious creative architects."[19] Obviously these relationships were mutually beneficial: corporations like Libbey-Owens-Ford spent money to have their products "endorsed" by association with leading-edge design, while architects received prestige and free publicity for their work.

Whether *Your Solar House* had a notable significance in its time is difficult to assess. A remarkable 50,000 copies were distributed,[20] but there are no known examples of any of the houses actually having been built. There may have been significant derivative effects. Within a few years, for instance, the *New York Times* noticed: "Almost every contemporary house these days seems to be a 'solar house' as well," although the loosest definition of that term surely applied.[21] *Your Solar House* did provoke some criticism in its time—in a glass industry publication. F. W. Preston complained that solar heating had numerous limitations: losses could outweigh gains; southern orientation was not always possible or desirable on a given site; solar houses did not control glare; and so on. He criticized both the book for providing a vague definition and the architects for missing the point: "Some of these are interesting, some may be practicable, but the reviewer feels that the fundamental principles are unsound, and that there is going to be a lot of grief if there is a sudden flight to house building of this type."[22]

Some *Your Solar House* designs have been revisited by scholars interested in their effectiveness as prototypes. A 1983 project by Katz and Olgyay examined four—Keck's for Illinois, Stubbins's for Massachusetts, Alfred Kastner's Washington, D.C., project, and John Gaw Meem's house for New Mexico—using early computer simulation methods with some critical assumptions. Meem's adobe house performed very well; the Keck and Stubbins designs offered modest savings; and Kastner's design required considerable energy use. They suggested that "misapplications" of solar principles, in this program and elsewhere, diluted the "solar house' label and led to its eventual decline.[23] Similarly, a 2006 study of Oscar Stonorov and Louis

Purdue solar house experiment by F. W. Hutchinson, 1945–46. *Progressive Architecture* (March 1947)

Kahn's Pennsylvania house found far more heat losses than gains, even in spring and fall, due to too much glass. The authors provocatively noted that the house would not be considered "solar" by today's standards, even with improved insulation.[24]

In retrospect *Your Solar House* appears to represent an end rather than a beginning. It failed to create a community of solar architects or to establish a consensus architectural language for the solar house movement after 1947. Poor timing contributed: energy conservation was imperative in 1945 when the project was initiated, due to wartime shortages, but by late 1947 the urgency was gone. Still the program showed that energy-related concerns could shape the architectural discourse, at least temporarily. Thus the evolutionary arc of *Your Solar House*—from the popular interest that prompted it, to its lack of tangible influence—points to an important and recurring historical theme: that mainstream architectural priorities tend to respond (often only symbolically) to energy costs, sometimes assisted by commercial interests.

Libbey-Owens-Ford saw *Your Solar House* as part of its larger "research program," which included the other publications discussed above and the IIT study of Fred Keck's Duncan House, plus a slide rule type of device "for designing solar houses" patented in 1946.[25] Additionally, the glass company sponsored a "full-scale experimental study" conducted by Purdue University mechanical engineering professor F. W. Hutchinson in 1945–46. Purdue built two houses side by side, identical except for the glazing. The object was to test whether passive solar homes gained more energy during the day than they lost at night. "During the past ten years," Hutchinson observed, "innumerable claims and counter-claims have been advanced concerning the solar house . . . Where, in this confusion of claim, opinion, and estimate, does the truth lie?"[26] The Purdue study promised to answer that question with a new level of methodological rigor. At this time the only existing "data" on direct-gain space heating came from the Duncan House study,

and Keck himself complained: "It was not a recognized engineering test because the owners of the house lived in it during the test and all factors were not under engineering control."[27] The larger issue, the lack of support for basic research in architecture, continued to irk Keck into the 1950s:

> What the construction industry really lacks is an experimental laboratory for testing. Most other fields have such facilities. Medicine, for example, is richly endowed in staff and financing to do basic research. Most industries have basic research laboratories. In the building industry a so-called research laboratory generally turns out to be a product testing laboratory, or a place where newer and more efficient machinery is designed to produce present products.[28]

Effectively, the first generation of solar house "research" had been sponsored by private clients like B. J. Cahn and Howard Sloan. In this context, and notwithstanding the commercial interests of Libbey-Owens-Ford, the Purdue project offered the promise of scientific objectivity.

Hutchinson decided the houses should be unoccupied, to avoid issues that plagued the Duncan House test. Hutchinson's solar house included almost twice as much glass as the "orthodox" house (22.5 percent of the wall area, versus 12 percent). Both were double-glazed; overhangs and sill heights matched. Period photos show the two houses stripped to their essential elements: walls, windows, roof slabs. Here was the degree-zero solar house, even more reductive in its expression than the prefabricated solar houses by Keck or Oren Thomas discussed above.

The results were inconsistent, and Hutchinson presented his conclusions in a manner that was particularly difficult to understand and littered with disclaimers. In the first trial, nine weeks in winter with no supplemental heating, the solar house saved 9 percent, as measured in degree-hours. These positive results were reported in newspapers nationwide, but Hutchinson warned the figures were "untrustworthy" and it would be "dangerous" to generalize.[29] For the second trial, the same period a year later, electric heaters maintained interior temperatures of 70°F. This time the solar house required 16 percent *more* supplemental heat than the orthodox house. Hutchinson again qualified the results; he emphasized that the weather had been "extreme" during the winter period, and noted that the solar house had saved 7 percent in the fall.[30] Careful readers could detect overheating, even in winter. When Hutchinson finally wrote an omnibus conclusion for a major architectural journal, he emphasized that large, double-paned, south-facing windows would admit more heat than they would lose in most American cities.[31]

Hutchinson's methods could be criticized and his conclusions interpreted in various ways. Engineer Maria Telkes complained that there had been no attempt to cover the glass at night (which would have improved the solar house's performance). Poor insulation may have posed another significant problem. Still, in a major summary to the engineering community, Telkes uncritically broadcast the most negative of Hutchinson's results—the solar house's 16 percent higher fuel bill in an extreme period—and called this finding "surprising," as if it applied generally.[32]

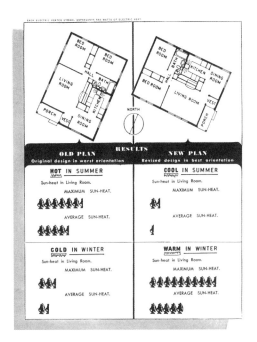

Illustration by Henry N. Wright, 1943. *House Beautiful* (September 1943)

Opposite: Ramirez House by Henry N. Wright, Milford, Pennsylvania, 1943–44. Interior glass removed. Photograph by Tom Solon

The study "must have disappointed" Libbey-Owens-Ford, as historian Frank Laird has noted, and Hutchinson ended up having a "skeptical view of solar energy."[33]

Through the late 1930s and the 1940s, Henry N. Wright found a notable middle ground between the solar house's promotion and his own effort to bring some technical sophistication to the architectural movement. He constructed an early heliodon at Columbia University in 1936 and collaborated with his father on solar studies for a Garden City–type housing project. (The father, also Henry, is well known for planning housing projects Sunnyside Gardens and Radburn with Clarence Stein. The son sometimes used his middle initial to distinguish himself from his father.) Together, with Columbia students, they investigated the spacing and orientation of buildings based on solar access. The elder Wright, in the last year of his life, recognized the heliodon as a major advance for town planning:

> "Of course, it is possible to make drawings in plan, section or perspective on which the angle of the sun may be plotted for different seasons and hours, but this is a laborious process which few architects would consider worth the time and effort. The use of the 'sun machine' has made possible a quicker and more simplified technique."[34]

Based on these studies, Henry N. Wright earned a grant from the John B. Pierce Foundation to study orientation and glazing strategies for individual buildings and facades. "In modern architecture," Wright argued, "the use of larger glass areas, often [leads to] disastrous results in terms of heating bills . . . these may be avoided only if windows are faced so as to receive a generous portion of winter sunshine." He continued:

> Full agreement as to solar orientation's objectives is still to be reached. There is, however, a growing realization that insolation is a mixed blessing: that the advantages of plenty of sunshine in buildings in the wintertime are equaled, if not exceeded, by its disadvantages in the summer.

It is striking to note how precisely Wright's concerns here corresponded to those being addressed by Fred Keck at the same time, though Keck proceeded more confident that proper orientation and shading would save energy. A building in New York City, Wright concluded, should include ample south-facing glass with shading, and that a west-facing orientation was "unquestionably the worst." He did not quantify solar gain, but developed "cotangent diagrams" that provided a new method of visualizing solar geometries, and two-dimensional shading diagrams like those Keck had devised at about the same time. Wright published these conclusions

and diagrams in considerable detail in *Architectural Forum*.[35] Ken Butti and John Perlin later concluded that "Wright reached thousands of readers with this message."[36]

Wright then expanded this study for a wider audience of homebuyers. He compared a typical small house plan in its "worst orientation" to the "best orientation," rotated to face south-south-west with some windows relocated. A chart showed the bad example would suffer nine times as much summer heat, but four times less winter heat, than the good plan.[37] This chart appeared in *House Beautiful* along with a column where Wright gave some rules of thumb, such as: "the solar radiation on a south wall is about five times as great in the winter as in the summer."[38] Never before had the general public been offered this level of solar literacy, and these efforts helped trigger important and enduring changes in the practice of architecture. For instance, *Architectural Record* published its first "Time-Saver Standards for Solar Geometry" in 1946.[39]

Wright's 1943–44 Ramirez House (Milford, Pennsylvania), demonstrated the challenges of using solar principles in a renovation project. The original building, a rustic summer retreat called Golden Spring, had been constructed in 1910 and suffered a serious fire in 1942. Wright made major changes to the original structure, including the removal of most of the second

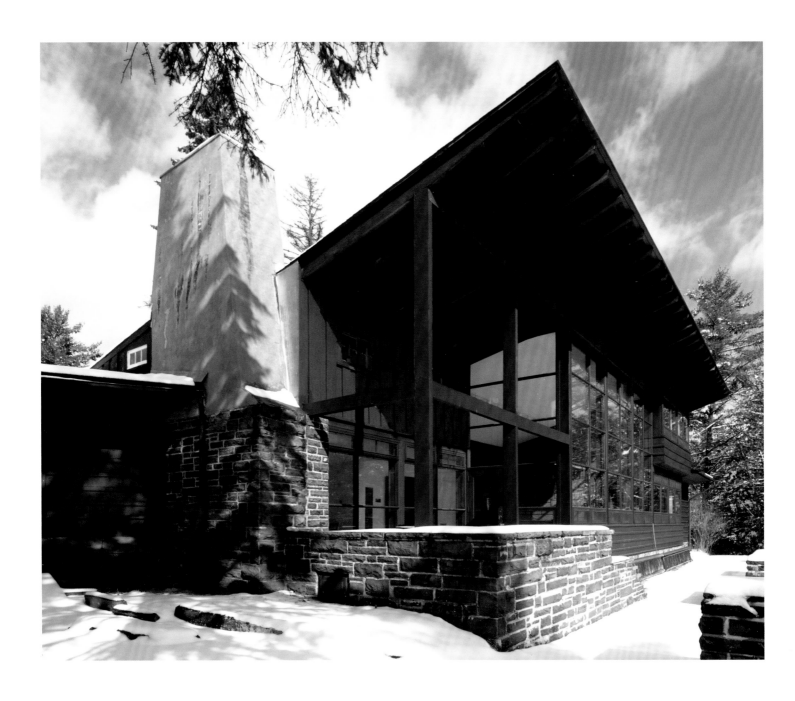

floor. But he did not attempt to alter the plan's most significant limitation: its main wing faced southeast. He created a "huge window wall" for this space and claimed "the sun has been harnessed to assist the traditional heating plant."[40] Even with insulated glass, Wright realized the eighteen-foot window wall would be cold at times and create downdrafts. To address this issue, he designed a novel "winter window," which consisted of an additional set of inner windows installed eight inches behind the main glass section, in the lower-third of the window wall—a kind of double-skin facade. This would funnel the descending cold air to pass over radiators he placed below and concealed. The extra layer of glass, which provided some passive heating effects in the cavity, was removed in the summertime, and the projecting roof created a 62-degree shading angle to address summer overheating.

Wright designed the Ramirez house at the same time he and George Nelson wrote the best-selling *Tomorrow's House* (1945), which included a chapter entitled "Solar Heating." The section mostly explained first principles of orientation and solar geometry, and included an interior photo of Keck's Duncan House with sun covering the living room floor. ("Notice how far into the room the low winter sun penetrates, bringing heat that cuts fuel bills substantially.") Then a new idea suddenly emerged—the concept of thermal mass—which Nelson and Wright called "the reservoir principle." *Tomorrow's House* includes what may be the first discussion of thermal mass in twentieth-century architecture:

> People who live in all-wood houses of the solar type have found that they tend to become overheated while the sun is shining and to cool off almost instantly when the sun goes behind a cloud. In houses with concrete floors the reverse happens. The floors absorb much of the solar energy while the sun is shining, and it may be hours, or even all night, before the floor cools down . . . This happens because the massive concrete has a greater capacity than wood for absorbing and storing heat.[41]

Although the Ramirez house included a massive stone base and fireplace, it had thin wood floors above the ground. When architect Joanna Kendig analyzed the structure in 2000–2001 she found it "does not contain sufficient thermal mass to balance its large window wall." In other words, it overheated at times. (Understanding of optimum mass-to-glass proportions would not exist until the 1970s.) Overall Kendig computed that the solar wing of the house received 12 percent of its energy from the sun. "It is a less-than-perfect solar design when judged by today's standards," she argued, due to its compromised orientation, limited insulation, and (then) inefficient windows.[42] She suggested a number of improvements, starting with new glazing and additional insulation. The Ramirez house was nominated to the National Register of Historic Places as a representative example of early solar design, and restored in 2008–9.[43]

Henry N. Wright also exerted considerable influence as the managing editor of *Architectural Forum* from 1942 to 1949. In the publishing world, only Elizabeth Gordon at *House Beautiful*

Ramirez House by Henry N. Wright, Milford, Pennsylvania, 1943–44. Photograph by Tom Solon

matched Wright's importance as a solar house supporter. Under Wright, *Architectural Forum* documented many major examples and did not shy away from "technical" issues. For example, the George Löf House in Boulder (to be discussed in chapter 6) was strictly an engineering system—not a work of architectural design at all—but Wright gave it a five-page spread, including graphs of data. Likewise, the magazine printed a detailed summary of the IIT report on Keck's Duncan House. When he left his editorial post in 1949, Wright wrote a solar heating primer for the seminal "Climate Control Project" of *House Beautiful* and the AIA.[44]

Above: George L. Rosenberg House by Arthur T. Brown, Tucson, Arizona, 1946. Photograph by Maynard Parker. Maynard L. Parker collection, The Huntington Library

Left: George L. Rosenberg House by Arthur T. Brown, Tucson, Arizona, 1946. *Progressive Architecture* (June 1947)

Opposite: George L. Rosenberg House by Arthur T. Brown, Tucson, Arizona, 1946. Photograph by Maynard Parker. Maynard L. Parker collection, The Huntington Library

Besides Fred Keck and Henry N. Wright, the other major architect to innovate within the solar house concept in the mid-1940s was Arthur T. Brown, who practiced, incongruously, in the desert southwest.[45] He built some of the first examples of an indirect gain system, or sunspace; he created numerous inventive shading devices; and he seems to have built the earliest transpired solar collector. He has been called "Tucson's pioneer of solar design."[46] Brown was probably directly influenced by Keck. He moved to Chicago in 1927 and worked in David Adler's office for fourteen months—possibly overlapping with Schweikher. In 1933, he worked for the Century of Progress Exposition helping to design auxiliary buildings, signage, and fixtures. There is no direct evidence that he met Keck, but he must have visited the House of Tomorrow. Like Keck his innovations are not well understood and little remembered. Brown's work should interest anyone building in hot arid regions today.

Brown seems to have enjoyed reflecting on two profound ironies. First, he spoke of his attempts "to use solar heat in a part of the world where the usual stress is to combat it."[47] And second, he conceded the misplaced economic moment, as he acknowledged: "I did these things at a time when gas was so cheap that people didn't have an interest in solar heating."[48] He does not seem to have been motivated by a deep-seated ideological critique, and in general he did not act the contrarian or the rebel. Rather, the logic of energy conservation apparently appealed to his pragmatic and scientific mind. His interest in solar architecture (like Keck's) began with a legendary "discovery," a happy accident. In 1945, he designed a home in Tucson for "Jardy"

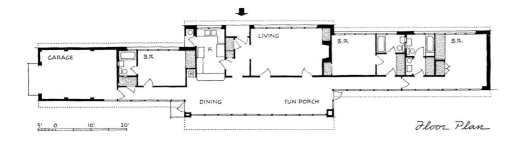

Floor Plan

Jardella. For aesthetic reasons, the client asked that the house be painted black. Later, Brown walked along the south wall and realized how much heat was stored and radiated back into the environment: "I could feel it five feet away . . . and I thought that the next time we do a house, we'll paint the wall inside the hall black so that we won't lose the heat."[49]

He fully developed the black "storage wall" at the Rosenberg House (Tucson, 1946). Brown had surely studied Fred Keck's linear floor plans, and he adopted the same basic premise: a long, narrow building running east-west—he used the term "in a line house"—with ample south-facing glass and shading devices. But Brown inverted Keck's typical orientation and placed the rooms to the north, and the single-loaded corridor to the south. In front of the corridor: floor-to-ceiling glass. Behind it: a concrete block wall, covered in plaster and painted dark, running the full length of the house. At the center of the plan, in front of the living room, the corridor widened to become a dining room and "sun porch," and Brown gave this section a taller roof with more glass to accommodate its depth.

Of course the corridors and sun porch would be heated directly by the sun, but Brown's true intent was to collect heat in the rear wall and radiate it later to the rooms on the north side. Essentially he sought to moderate the diurnal temperature swings in those spaces. This strategy would later become known as an *indirect-gain* system, though that label did not exist in 1946 and Brown did not cite any precedents for his idea. More pointedly, because Brown's concept allowed the corridors and sun porch to overheat and overcool, this represents an early *sunspace* (again a term that was coined later). The Rosenberg House may well be the first example of this strategy anywhere. Brown made the storage wall eight inches thick because he believed heat would move through it one inch per hour, so it would collect heat for approximately eight hours per day and emit it at the same rate each night. Interestingly, though it functioned as a storage wall, Brown also called it a "barrier wall," and said it "enables the owner to be in or out of the sun as the weather—or his pleasure—may dictate."[50] This emphasis on variability appears a striking critical insight, particularly in the late 1940s, when mainstream architecture and engineering practices focused almost exclusively on producing uniform temperatures with mechanical systems.

The system performed well. Temperature readings were collected by the owners on a cool winter day in 1947, showing that the living room remained comfortable while the sunspace overheated:

	10:00 AM	2:00 PM	6:00 PM
Outside (north wall)	50°	62°	59°
Solar wall	94°	102°	81°
Inside (living room)	72°	72°	72°

After the first winter, Brown reported: "It has not been necessary to use the furnace at night, after a clear day, or in the morning, after nine o'clock."[51] Decades later, when Brown was asked if he would change anything in the Rosenberg House retrospectively: "he replied that he might

Victor Hirsch House by Arthur T. Brown, Tucson, Arizona, 1949. *Better Homes and Gardens* (February 1953)

cut down the number and size of the openings in the solar wall to retain more mass; but on the whole, he is pleased with the house's design and performance."[52] The system would have performed even better if the glass had been covered with insulating curtains at night, and if Thermopane had been used. (The glass was single-pane with continuous metal frames.)

Like Keck, Brown recognized the need for control. "Shade is very important on the desert," Brown wrote. "There is, sometimes, a 25°F difference between sun and shade."[53] The Rosenberg House included a system of overhangs consisting of angled metal louvers, an idea he might have borrowed from Libbey-Owens-Ford's 1944 brochure *Solar Houses: An Architectural Lift in Living*. He also recognized that solar houses required natural ventilation and used Keck-style convection vents and hopper doors.[54] And Brown followed Keck claiming that he did not work from prescriptive aesthetic objectives. He remembered a remark from a critic all his life: "Never design in a style. If you have to design in a style, remove everything that makes it a style."[55] Still, Brown's Rosenberg House showed an uncanny similarity to the Sloan House, particularly in the central uplifted roof that reached for the sun. Perhaps Brown believed Keck had created an appropriate expression for the emergent solar house.

In the Hirsch House (Tucson, 1949), Brown refined the storage wall, sloping its base to catch the inclined rays of the winter sun. Period photos show the wall-window geometry in the hallway area working perfectly, and the wall's shape—sixteen inches thick at the base—provided

more thermal mass than a straight wall. (More mass generally translates to more storage, although the relationship is not linear; there are diminishing returns where additional thickness may not make sense.) Again, the plan was one room deep, and the storage wall would provide indirect gain to the north-facing bedrooms behind it. For the living room, however, he abandoned the sunspace idea and designed this room to operate with direct gain alone.[56] "The solar wall worked fairly well, sometimes too well," Brown remembered. "Victor [Hirsch] told me there should be some way to control the amount of heat that was brought in by the wall."[57] After this episode, the architect invested even more creative energy in rejecting solar heat. The Ball-Paylore House, discussed earlier for its plan-geometry, included novel "revolving porches." Likewise, Brown's buildings for the Tucson Chamber of Commerce (1952) and Tucson General Hospital (1963–70) featured absolutely original shading devices which transformed a prosaic need into a major architectural feature.

Brown also made a major contribution to the history of solar architecture with a system which did not admit direct sunlight into the building at all. In 1947–48 he created a "solar roof" system for the Rose Elementary School (Tucson). Architecturally, Brown organized the building with a Bauhaus clarity: three one-story rows of classrooms spaced repetitively north to south. Each building was one-room deep and stretched "in a line" east to west. South-sloping shed roofs gave the profile a broken sawtooth pattern, and each classroom contained a large amount of north-facing glass, excellent for daylighting. Brown used overhangs to create outdoor corridors (reminiscent of traditional *portales*) and to shade the south walls.

The "solar roof" consisted of hollow construction—heavy-gauge aluminum pans, a shallow pan inside a deep pan—that formed parallel air ducts heated by the sun. At the ridge, a horizontal duct with fans distributed the warm air to each room. In winter, this system would preheat outdoor air by 10–15°F. Storage of heat was not provided because the school would only be occupied from 9 a.m. to 3 p.m. A furnace could provide auxiliary heat on cloudy days. In summer, the heated air was exhausted at the ridge, keeping the building cool by convection. In the end the solar roof provided 86 percent of the school's heat in the first ten years of operation, and effectively "kept the Rose School warm in winter and cool in May and September—the two hottest months of the school year."[58] It was the first solar-heated public building in the United States.

The origins of the solar roof are unknown; Brown may have invented this system. (Primary sources are limited, and he did not discuss his influences.) Richard Neutra's Beard House (1934) is a possible source. Here, Neutra designed south-facing cellular steel walls with air vents at the top and bottom. The solar heat would create a convective loop and "minimize heat transmission" through the insulated interior wall. The walls did not capture the heat generated, and Neutra called it a cooling system. If Brown was aware of and inspired by this example he still transformed it significantly. In any case, the solar roof clearly prefigured the transpired solar collector, which remains an effective and popular technology. The Rose School's solar roof worked well for ten years but was removed when the building was expanded in 1958. In discussing the project, *Architectural Record* uncharacteristically swerved into a broader critique of the prevailing trends, giving importance to Brown's creative and critical contribution: "We are building into our structures increasing quantities of mechanical and electrical equipment . . . In a way our progress is almost circular, like the route of a dog chasing his tail."[59]

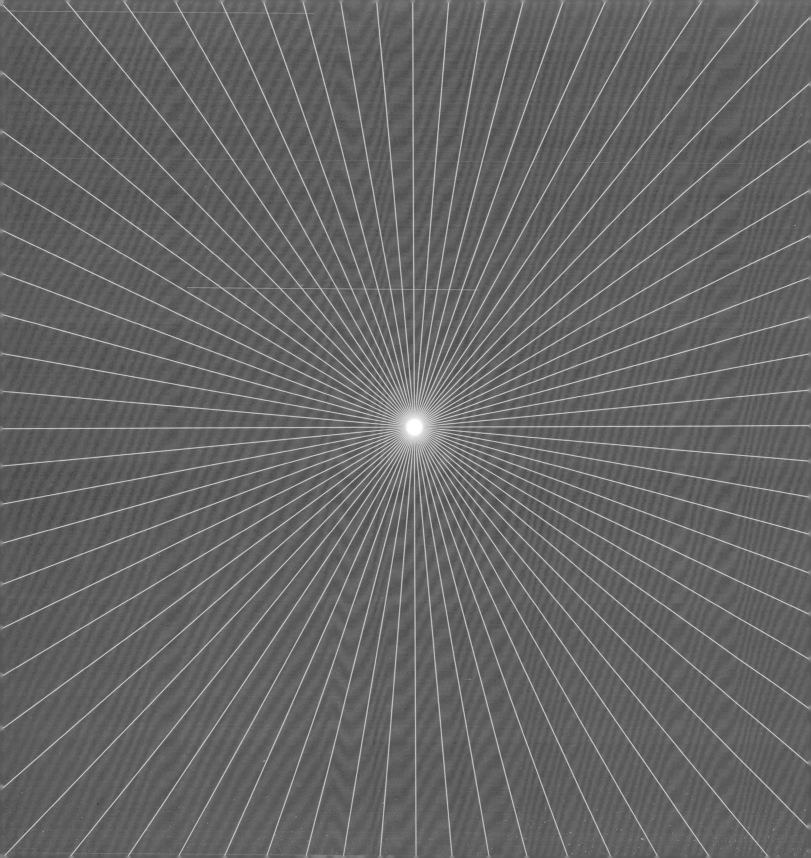

CHAPTER 5

HOYT HOTTEL: A SKEPTICAL INNOVATOR

Nature teases us with a solar incidence on the earth so enormous that we feel impelled to do something about it, and so dilute that we don't quite know how.

—Hoyt Hottel (1954)[1]

At the same time that Fred Keck developed his conception of the solar house using what would later be called "passive" strategies, a group of engineers at the Massachusetts Institute of Technology (MIT) created a different kind of solar house using rooftop collectors and water storage tanks. It was the first sustained and rigorous scientific inquiry into the basic problems of collecting and storing solar energy. Hoyt Hottel, a chemical engineer whose true expertise lay in combustion processes, led the MIT team. Hottel dedicated much of his career to solar heating systems despite the fact that he maintained "an informed pessimism" about the commercial feasibility of these systems to the end.

It is well known that industrialist Godfrey Lowell Cabot sponsored MIT's solar energy research, but in fact Vannevar Bush, MIT's vice president and dean of the School of Engineering, initiated the effort. Bush is remembered as the first director of the Manhattan Project and for shaping military- and industry-related academic research, but not for his role in solar energy. (A major biography does not even mention the Cabot project.[2]) In 1936—prior to Cabot's involvement—Bush wrote a ten-page memo entitled "Power from the Sun" to MIT President Karl Compton:

> The subject of sun power warrants serious study . . .
>
> [We] must ultimately learn to use sun power directly, or else face a gradual increase in the cost of power, and ultimate exhaustion of stored energy in fuels.[3]

Bush did not discuss space heating or building a house, but he did show extensive knowledge of flat-plate collectors, or "heat traps" (used for water heating in California and Florida), and the fundamental scientific issues that needed to be explored. A year later, MIT asked Cabot for a substantial gift, and Bush outlined three major areas of research that MIT was well suited to study: sun engines (to deliver mechanical power); photoelectric cells and thermopiles (to produce electricity); and conversions of solar energy to chemical energy.[4] Again Bush described a flat-plate collector in some detail—almost exactly the collectors that would be used on the first solar house—but no demonstration dwelling was mentioned and MIT's architecture department was not involved. Cabot found the report "very interesting" and in April 1938 gave MIT an endowment worth approximately $650,000. Bush left MIT before the first solar house was built, and thus never participated in the development of his idea, but he remained an interested observer through the 1950s.

Two points bear emphasis here. First, the benefactor, Cabot, did not specify the construction of a solar house, and he initially played a relatively hands-off role in the research. (Later he would show a great enthusiasm for the subject and, at times, attempt to influence MIT's work.) Second, Bush's role marks the first of several significant intersections between the solar house and the Manhattan Project, or the "military-industrial complex" in general. From its beginnings the solar house has included a tension between individual creativity and institutional work. This is related to the "schism" between architects and engineers, though not exactly the same. (Peter van Dresser later complained: "We have a marked tendency to 'attack' the 'problem' of solar construction in the same spirit we set up the Manhattan Project."[5])

Though Hottel ultimately became the protagonist in this story, he earned his role somewhat inadvertently. How did responsibility for the Cabot program fall to a young chemical engineering professor? Hottel had been surprised to be invited to the first meeting to decide how the endowment should be spent. He "sat up all night working" on calculations of the performance of a flat-plate collector: "It turned out that I was about the only person who had any concrete ideas about what we might do . . . So, I was made the rather too young chairman of the solar energy committee that was set up to decide how to spend the income from Dr. Cabot's gift."[6] Hottel would effectively control the endowment from 1938 to 1964, and he consistently sought to maintain "a 50-50 balance" between fundamental and applied research. At one point he labeled the Cabot program "Harness for Apollo's Horses," but the name did not stick.[7]

In February 1939, Hottel described a plan to build "an experimental solar energy research laboratory and an accompanying tank storage system" to collect the sun's heat for space heating.[8] Simply stated, this building would be the first of its kind anywhere. The MIT project was later recognized as "the prototype for most of the . . . systems on the market and in houses today,"[9] and in retrospect that assessment appears perfectly accurate. Certainly the breadth and depth of the solar house movement in the 1970s—including the solar White House—would not have been possible without the efforts begun by Hottel in 1939.

Did Hottel build the first "solar house"? This is a question of semantics. Though the MIT project predated Keck's Sloan House by a year, it was not labeled a "solar house" at the time, either in publicity or in any internal documents. In fact, Hottel's structure was not an actual dwelling, as it contained only two rooms: an office and an instrument room. At MIT it was called Building 34, and its location—on the "back lot" of campus near the steam plant—confirmed its status as a laboratory rather than a showpiece. Beyond semantics, the MIT project did not include the architectural features that came to define the solar house in the early 1940s. In short it was a site for basic scientific research, not an architectural proposition. Architectural "authorship" of the structure is not known, but Hottel probably made the schematic sketches. He called it "a strange-looking little building."[10] By convention it is now called MIT Solar House I, an instance where the label "solar house" has become more inclusive over time.

The experiment had two basic goals: to test various types of flat-plate collectors and tilt angles, in order to gauge their efficiencies and to compare theoretical to actual performance; and to test the long-term storage of heat in a large volume of water, again measuring the tangible results against the mathematical predictions.[11] "Long-term" meant seasonal—heat would be collected in summer and "hoarded away" for the winter. This required an extraordinarily

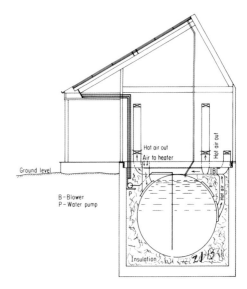

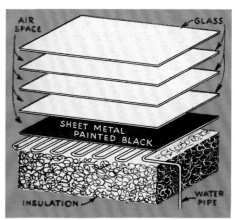

Top: MIT Solar House I, 1939. *Scientific American* (June 1942)

Above: Flat-plate collectors for MIT Solar House I, 1939. *Popular Science* (February 1940)

large tank: 17,000 gallons for a space of only 558 square feet. In a cross-section view, the basement water tank appears almost cartoonishly large in proportion to the house above.

"The house was designed with no consideration for economics at all," Hottel emphasized. He purposely oversized the system "in order to better follow the experiment and check up on what you can do about storing heat in the summer and using it in the winter. Preliminary computations said it wouldn't be feasible, but we wanted to find the invisible effects that went on."[12] The notion of "invisible effects" provides a crucial conceptual bridge between the work at MIT and the experimental work of architects such as Keck. While Hottel's problems generally intersected very little with Keck's problems, they both understood that a building was apt to perform differently than theory would predict, because the interactions were so complex relative to the knowledge of the time.

Fourteen flat-plate collectors, or "heat traps," covered the roof (408 square feet total, about three-quarters of the floor area). Each collector was essentially a shallow box, consisting of three glass plates separated by airspace, a black-painted copper plate backed by copper tubes of water, and 5½ inches of mineral wool insulation. The basic idea was to heat the plate, thereby heating the water while minimizing other heat losses. Later this general type of apparatus was sometimes called "the Hottel collector." MIT I also studied the optimum tilt angle for collectors. Its roof slope (a shallow 30 degrees from horizontal) conforms to practically none of the "active" solar houses that followed. The low slope reflected the goal of summer collection and long-term storage. Virtually all subsequent houses of this type aimed for winter collection and therefore had a higher tilt angle.

The house was well insulated by standards of the time, with 3½ inches of rock wool in the wall and 4 inches of mineral wool in the ceiling. There would be no losses through the floor. Hottel estimated that the structure corresponded to a moderately insulated six-room house, in terms of heat required per volume. When heat was needed, it would be transferred from the storage tank to the interior spaces by blowing room air directly over the surface of the metal tank. The system as a whole, with fans moving air and pumps circulating water, could not operate without a fair amount of power. Due to the need for major electrical and plumbing equipment, this scheme would later represent an "active" system, though that language was not used until the 1970s.

The structure was built from June to October 1939, and the systems caused difficulties during construction. The original cost estimate was $6,000, but by June that number had ballooned to more than $10,000,[13] and there were further overruns during construction due to problems installing rock wool insulation around the tank.[14] Daniel Barber has concluded that the system costs were "three times the initial cost of a comparable fuel-based system, not including operational maintenance."[15] Hottel later recalled an additional problem:

> At solar noon on the first day of occupancy of the new structure Dr. Woertz
> came running, red-faced, to tell me the roof did not face south! I thought he

had gotten mixed in converting Eastern Standard to solar noon. No; the Institute's Buildings and Power Division had put the compass correction on backwards. We were chagrined but of course able to allow for the error.[16]

The building was misaligned by about seven degrees. The structure was finished by November, and MIT's publicity image shows research associate Byron Woertz (who had just completed his doctorate as Hottel's student) standing on the roof inspecting a collector. It appears to be the only surviving photograph of the structure.

The system worked well, keeping the interior spaces at 72°F throughout the first winter (1940–41) without any auxiliary heating, and eventually for three years. You could call it the first 100 percent solar-heated building anywhere. The electrical energy was not recorded. The "heat traps" collected enough solar heat that the tank registered 195°F by September, and after a winter of extraction the water measured 127°F.[17] Hottel later called the performance "satisfactory." The method remains perfectly serviceable today. You could replicate MIT I and there is little doubt it would work well. With modern insulation and tight construction, and a lower interior set point, the system could be downsized considerably, or the floor plan enlarged. (Researchers in Toronto successfully completed an MIT I–inspired project in 1960.[18])

The project established the basic scientific principles of flat-plate collection. In general the experimental data correlated well to the calculated predictions (within 1 percent). Indeed, when major discrepancies occurred, the team discovered an error in the Weather Bureau's method for measuring insolation with pyrheliometers.[19] Additionally they concluded a collector loses efficiency with greater temperature differences between the absorber plate and the outside air. Much additional detail is found in a 1942 paper by Hottel and Woertz, which is universally considered the first definitive paper on flat-plate collectors.[20] In it they established the first calculation method for heat collection that accounted for reflection, absorption, and conduction loss, allowing for various numbers of glass layers and angles of incidence, various air and water temperatures, and of course solar intensity.

Misinterpretations of MIT I later frustrated Hottel, particularly that the main conclusion was understood to be that long-term (seasonal) storage was too expensive. Fifteen years after the structure was built, Hottel still felt compelled to inform his peers: "No claim was made that such storage was economically sound, and economic analyses of the time in fact produced a firm conclusion that long-time storage was not practical." And he lamented that the project "unfortunately served to overemphasize, in the public eye, the importance of heat storage in space heating."[21] The true importance of MIT I is now easy to perceive: its schematic essence of roof-mounted flat-plate collectors and water and storage tanks was found in thousands of solar houses in the 1970s and '80s, and those designs relied on equations and fabrication details developed by Hottel and his team.

Hottel was skeptical by nature and especially fearful of creating false expectations about the promise of solar energy. He often complained that MIT's reputation would be tarnished by too-optimistic media reports. In a May 1940 lecture at Harvard, just as he had begun collecting data at MIT I, Hottel gave powerful and witty voice to his internal doubts. To capture the full flavor of Hottel's "mood" requires quoting at length:

> A study of the literature on solar energy utilization has convinced me of the existence of an unalterable tradition among speakers and writers on the subject. One must always begin such a discussion by expressing the earth's reception of solar energy in units no one has thought before to use, the more startling the better. In keeping with this tradition, I shall mention a few old figures and add my own. The earth and its atmosphere intercept the equivalent in energy of 21 billion tons of coal per hour; six million tons per second; the equivalent in three minutes of the annual American energy consumption of about one billion tons; energy at a rate sufficient each year to melt a layer of ice 114 feet thick; on an acre at noon the equivalent of the discharge of a healthy stream from a garden hose spouting fuel oil instead of water.

> Having made the conventional beginning, let me add what many of you know; that figures such as these are almost irrelevant to the problem of practical utilization of solar energy. They have attracted uncounted crank inventors who have approached the problem with little more mental equipment than a rosy optimism. Now, an informed pessimism is sometimes the healthiest mood in which to approach an engineering problem; and I want to use a little space in an endeavor to put you in that mood. Consider a solar power plant utilizing one acre of land, and operating on the principle of conversion of solar energy to heat in steam used to run an engine. There is incident at noon, normal to the sun's rays and outside the earth's atmosphere, 7400 horsepower of solar energy. On a clear day, of this quantity about 5000 horsepower arrives at the earth. Allowing for the efficiency of collection of the sunlight as heat in the working fluid to be used in the engine, the quantity drops to about 3300 horsepower. Utilizing the highest achieved efficiency of conversion of solar heat to useful power (results of Dr. Abbot's experiments), the horsepower output drops to 490. These calculations have so far all been on the assumption of normal incidence of the sun on the collector systems. To achieve this the collector must be mounted to turn with the sun and must be far enough from its neighbor not to shade the latter in morning or afternoon. Introducing a ground coverage factor of one-third to allow for this, the output is cut to 163 horsepower. But this figure applies only to the hours when the sun shines

with full intensity. Converting to a 24-hour basis of operation on clear days in summer in Arizona, the output drops to 83; or in winter to 46 horsepower; or for the year to 68 horsepower. Passing on to the average year of New York weather, the output is down to 30 horsepower. Even if one stops at a reasonably attainable value of 50 horsepower in Arizona, that figure is 1/150th of the original 7400 horsepower.

For rough orientation as to the meaning of these figures, suppose the possibility of a 50 horsepower steady output from an acre in Arizona be accepted. To evaluate this power, let it be assumed that electric power can be produced in a large modern steam plant at a cost of 0.6 cents per KWH, or $53.00 a kilowatt year, making the output of our one acre worth $1900 per year. In the absence of knowledge of labor costs, maintenance, etc., one can only guess the capital value of such an output. Capitalization at 15 per cent is almost certainly overoptimistic, and even that yields but $13,000 to spend on the entire plant, or about $2.60 per square yard. Since the ground coverage is but one-third, $8.00 are available to build each square yard of reflectors, mounts, and accessories. The result is one so often encountered in engineering projects: indecisive. It may be possible to build a plant for such an amount; much more exact knowledge of performance and costs is necessary than was at hand in making the above rough estimate. What I have particularly wanted to emphasize by this preliminary consideration is perfectly obvious to the engineer, namely, that solar power is not there just for the taking!

He concluded by calling for a long-range program of fundamental research which should be "divorced almost completely for the time being from any considerations of a practical nature."[22]

World War II interrupted MIT's work, but Hottel found that time had allowed some "conclusions to gel." When he returned he decided to "enlist" the Department of Architecture in the project because, he recalled: "Solar houses were not just problems in economics. They had to be lived in, and architects were better at this than engineers."[23] Nothing in Hottel's direct experience at MIT I would have prompted such a conclusion; nobody criticized the project for its architectural deficiencies. Hottel, then, must have been attuned to the larger "solar house" trend and felt compelled to participate. Most immediately, the *Boston Globe* had run a short feature on the Green's Ready-Built project by Keck in June 1945. Within a week, the newspaper received "so many queries" from readers that they asked Hottel and others at MIT whether a solar home was practical in New England. (Hottel did not comment specifically on Keck's work but reiterated what had been learned at MIT I.)[24] Just a few weeks later, Lawrence B. Anderson joined Hottel's team from the Department of Architecture, and Hottel told Cabot of plans to build a house which would be used temporarily as a laboratory and then sold on the market.[25]

Hottel's other major initiative after the war would ultimately supersede the first. A new focus on economic feasibility meant that long-term storage would be cast aside; the next house would collect and store enough heat for twenty-four hours. Then, in October 1945, Maria Telkes proposed a wholly original idea. (Telkes had been hired by Hottel as a research associate for the Cabot project in 1939.) In a detailed report, she advocated placing containers of storage material directly behind a vertical south-facing glass wall.[26] The concept possessed a beautiful simplicity, with no expensive underground tank or plumbing systems, only a few fans for air movement. Hottel must have agonized; would he forsake the proven technology of flat-plate collection, for which he was world's leading authority? He replied that "the idea looks very good, and Dr. Telkes' contribution may make a big difference in the outcome of our project."[27] Excitement at MIT rallied around Telkes's storage wall concept, but the engineers believed this idea needed to be studied in isolation from the architectural issues. Hottel said: ". . . we came to the conclusion that we did not, after all, know enough to build a house for occupancy without some preliminary experiments, if the new southwall storage idea was to be embodied in the plans."[28] It would be a full decade before MIT would build a house specifically to be marketed to the public.

As it developed, MIT II would not embody exactly what Telkes had proposed. She had suggested a house heated by a uniform "wall" of containers of Glauber's salt behind south-facing glass. Glauber's salt is a "phase-change material," meaning it melts and solidifies at an advantageous temperature during heating and cooling. This process—known as heat-of-fusion—captures and releases large amounts of energy. In theory, Glauber's salt holds eight times the amount of thermal energy as water (per volume). Three to four average days of solar gain would be contained. Instead, the project team wanted to test different storage strategies, which led them to create seven thermally isolated "cubicles" of identical footprint and glazing area. The structure, built between September and December 1946, was even less a "house" than MIT I. Hottel later called it "nothing more than a series of parallel cubicles in which different experiments on heat storage could be carried out simultaneously; it was an unoccupied building."[29] Essentially it appeared as a modest shed with clapboard siding and large sheets of south-facing glass, though curiously it was given an honorific location on Memorial Drive. A newspaper described it as "a queer-looking, one-story structure on the Cambridge bank of the Charles River."[30]

The cubicle concept allowed simultaneous tests where many variables could be studied, promising to "concentrate seven years of research in one year."[31] One compartment had no storage wall and "uncontrolled" solar gain; another had triple-pane glass, as opposed to the typical double-pane. Various types of chemicals and liquids could be contained in one- or five-gallon cans (painted black) to build walls four- or nine-inches thick. Some walls would heat the space by radiation alone, others would have forced convection. At night the glass would be

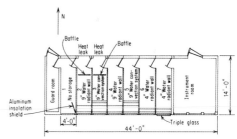

MIT Solar House II, 1946. Acme Newspictures. Author's collection

MIT Solar House II, 1946. *Heating, Piping, and Air Conditioning* (March 1950)

covered by double curtains with aluminum coatings. At one point, the engineers considered placing a thirteen-inch brick wall in one compartment, but apparently this did not occur; it would have been a proto-Trombe wall.[32] Hottel's press release of December 1946 explicated the difference between this and "the usual solar house," which did not provide storage.[33]

The MIT team—Telkes excepted—quickly discounted Glauber's salt and similar phase-change chemicals. They found the salts would separate and stratify when melted, reducing their efficacy to about the same as water. So the research narrowed to various configurations of water walls, with data collection in 1947–48. The *Boston Globe* reported anecdotal results: ". . . we dropped in to see what goes on when the outside temperature is low but the sun is shining. At 2:30 o'clock the outside temperature was 19 degrees. But in the 'controlled' cubicles the thermometer stood at 68 degrees. The 600-watt auxiliary electric heaters in each, which go on automatically when the temperature drops below 65, had not been on since 8 o'clock that morning." It was 101°F in the uncontrolled cubicle.[34]

Overall the water walls provided 38–48 percent of the required heat, but Hottel was especially disappointed by the large amount of heat lost through the glass: 71–84 percent of the amount collected. "It dawned on me," Hottel recalled, "that I had not taken into account the enormity of leaks in such a system . . . a ten-foot vertical hot chimney sits next to a space which is cold. The buoyancy forces available to push cold air through small leaks are large."[35] The broader lesson—that solar gains are easily offset by a leaky envelope—is uncannily similar to the major conclusion of the 1941 IIT test at Keck's Duncan House.

In the official project report, Albert Dietz and Edmund Czapek included other findings that would have interested future solar builders. All types of storage walls performed better than the "direct-gain" room. A thicker storage wall, of course, collected more heat than a thinner one, but "increasing the thickness . . . does not increase the efficiency proportionately." Also triple-pane glass increased the net solar gain by about 15 percent compared to double-pane. (Combined, these effects meant a 4-inch water wall behind triple-pane glass slightly outperformed a 9-inch water wall behind double-pane.) The global conclusion was to separate collection from storage; with remote storage they projected to achieve 70–130 percent solar heating.[36]

Hottel seems to have interpreted the results too harshly, and apparently disowned the project. (There is no reasonable explanation for his absence as an author on the Dietz/Czapek paper.) For all of Hottel's attention to economy, it is especially curious that the costs of these systems were never compared to the savings.[37] Later he consistently minimized the project, in one case reducing the findings thus: ". . . a south vertical water wall is no place to store heat on a cold winter night in New England."[38]

Interest in this technology would resurface in the 1970s and '80s, when David Bainbridge celebrated the MIT project for introducing "what was probably the first water wall in the world." He believed they had achieved "a very good performance for the cost." But he also launched a penetrating critique: "Rather than continue with these experiments . . . the investigators opted to return to costly and unreliable active solar systems."[39] There would be no other research on water walls in the 1950s or '60s. It is fascinating to consider how the course of history might have changed had Hottel responded favorably to the results at MIT II. For their part, Dietz and Czapek believed the findings from MIT II still held relevance in 1977. They reprinted their 1950 paper, practically verbatim, again without discussing the economics.[40]

Hottel's disengagement from MIT II apparently irked the benefactor Godfrey Lowell Cabot, who complained to MIT's president, Karl Compton: "I would like to see this solar energy research entrusted to someone who would give more attention to it." Cabot in fact had been meeting with Maria Telkes, who was embittered by the arrested Glauber's salt experiments. (She said they were not carried out to her specifications.) Cabot was impressed with her "practical" outlook. Compton replied that Hottel was overworked, that the whole Solar Energy program should be reviewed, and "it may be advisable to find a new chairman."[41] Suddenly Hottel found his leadership in jeopardy, and Telkes emerged as a nemesis.

Hottel responded cleverly by returning to his initial postwar agenda, shifting the attention from engineering to architecture. He worked with Anderson to propose a new "Solar House"—the first MIT project conceived as such. It would be a demonstration of livability. In the internal prospectus, Hottel said nothing about the proposed engineering systems but emphasized that it was a Department of Architecture project, with "the objective . . . to indicate how pleasant living conditions can be in such a house."[42] Hottel must have imagined the spectacle of a young attractive family living in a solar house on campus.

Anderson decided that the solar house should be a student project, and he developed a competition brief for a 600-square-foot house that would be "available to some MIT student veteran and his wife." The new house would be constructed adjacent to MIT II on Memorial Drive. The initial program called for *both* a storage wall behind the glass (concrete, masonry, or water) and flat-plate collection: "The architectural problem is that of reconciling the form of this collection and storage equipment to the usual and familiar requirements of a small dwelling without sacrifice to either."[43] At some later point (records are spotty), the project was redefined in two important ways. First, a significant architectural constraint: MIT III would be renovated in-place from the shell of MIT II. Second, the storage wall seems to have been dropped in favor of flat-plate collectors, surely Hottel's imperative.

J. Frank Haws won the student competition in late 1947 and developed the plan in detail through 1948. His design accepted the simplicity of the box, and capped it with a distinctive A-shaped roof narrower than the house itself. The steep collector angle (57 degrees) was supplied by the engineers, but Haws added the novel idea to cover the front flat portion of roof and overhang in aluminum, which would reflect additional radiation up to the collectors. Haws's most sophisticated design work appeared in the reorganization of the south facade for direct gain. He computed the optimum ratio of south window area to total heat loss area (1:7) and designed a ribbon of triple-pane insulated glass with appropriate shading. He showed by calculation that the south windows would provide 41 percent of the seasonal heat requirements, and he added mass to the floor to promote "increased heat lag" and prevent daytime overheating.[44] For the honor of being the first person in history to realize a project marrying architectural design and a mechanical solar heating system, Haws earned a $50 prize. (He later partnered with Oscar Stonorov for fifteen years, but apparently did not design another solar house.) Haws's final construction drawings were dated October 1948, and the project was built by December.

MIT III immediately attracted nationwide attention. It was "promoted and received as an unmitigated success," and the house "caught on as an icon of fuel-efficient living," according to Daniel Barber.[45] Numerous press reports highlighted the domestic life of the residents (third-year student Harry Reid, his wife, June, and son, Toby) and the interruptions to their life from passersby and the researchers. Harry became an educated and charismatic spokesman for the

MIT Solar House III, 1948. Courtesy MIT Museum

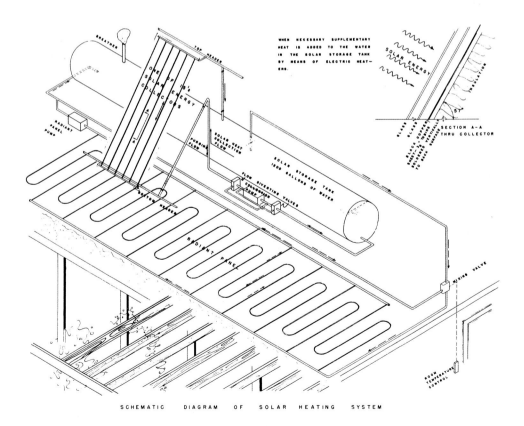

solar house. A lengthy full-color feature in the *Saturday Evening Post* also took a larger view of energy use, and conveyed a sense of consequence:

MIT Solar House III by Frank Haws, 1948. Courtesy MIT Museum

> On its performance might depend the feasibility of mass-production solar houses, a development which would greatly reduce our present annual fuel consumption—not to mention our staggering national fuel bill.[46]

Hottel foresaw the positive publicity, and again sought to temper enthusiasms: "It is not now presumed that solar heating will be economically feasible in a climate as cold as that of New England, but the results should serve to indicate under what conditions of climate solar heating is competitive with fuel oil, gas or coal."[47]

Hottel's system at MIT III in many ways functioned like the system at MIT I, though the storage tank was downsized considerably and moved to the A-frame attic. Water again served as the circulation and storage medium; Hottel contemplated nothing else and by this time he had managed to effectively exile Maria Telkes from the project. Again the design included about 400 square feet of collectors for about 600 square feet of interior space. The 57-degree tilt angle was selected to face the midday sun in mid-November and mid-February, and it was recognized that a variation of 8 degrees each way "makes little difference." For the first time, the team proposed "a convenient rule of thumb" for collector tilt: the latitude plus 15 degrees.[48] In a new twist, the insulated 1,200-gallon tank would feed radiant panels in the ceilings below, rather than producing hot air. There were no ducts or fans.

"The house is basically a compromise between theory and practice," *Architectural Record* concluded, because it did not attempt 100 percent solar heating.[49] The system would accommodate 90 percent of the conditions in a typical Boston winter; an economic analysis had figured an "oversize" system would be too expensive. To account for the extreme cold spells, electric immersion heaters were placed in the tank. One team member later criticized that the storage tank was "poorly located in the attic" and it was not designed to encourage temperature stratification in the water.[50] Another noted that locating the storage within the living space would save an additional 16 percent, but "this improvement, however, is not wholly available because the storage heat loss will add heat to the living space at a time that coincides with an already over-satisfied thermal condition."[51] The system later struck Bruce Anderson as inefficient overall because only 30 percent of the solar radiation which struck the collector was eventually used for heat.[52]

At MIT III the system's performance was mixed. "During one of the best days, March 2, nearly half a million Btu were stored. This would take care of two sunless days with the outside air temperature at about 30°F."[53] Overall the Reid family was heated 76 percent by the sun in 1949–50 and 75 percent the following winter, but there had been plumbing problems. In 1951–52, with those problems fixed, the performance improved to 82 percent.[54] It never achieved the 90 percent for which it had been designed. Just as Haws had predicted, a substantial portion of the house's heat came directly through the south windows. Hottel's doctoral student Austin Whillier found the south windows contributed 42 percent of the heat gained in the winter of 1950–51, but he then qualified this finding: ". . . in actual fact much of this energy is wasted because it causes overheating of the house."[55] The next season, Whillier changed his computation method and insisted the windows only contributed 11 percent toward the heating load.[56]

The data from the collectors proved to be "in substantial agreement" with calculations, according to Hottel.[57] Therefore the project validated further the equations he had published in 1942, and it cemented his status as the world's leading authority on flat-plate collectors.[58] In the end it appears Hottel executed a brilliant subterfuge, using the architecture department and the Reid family to create an attractive Trojan horse which would accommodate his experiment and distract from controversies about his leadership.

MIT III remained in operation until a fire in the attic in December 1955. An electrical wire for one of the auxiliary water heaters began to smolder. Firefighters responded to the smoke by destroying the roof, and fire erupted when fed by oxygen. The house could not be saved. Hottel, a combustion expert, immediately wrote a six-page memo to the MIT administration. He found "no evidence that the [solar heating system] would have contributed to the fire, and uncovered no weaknesses which should affect the design of the next house."[59] In fact the fire barely interrupted MIT's momentum. The "next house," MIT IV (to be discussed in chapter 7), was already on the drawing boards at this time.

"We conclude," Hottel said in 1950, "that solar-heated houses in New England must be unusually well insulated, or the collector must be larger or most efficient. All these things, if they can be achieved at all, involve tremendously increased building costs. The problem is not easy." He said he thought solar houses would become feasible in about ten years.[60] MIT III had cost $22,000 (including furnishings but not land), though this figure was not disclosed at the time. By comparison, new tract homes in the Boston area, with land, ranged from $6,600 to $10,000.[61] There is no evidence that Hottel and his team performed a full cost-benefit analysis for MIT III. This is, again, difficult to understand given the program's acute rhetorical emphasis on economics. Such an analysis would be tremendously informative, because Hottel never clarified what he meant by "feasibility" in terms of payback period, system lifespan, maintenance costs, future energy costs, and so on. Lawrence Anderson gave some broad context to these issues when he later reflected on MIT III: "At that time the price of heating oil was very low; it would be impossible to make solar heating pay off economically." But, he said, "we knew that it was a hedge against the future."[62]

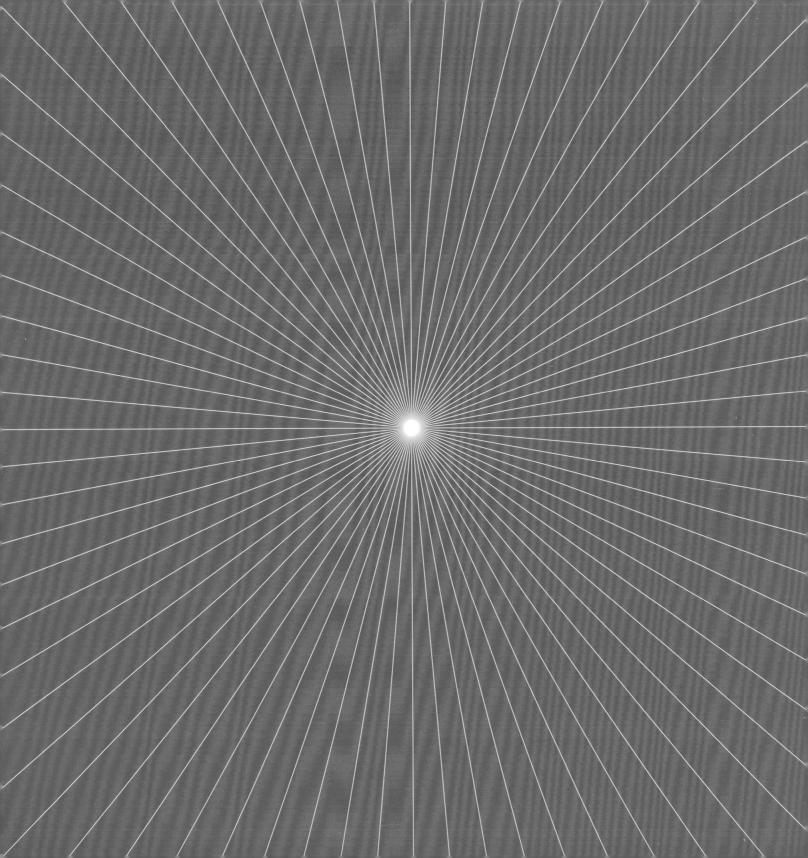

CHAPTER 6

TWO OPPOSED ATTITUDES: THE SCHISM

By the late 1940s the nascent solar house movement had produced two competing concepts: the architects' type, where windows admitted solar heat, and the engineers' concept, which used mechanical "heat traps" and storage systems. A newspaper noted that "the engineering approach to solar houses clashes head on with the architectural concept," but forecasted that "a new type of architecture" might emerge if solar architects and engineers could work together[1]

The architects' view was nicely summarized by the Libbey-Owens-Ford pamphlet "Solar Houses: An Architectural Lift in Living," which articulated three fundamental principles: orientation, large windows, and sun control.[2] The engineering position could too be summarized in three points:

> To have a sun-heated house, you must solve three problems. First, find a way to trap the sun's heat—or a sizable amount. Second—far more difficult—find a way to *store* peak heat for use at night and in bad weather. Third, do these things with apparatus not too complicated, too bulky, or too expensive.[3]

At times, the gulf between architects and engineers appeared quite wide. When Fred Keck visited MIT in 1950, he apparently did not know of *any* of the MIT projects (I through III); Hoyt Hottel remembered this clearly decades later.[4] Conversely, engineers criticized the overheating problems often experienced in architects' solar houses.[5] One engineering publication spoke almost disdainfully of "the commonly referred to 'solar house' . . . buildings with large sun-facing window areas but no collectors per se or storage facilities."[6] At this early stage of the solar house's development there was little communication between the two disciplines and therefore almost no movement toward what might be called integrated design.

The solar house movement therefore helps to illuminate an important historical issue, which Sigfried Giedion famously called "The Schism Between Architecture and Technology." The discipline of architecture, in this view, excludes "technical" issues, which are to be solved by engineers. Giedion identified the origins of this schism in the French academic system, specifically Napoleon's 1804 creation of the École des Beaux-Arts (for architects) apart from the École Polytechnique (for engineers): ". . . two opposed attitudes, each extreme and each represented by an official institute."[7] Giedion and many others, from Labrouste to Le Corbusier, believed the schism to be a tremendous problem for architects, who were at worst reduced to the trivial role of decorating surfaces. Certainly the lack of technical innovation in *Your Solar House* represented one tangible consequence of the schism.

Significantly, Giedion formulated his notion of the schism in 1938–41, just as the solar house movement emerged, and just as a larger discourse acknowledged the rapidly growing sophistication of modern buildings. Paul Zucker presciently argued: "The organization of the highly integrated complex of technical, social and artistic problems which a modern building or group of buildings necessarily represents, can be achieved only by teamwork."[8] (This discourse would lead to the rise of "systems thinking" in the 1950s.) Because of its complexity and small scale, the solar house would eventually provide a perfect opportunity to innovate via interdisciplinary teamwork. But in the 1940s, the schism remained a powerful burden. In terms of expression the principle question became: Is the solar house a machine or organism?

The early work of George Löf highlights some problematic effects of the schism. Löf, a chemical engineer, had been a graduate student of Hoyt Hottel during the MIT I experiment and had examined data from the house. In 1943 at the University of Colorado, Löf established a solar house program of his own, and then found substantial funding from the U.S. War Production Board. Fuel shortages were a military concern, and Butti and Perlin noted the irony that World War II interrupted one solar program—MIT's—while creating another.[9] An engineer working with the agency, Kenneth Miller, had conceived a new type of flat-plate collector, consisting of overlapped glass plates encased in a box with a glass cover, and Löf set out to explore this type of "heat trap" as a method for space heating using air, rather than water, as the circulation medium. They began with bench-scale experiments using lamps, then in 1944 Löf and his team built a larger collector on the roof of a campus laboratory building. After positive results from these tests, Löf decided to place collectors on his own home, a nondescript "five-room bungalow" in Boulder. Löf reported:

> The three principal purposes of the Boulder solar house were to:
>
> 1. Determine with what success a solar heating system of this type could be installed and used in an existing house heated by conventional means.
>
> 2. Ascertain and eliminate the operating problems associated with a solar heating system in a typical home, and particularly in combination with a standard heating system.
>
> 3. Measure with as much accuracy as possible under the circumstances actual and potential fuel savings by use of solar energy.[10]

The project, completed in 1945, certainly earned historical significance as the first house heated by a solar-air system. (It was recently called, erroneously, "the nation's first solar-heated home."[11]) It also appears significant in retrospect for its status as a work of engineering alone, without any architectural contribution or even a sense of its absence. Like MIT I, the building was seen as a generic armature to support novel mechanical equipment. (Unlike MIT I, however, this house would be fully inhabited, by Löf and his family.) The quotation above notwithstanding, Löf usually spoke of "solar heated houses" in this period, to distinguish the engineering enterprise from the direct-gain "solar house" being popularized by architects.

The Boulder bungalow carried an obvious constraint: its fixed roof slope of 27 degrees. Löf recognized that a 43-degree tilt would be "optimum for heat *collection*" at this location, "but not necessarily for heat *use* in a house" (his emphasis).[12] He actually would have preferred a 47-degree tilt, inflected toward the lower winter angles, because excess heat would be gathered in fall and spring, and there was no long-term storage. He calculated that the collectors at 27 degrees would be 92 percent efficient compared to the optimum, and he accepted this compromise. The collector area measured about 460 square feet and occupied about one-third of the roof.

Löf and his team designed the collectors to be "produceable on a factory basis, and suitable for installation in a new dwelling without extensive fabrication at the site."[13] (Recall that Hottel had called for "fundamental research . . . divorced almost completely . . . from any considerations of a practical nature" just a few years earlier. Here the funding agency sought applicable results.) The earlier experiments had established the best values for some critical variables, such as the amount of overlap for the plates of glass and the spacing between them.[14] The panes were partially blackened in the area which would lie beneath two other clear surfaces. By this arrangement, air would enter the chamber, pass between the plates, and be heated by as much as 110°F. Löf said the overall efficiency matched the Hottel-type water-circulating collector. The experiments also found that heat recovery in the collectors increased with the air rate, and that nonreflective glass performed much better than ordinary glass.[15] Interestingly, he determined (based on the earliest lab experiments) that wood should not be used to frame the collectors, but in the 1970s he was frustrated "to see that . . . people are still discovering that."[16]

Why would Löf even consider air as a medium for heat transfer? Water can store three thousand times as much heat by volume than air, and Löf understood this physical property well. But he also recognized that most homes already included a system of ducts and fans and therefore hot air produced by solar energy could be delivered directly to the occupants. No extra plumbing systems were required. Automatic controls triggered a conventional furnace when needed. "This was the first time," Butti and Perlin noted, "that anyone had integrated an active solar-heating system with an existing house-heating system."[17] Initially, the system had no ability to store heat for use at night. To give the system a summertime function, Löf designed it to produce domestic hot water when space heating was not needed.

In its first winter, the Boulder house saved approximately 25 percent in fuel consumption, but there had been significant problems of glass breakage due to thermal expansion and leaky air ducts. With improvements the savings approached 50 percent late in the heating season.[18] Löf believed he could achieve 55 percent, and higher numbers in the southwest, but said it was impractical to consider eliminating the furnace. The costs were not relevant, Löf said, due to "much trial and error, meticulous hand labor, excessive instrumentation, and other factors."[19] But in 1947 *Architectural Record* reported that this system, if mass-produced, could cost about $500 and that such an effort could commence within the next twelve to eighteen months.[20] (No mass production would occur until the 1970s.)

In 1945, Löf applied for a patent that described the Boulder house and a few variant features which had not been developed yet. "Solar heating systems," he wrote, "are now recognized as a possible adjunct of future home building." Löf's patent documents describe two types of overlapping-plate collectors in detail: the air-type used in Boulder and a never-built second design which would use fluid as the circulating medium. The patented system included storage in the form of a bin which would be "filled with a heat absorbing and retaining material which preferably is a loose or spaced solid, such as sand, gravel or stacked brick, but which may be a fluid, such as tar, oil, water or the like."[21] In the laboratory, Löf's team conducted extensive tests on the heat-exchange and storage characteristics of gravel beds, with much attention to the size of gravel and resultant spacing. And based on economics, Löf determined the optimum size for a "heat storage bin" to store a single day's collected heat for use at night. Then he added such a system to the Boulder house. In August 1947, two MIT engineers visited Löf on a cross-country solar tour and found workers busy installing a horizontal nine-ton gravel storage system in the basement.[22] Though the problem of glass breakage continued, the gravel storage improved overall fuel savings to about one-third.[23]

Much later Löf characterized the Boulder house system as "the first solar air heating system" and "the first retrofit solar heating system of any kind in the world."[24] But in the nearer term, the issue of architecture versus engineering arose again. When he left the University of Colorado, in 1948, Löf was forced to deconstruct the solar equipment "when Realtors found they couldn't sell the house with its unconventional glass panels."[25] The lack of aesthetic resolution between the traditional architecture and modern machinery seemed troublesome. Löf realized the engineered

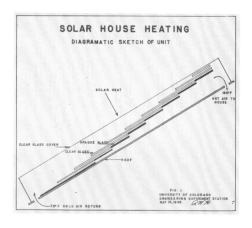

Flat-plate collectors for Löf's "Boulder House." "Solar Energy Utilization for House Heating," report PB 25375, U.S. Office of Production Research and Development, 1946

Opposite: George Löf's "Boulder House" (system installed 1945). Carnegie Branch Library for Local History, Boulder Historical Society Collection

"Dover Sun House" by Eleanor Raymond and Maria Telkes, Dover, Massachusetts, 1948. Author's collection

solar house needed a higher level of design, and he began to envision "a modern house, planned from the start as a solar heated dwelling," as the next logical step.[26]

In 1948, Maria Telkes broke from the confines of MIT and developed the seminal "Dover Sun House," perhaps the most widely published solar house ever. It was intended to be the first 100 percent solar-heated house—with no backup heater. (She remained a research associate at the Institute but no longer participated in the solar house program.) Despite the negative experience with Glauber's salt at MIT II, Telkes still believed that the phase-change chemical could perform well. She had already designed a house which demonstrated "the feasibility of an entirely solar-heated house in the vicinity of Boston."[27]

To realize a Glauber's salt experiment at full scale, Telkes needed to find another source of support. She had previously consulted with Boston architect Eleanor Raymond on a small project; together they approached Amelia Peabody and "presented the possibility of constructing one of the first houses heated by solar energy."[28] Peabody, a sculptor, heiress, and "Proper Bostonian,"[29] decided after some consideration to provide both the site and funding for the project. She was "interested in experimenting," as demonstrated by earlier collaborations with Raymond on the 800-acre Peabody farm in Dover: the Plywood House (1940) and Masonite House (1944).[30] Peabody did not bring a personal commitment to solar energy. She said: "Things just came along to be done and I did them"; and a journalist noted: "There was no particular philosophy back of it, or at least none that she can think of."[31]

It is fascinating to consider Maria Telkes's position at this time, and the larger social history represented by her success. She came to MIT as a Hungarian immigrant, with a Ph.D. in physical chemistry from the University of Budapest, and joined the solar energy project in 1939. During World War II she had successfully developed the Cabot project's greatest practical achievement: a solar still used to produce fresh water for aviators downed at sea. A million were produced, and she personally impressed Cabot. Then, after proposing the storage wall concept for MIT II (a reasonably successful project despite Hoyt Hottel's negative appraisal), her strong opinions alienated her colleagues, and she was effectively removed from the group. But she barely slowed down, and rallied support from another of the most established patrician families of New England to move ahead with her work. This distinctive charisma later earned her the nickname the "Sun Queen."[32] The Dover Sun House would be recognized as "exclusively a feminine project,"[33] and issues of gender give the building a wider importance.

Initially Raymond and Telkes explored a wall of Glauber's salt behind south-facing glass, akin to the water-wall systems at MIT II. Raymond found this type of system too restrictive because it would require a narrow linear plan and block all views to the south. (Here Raymond anticipated the limitations of the Trombe wall before it existed.) She urged Telkes to devise a system of rooftop collectors. A fully developed February 1948 scheme included flat-plate collectors built into

the roof at a tilt angle of approximately 45 degrees. This "Sun-Heated House" would have been a humble structure with a fairly compact floor plan. A combination of gable- and upturned-roof sections would shield the collectors from view. With simple additive forms and clapboard siding, the design resembled the vernacular houses that Raymond loved and documented in *Early Domestic Architecture of Pennsylvania* (1931). In the floor plan a new idea emerged: the heat storage would be placed between the rooms, rather than in an attic or basement.[34]

By August 1948 the architect and engineer decided to position the collectors vertically and place them *above* the south wall of a single-level plan. Why did Telkes return to the concept of vertical collectors? She acknowledged the "optimum winter tilt" would be 60–70 degrees, but she worried about snow accumulation and believed the vertical surface "could even receive additional sunshine reflected from the snow on the ground."[35] By moving the collectors to the attic level, they "could occupy an entire south wall" and offer the architect "as many and as large windows as might be desired."[36] This was the fundamental conceptual breakthrough that produced the Dover Sun House's novel shape.

Still, Telkes's design required 720 square feet of collector area, and this triggered a number of architectural problems for Raymond. First, the south wall needed to be unusually tall and dominated by the collectors, hardly the modest profile she preferred. Moreover, those collectors would appear "forbidding black" if designed with clear glass; in the least they would be too heavy visually. Raymond created a "visor" over the first-floor windows, intended to shade those windows and to "break the sheer height of the south wall of the house and to express the break between the first floor windows and the second floor continuous glass wall." Then she worked with Telkes to specify "Pointex" glass for the collectors, which would reflect the sky without compromising heat transfer. How to reconcile a tall south wall with a one-story house? "The steep shed roof was accepted as the cheapest and simplest form," Raymond said.[37]

Additionally, the plan needed to be long and shallow (72 by 17 feet), a "logical result" of controlling factors, but which Raymond found both difficult and uneconomic. In general terms Raymond handled the south-facing linear floor plan much like Fred Keck, placing a corridor on the north as a climatic buffer. (The influence of Keck can also be seen in the screened ventilating louvers above and below each fixed window.) But Raymond's plan lacked the spatial refinement found in Keck's finer plans; his *Ladies' Home Journal*/MoMA project provides an excellent counterpoint. With all of these difficulties and a strong sense of compromise, Raymond said, "I found the large glass collector plate a hard design taskmaster."[38] Telkes developed a different view: "Her part as the architect was to convert a heating method into an actual home. I resolved not to interfere in any way with her plans as an architect, but to incorporate the heating system into her design. It was a very pleasant task, and the collaboration was unusually perfect and without any misunderstanding."[39] The stark difference in attitude here was, again, symptomatic of the schism.

Telkes's system for the Dover Sun House embodied a new method for collection, storage, and distribution, assimilating techniques from MIT I and from Löf's experiment in Boulder, as well as original ideas. The collectors consisted of two panes of glass (spaced one inch apart), a black sheet of galvanized iron, air circulation space, and an insulated panel at the back. Like Löf, she used air to circulate heat from the collectors to storage. In this case, three "storage bins"—essentially closets within the floor plan—contained five-gallon metal drums of Glauber's salt. The drums were stacked vertically and placed one inch apart to allow proper air circulation. By locating the storage within the living space, rather than in an attic or basement, Raymond and Telkes's scheme offered a major improvement over previous projects, because ambient heat "losses" would not be lost but remain in the control volume. Telkes calculated that a storage tank would lose 25 percent of its average daily solar heat collection, even if insulated.[40]

When solar energy heated the collector plate to 100°F, a thermostat would trigger circulation fans, pushing hot air through ducts to the storage bins, where the salt would absorb the heat and melt. The heat-of-fusion phenomenon would allow the Glauber's salt to store and release much more energy than water or rock. Each room contained its own thermostat and fan. If a room fell below 70°F, its fan would draw air from the space to circulate around the containers of salt, and warmer air would be returned to the space. (Fresh air was supplied "passively" by a leaky envelope, here and in virtually every project before the 1970s.) The only power used by the system was the electricity to run the twelve fans; since no fluids were moved there were no pumps. Raymond's biographer Doris Cole noted: "It was a 'home-made' operation piecing together the parts they could find at that time. In view of this, it is remarkable that the experiment was so successful, both technically and architecturally."[41]

The house required a significant amount of storage space, because Telkes designed the system to capture enough energy for an extreme cloudy cold spell. To determine the amount of storage, Telkes of course needed to calculate the structure's heat losses. These computations reveal, again, a sense of how engineering knowledge has evolved over time. Telkes's procedure was a bit more sophisticated than William Keck's. She used different values for windows in the daytime versus the nighttime, due to "double aluminum painted shades" that would be drawn after sunset. Losses through the concrete floor slab were included, following a new recommendation by the National Bureau of Standards.[42] She then designed the system to hold twelve days' heat requirements (3,500 gallons of Glauber's salt) and the storage comprised about one-twelfth the interior volume of the house. (The attic space behind the collectors represented a tremendous amount of additional excess space. Raymond later suggested an improvement where the collectors could be placed *below* the first level on a south-sloping site.)

In summer, the Dover Sun House's heating system would "work in reverse" to cool the interior, a feature which Telkes described as "something totally new and different."[43] At night, the collector plates would cool by radiation, and the system distributed cool air to the storage bins. Additionally, the galvanized metal roof included airspace for natural convective cooling, so that the attic did not overheat. One day a *Boston Globe* reporter found: "The temperature was 100 degrees in the shade on the north side of the house. But inside 'Sun House' it was a cool, comfortable 75 degrees—without any fans blowing, either."[44]

Popular Science, March 1949

Life, May 2, 1949

Construction costs totaled $45,000, including about $8,000 for the heating system, making Peabody a "patron" in the true sense of that term.[45] Eleanor Raymond recalled her first visit when the house was completed in December 1948: "When the door opened to me on Christmas Eve and I was greeted with a flood of warm air that I knew had to have come only from the sun, that was really thrilling."[46] The Nemethy family (cousins of Telkes) occupied the house and found it operated "comfortably" for its first two winters (1948–49 and 1949–50).[47] They also appreciated the indoor air quality: "The solar house proved easy to keep clean—after all there was no furnace!"[48] (The Reid family at MIT III also mentioned health and hygiene as a benefit.) "It is a new way of living," Telkes wrote, "without the hazards of fire, smoke, ashes and the annoyance of fuel difficulties and fuel bills."[49] By March 1949 she declared the experiment "a success" in newspapers across the country.

No other solar house received as much publicity as the Dover Sun House.[50] *Life* magazine proclaimed it: "World's First Sun-Heated Home," and predicted it "may turn out to be historic."[51] Front-page articles were common in New England newspapers. Some reactions appear humorously overstated in retrospect:

> This is the house we've all been moving toward since we heirs to Promethian [sic] fire have been turning this side and that to the consoling warmth and crept shivering to bed. What compounded miseries men (particularly) have suffered because of the sun's delayed benefactions to householders![52]

The house's unusual appearance also provoked quite a few funny comments. Readers would find it "bears no resemblance to anything that New Englanders have seen in terms of houses," or resembles "a modern house with superimposed chicken coop."[53] Reactions such as these surely stemmed from the building's unusual form and the visual dominance of the collectors, and today it is easy to agree with the sentiment that Raymond did not fully succeed in finding a pleasing or graceful expressive form.

Some news reports framed the Dover Sun House specifically in reference to fossil fuel consumption. Telkes, unlike most engineers, made a special effort to explain the energy economics in terms homeowners would understand. She noted that a "standard house" in the Boston area would burn 1,000 gallons of oil in a winter, which cost $150 a year and demanded a furnace. This could be replaced by 28 tons of Glauber's salt, which would "cost $240 and require nothing but insulated bins."[54] Elsewhere she translated the house's solar production to 140 pounds of coal on a clear winter day. Indeed, conventional fuel sources could be portrayed as burdensome by contrast:

> While other Doverites are filling their oil tanks and coalbins with high-priced fuel, and calling in high-wage servicemen to check their complicated heating mechanisms, Dr. Nemethy's winter precautions will be vastly simplified. All he will do is to scan the skies hopefully for sunny weather . . . Other than that, it will not cost him a cent to heat the house.[55]

This last claim was demonstrably false, as the operational expenses were significant. Daniel Barber has recently revealed that Raymond and Telkes measured the system's fan power and found an "almost quadrupling of electrical costs during the heating season."[56]

The "schism" between architecture and engineering emerged in the subtext of some accounts. *Architectural Record* now explained: "It is not a solar house as the term has been used commonly in recent years to describe a house with large windows. It is the genuine article—a house depending entirely on the sun for space heating."[57] This statement, of course, again implied that the architects' solar house was not "genuine," and it represented an apologia for using the label indiscriminately in previous years. As for the Dover house's "architectural" solar heating, direct-gain from the south-facing windows contributed 25 percent of the total heat gained in a typical winter month.[58]

The system ceased to operate properly in the third winter, as Esther Nemethy described in an interview with Butti and Perlin:

> Both I and my son had very bad colds and there was a snow storm and there was no heating in the house. I called up Mrs. Peabody and said, 'I'm sorry, we love Dover, we love you, we love the house, but I'd rather move out from here unless you install electric heaters or do something![59]

What went wrong? First, the metal containers corroded and leaked, a messy problem that should have been anticipated, but one which could be easily remedied. More seriously, Telkes believed that the Glauber's salt could melt and solidify repeatedly and continuously while retaining its integrity.[60] Just as had occurred at MIT II, the chemical stratified into solid and liquid layers. In order to work properly, these layers needed to mix as they cooled. Degradation also came from the phenomenon of supercooling. As a result of supercooling and stratification, the heat-of-fusion process did not occur, and the Glauber's salt basically performed like water. Telkes believed that these problems could be addressed with different admixtures, and she "saw them as topics for research, not serious impediments."[61] In any case, Peabody removed the solar heating system and replaced it with a conventional furnace in 1953.

Today the Dover Sun House presents many interpretive challenges and sustains multiple readings. You can claim it was the world's first completely solar-heated residence, and you can say with equal conviction that it failed. Some accounts emphasize that the house was self-sufficient for two winters, and some say the experiment was inconclusive. Existing interpretations are colored by gender issues, personal and ideological biases, disciplinary turf battles. Hoyt Hottel—the pessimist—criticized Telkes's design for masking the Glauber's salt problem by oversizing the storage.[62] He became frustrated that the Peabody house was sometimes misunderstood as being affiliated with MIT. (Telkes was correctly identified as an MIT researcher in most reports.) He later complained that Telkes's tendency "to overlook clear evidence of inadequacy of a device . . . and to promise the moon was one of our biggest problems."[63]

For her part, Telkes boldly aligned herself with Henry Ford to discuss the project in a larger context of technological development: "The Dover house is the 'Model T' of the sun-heated houses, and during the next ten years we will probably see just as much improvement as during the first ten years of automobile construction."[64] A key distinction between the automobile and the solar house was consumer demand. For the solar house, the availability of cheaper fossil-fuel sources of heat suppressed that demand, though it was perfectly reasonable for Telkes (and others) to expect a growing market, given the positive publicity for the solar house and the fresh memories of wartime fuel shortages. Indeed, Telkes saw solar energy performing at a larger scale: "I envisage the day when solar heat-collecting shelters, like power stations, will be built separately from the houses . . . One such solar heating building could develop enough heat from the sun for pumping into an entire community of

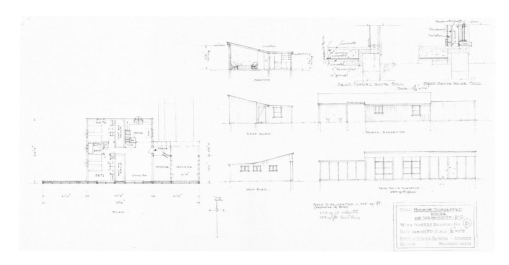

"Sun-heated Minimum House" by Eleanor Raymond and Maria Telkes (unbuilt), 1950. Eleanor Raymond Collection, Special Collections, Frances Loeb Library, Graduate School of Design, Harvard University

surrounding homes."[65] Here Telkes's sweeping and optimistic vision stood in sharp contrast to Hottel's "healthy pessimism."

Raymond and Telkes next proposed a "Sun-heated House" for the Federal Housing Administration (FHA), intended for a middle-class price of $10,000. It included three types. Types A and B attempted to reconcile a squarish floor plan, to minimize heat loss, with a broad facade, to maximize collector area. Raymond preferred a compact plan with the heat source at the center, due to her deep understanding of vernacular houses in the region. Plan C, the logical conclusion, was a two-story house. Clearly Raymond saw the linear plan of Dover as a design issue worthy of revisiting. When Telkes published this project, she chose type B only, and called it the "Sun-heated Minimum House," omitting mention of the FHA.[66] Type B was almost comical in its facade-plan incongruence. The project was never realized, and neither Raymond nor Peabody made any subsequent contribution to the solar house.

The Dover Sun House inspired a few interesting followers. MIT engineer Ranulf Gras planned a house in the Boston suburbs which was meant originally to have a Glauber's salt storage wall behind glass—much like Telkes's original vision for MIT II. Gras joined the Kendal Common cooperative in 1948, and his plan included "one complete elevation covered with black glass panels, which was to face the cul de sac." The design was rejected by the community for being "out-of-place," and Gras dropped out.[67] Finally, in 1956, Gras built the house in the Brown's Wood neighborhood in Lincoln. Although he had still planned to use Glauber's salt as late as 1955 (well after the Dover Sun House had failed),[68] he finally built a wholly original storage wall, two stories tall, consisting of black-painted corrugated metal, a wide airspace with fan-driven convection, and pumice blocks. The system provided approximately 50 percent of the heat required and it operated for decades.[69] David Fixler called it "a very early version of a passive solar trombe-wall house."[70] Even though it did not finally employ Telkes's system, the Gras house adopted the general aesthetic of the Peabody house: a bold two-story wall of panels capped somewhat awkwardly by a sloping roof.

In 1953, in New Mexico, Lawrence Gardenhire attempted to use a system similar to the Dover Sun House, and likewise experienced frustration. In a new aesthetic strategy, this project included tilted flat-plate collectors above the south and west elevations, appearing a bit like a solar mansard roof. As in Dover, solar-heated air was delivered to a storage room full of containers of Glauber's salt, and here too the chemicals stratified and lost their effectiveness. More than three years later Gardenhire reported: ". . . this problem has not been solved and the amount of active chemical is very small. It is hoped that this problem can be solved by proper mixing of the chemicals and a better shape of the storage container."[71] From afar, Austin Whillier (formerly of MIT) complained that the Dover Sun House had led to at least four other instances "where chemical heat storage has been attempted, but found unsatisfactory." He emphasized that Glauber's salt "must be continuously stirred during cooling" and he suggested mounting the containers on a wheel which would be slowly rotated.[72] (Such a device was built in the 1970s by General Electric engineer Carlyle Herrick.[73]) Whillier had also visited a University of Toronto solar house using Glauber's salt in 1954. "Like so many others they were misled," he reported. "They wasted at least six months in fruitless effort in this direction, and finally gave up in disgust."[74]

Telkes continued for years to experiment with additives to improve the chemicals; in fact she worked as late as 1978 on the precise problems encountered at Dover and by Gardenhire.[75] Additionally, among her fifty patents, she invented a shipping storage container using the phase-change material to maintain a constant temperature regardless of extremities in exterior temperatures. This was a military project for shipping Polaris, Minuteman, and Apollo guidance systems.[76] And she remained an expert in solar distillation systems for fresh water. Her contributions to later solar buildings—the Princeton Solar Lab with Aladar Olgyay (1958) and the University of Delaware's "Solar One" (1973)—will be discussed in later chapters. Both used Glauber's salt.

In 1950, MIT hosted a great summit meeting of solar architects and engineers, where participants specifically recognized the need for an integrated approach to the solar house's technical and aesthetic challenges. The six-day "course-symposium," entitled *Space Heating with Solar Energy*, attracted more than a hundred attendees, and the roster reads like a solar house hall of fame.[77] The importance of this event should not be underestimated, akin in architectural history to the CIAM meetings or the Congress for the New Urbanism. While the solar house effort already had a name, a powerfully distilled concept, and significant publicity, in Cambridge it gained a sense of organizational momentum. With internal disputes, alliances, and efforts to establish common ground, it resembled a maturing movement.

1950 MIT Symposium Proceedings (published 1954). Author's collection

The symposium received an unusual degree of press coverage for what was essentially an academic conference. To a wider audience, Hottel adopted his usual role as pessimist. He declared that the participants "are approaching the subject with far greater caution than have some 'heating by the sun' articles in popular magazines." Solar houses had achieved "varying degrees of success."[78] Internally, the symposium revealed a fundamental weakness in the movement at this stage: the inability to quantify these "varying degrees of success." It was difficult to compare an air-gravel system (Löf's Boulder house), a water-water system (MIT III), an air-salt system (Dover Sun House), and a direct-gain system (Keck's Duncan House). Even a few years later, Hottel's top student, Austin Whillier, concluded: "While these houses have yielded much useful information on the particular designs used, they do not permit evaluation of their relative merits."[79]

Although most presenters at the symposium summarized the results of earlier work, a few proposed new ideas. Raymond and Telkes announced their plans for a $10,000 solar house, as discussed above. George Löf presented a model of a ranch-style solar house, designed in collaboration with architect James Hunter, which was "suitable for construction throughout the Southwest, from Texas to Los Angeles."[80] It included an "active" system of flat-plate collection and gravel storage, plus direct gains from a south wall of glass. It would cost about $25,000, and solar would supply 70–90 percent of the heat requirements. The project was not realized in this original form, but it initiated a long collaboration between Löf and Hunter, culminating in the 1956 Löf House.

The head of MIT's architecture department, Lawrence Anderson, also unveiled some provocative designs at the 1950 symposium. Following Telkes, he concluded that heat storage should be located within the house envelope, and he displayed a student project featuring a large cylinder (for heat storage) in the middle of a rectangular open plan—a witty play on Philip Johnson's Glass House. But in a most striking piece of analysis, Anderson created a taxonomy of solar house types, classified by the shape in cross-section, which included a number of hypothetical schemes that suggested sloped walls and earth-sheltering. The goal was to compare the ratio of collecting surface to total envelope.[81] These investigations eventually led to MIT IV, but more immediately to an astounding "idealized house," formed by a circular section sliced by an angular plane. Anderson labeled the idea "Dwelling in Northern U.S. showing hypothetical disposition for maximum solar heating advantage," and he meant it as a serious proposal in presentations to both scientific and popular audiences.[82]

The symposium also launched a side-project that would eventually generate significant effects for the broader movement of climatic architecture. Victor and Aladar Olgyay, working for the MIT School of Architecture, created an exhibit for the symposium called *The Temperate House*, which studied climate control in relation to house-types and construction techniques. The study was later published by *Architectural Forum* and in book form by the U.S. Housing and Home Finance Agency.[83] With further development these studies became the foundation for Victor Olgyay's seminal *Design with Climate* (1963). Eventually, this work was understood as a means of repairing the schism between architects and engineers:

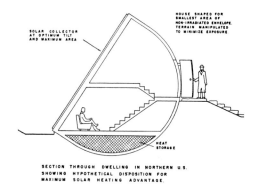

Solar house studies by Lawrence Anderson, c. 1954. Farrington Daniels and John A. Duffie, eds., *Solar Energy Research* (Madison: University of Wisconsin Press, 1955)

Opposite: Libbey-Owens-Ford's "Solarometer" at the 1950 MIT Symposium. Left to right: Lawrence Anderson, Maria Telkes, W. J. Arner (of Libbey-Owens-Ford), Fred Keck. Courtesy MIT Museum

> Much has been written recently of "the two cultures," and of the need to bridge the gap between them. Building scientists may be seen as being on one side of the "gap" and architects on the other, and in this sense *Design with Climate* may be seen as an attempt to bridge the gap by making architects aware of scientific information which can help them to design better buildings, and by helping them to understand it.[84]

Anyone attending the 1950 symposium would have detected the schism as a major theme. In his opening address to the symposium, Hoyt Hottel confronted the issue explicitly:

> In bringing together representatives of the architectural and engineering professions to discuss solar housing, one has the difficult problem of measuring merit in two sets of units: the dollar suffices so long as the subject is solar heating, but if the subject is solar housing there are included such considerations as cleanliness, health, freedom from concern over oil shortages or coal strikes, and aesthetic satisfaction. It is because of these dollar-imponderables that the problem is so much more an architectural than an engineering one. Other things being equal however, the architect who uses the sun to achieve the lower heating cost has done the better job.[85]

Rather than continuing to explain or probe this immensely interesting topic, Hottel unwittingly underlined the problem by moving quickly into a discussion of solar radiation data and collector efficiency, complete with graphs. In general the presentations fulfilled the common stereotype: the engineers overly concerned with data, and the architects unwilling to address technical issues, as if a translator were needed. Even Fred Keck discussed only "the cultural and psychological aspects of living in a solar house," apparently having checked his identity as an architectural engineer at the door.[86]

Still, the meeting genuinely prompted a questioning of the centuries-old implications of Giedion's schism. When George Löf reflected on the meeting's significance, he noticed "the clear indication that the solar heating problem is closely associated with an architectural problem."[87] Outside the academy, American building practices in general rushed toward methods that would perpetuate the schism by using mechanical systems to solve architectural problems and treating a building's environmental needs independently from its aesthetic expression.

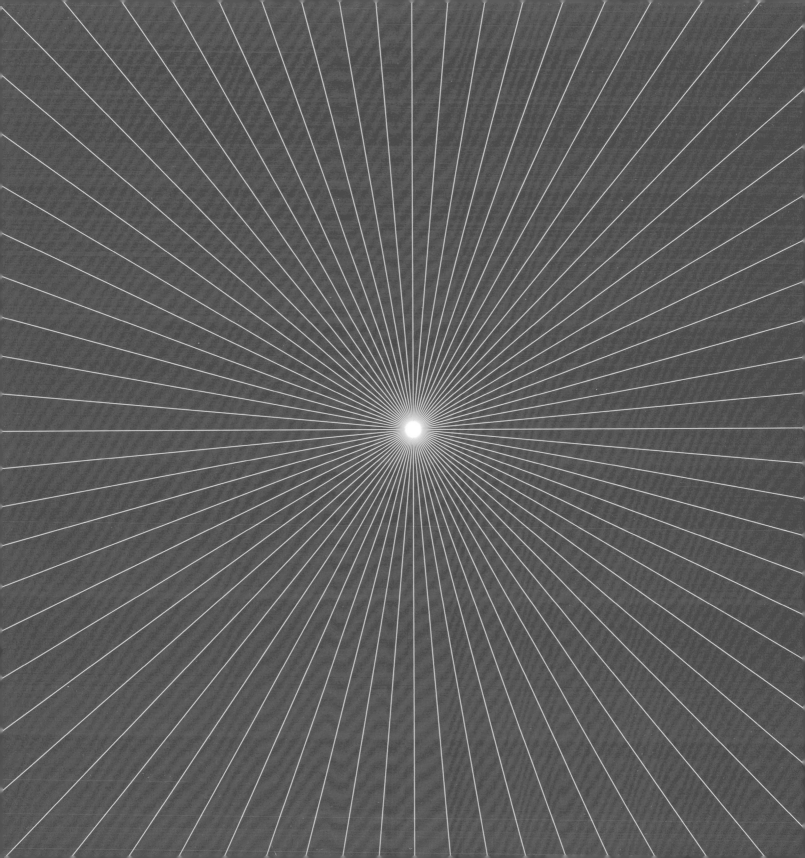

CHAPTER 7

CONCERTED EFFORTS: INTEGRATION

The architectural problem of the flat-plate solar collector is one worthy of multiple attack . . . It is true that solution lies in the concerted efforts of all of the design professions.

—James Hunter (1955)[1]

Designing a solar house requires close cooperation between the architect, the heating engineer, and the prospective occupant; the house finally decided upon will be the result of numerous compromises by all concerned.

—Austin Whillier (1955)[2]

After the grand conclusion of the 1950 MIT symposium, "the clear indication that the solar heating problem is closely associated with an architectural problem," integration of architecture and engineering became the dominant theme of the 1950s. Earlier, both MIT III and the Dover Sun House had represented tentative steps in this direction, in the limited sense that the architectural design had been constrained by the engineering requirements in each case. Still, until the mid-1950s, the solar house movement lacked a true example of integration, where the two disciplines worked together to transcend constraints. Three seminal projects realized in 1956–57—the George Löf House in Denver, MIT IV outside Boston, and the Bridgers and Paxton Building in Albuquerque—pointed to the possibility that the solar house could reconcile the epic schism of Giedion.

In Colorado, engineer George Löf had begun working with architect James Hunter in 1949, and their partnership can be characterized as the first effort in the solar house movement to aspire to an integrated design process. Löf and Hunter proposed a ranch-style solar house, originally meant for the Los Angeles area. Why such a benign climate? Löf said the solar equipment "might easily justify itself" there. They chose the "ranch house image," according to Hunter, in order to make the solar house "palatable and acceptable" to the house-buying public at that time.[3] The low roof slope was not optimized for winter solar heating, even at the lower latitude of Los Angeles. By placing architectural marketability ahead of engineering performance, the project would be more than a science experiment. Hunter integrated the collectors by setting them flush with the conventional roofing.

During the design process, Löf and Hunter "moved" the hypothetical house to Dallas, and then again to the Denver area. They did not alter the architecture significantly, and they kept the ranch-style roof with its low slope. Löf used solar heating equipment similar to his earlier Boulder project: an air system with overlapped-plate collectors, a gravel storage bed in the basement, and a conventional furnace for backup. He calculated that such a system could provide 70–90 percent

SOLAR-HEAT COLLECTORS on a model of his house are pointed out by Dr. George O. G. Löf. On the finished house (photo at top) they are less noticeable, blending agreeably with its lines.

George Löf with model of his "Denver House" by James Hunter, 1956. *Popular Science* (February 1958)

of heating needs from the sun, even in Denver. Still, he acknowledged it "might not cut heating costs much" there due to cheap natural gas.[4] Hunter provided for direct-gain through south windows, but it is unclear if these gains were accounted for in the engineering design. At the 1950 symposium Löf and Hunter displayed a model and announced "blueprints were ready for a solar house suitable for the southwest area bounded by Denver, Los Angeles, and Texas."[5] It would include 2,000 square feet of living area and cost $25,000. Apparently they found no demand.

Hunter found the ranch-style roof form to be a "straight jacket" [sic], and in about 1955 he and Löf abandoned the 1949 scheme and "attacked the problem with new vigor." The resulting process raised immensely interesting issues about "style" and the solar house. Their solution—a flat-roofed house—responded to contemporary trends in the larger world of modern architecture, but not necessarily in the solar house movement. Hunter preferred the flat roof because "[the solar house] must be the very best and timeliest architecture within our ability." What about the tastes of homebuyers? "We feel now that the American buying public was, and is, far more discriminating in its evaluation of architecture than the speculative builder supposed."[6] The house was later celebrated in the *New York Times* for its "modern lines."[7]

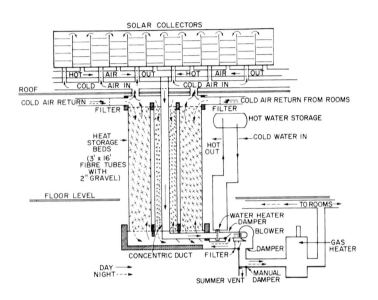

SOLAR COLLECTORS

HOT — AIR — OUT | HOT — AIR — OUT

ROOF
COLD — AIR IN | COLD — AIR IN

COLD AIR RETURN | COLD AIR RETURN FROM ROOMS
FILTER | FILTER

HOT WATER STORAGE

HEAT
STORAGE
BEDS
(3' x 16'
FIBRE TUBES
WITH
2" GRAVEL)

COLD WATER IN

HOT
OUT

FLOOR LEVEL

TO ROOMS

WATER HEATER
DAMPER
BLOWER
DAMPER
GAS
HEATER

CONCENTRIC DUCT | FILTER

DAY →
NIGHT ---→

SUMMER VENT | MANUAL
DAMPER

The concept of placing sloped collectors on a flat roof with an independent supporting structure was essentially novel and transformative, but it largely avoided the true complexities of the problem, as it allowed each discipline to dodge major constraints imposed by the other. At the very same time, integrated design teams at MIT and in Albuquerque pursued tilted-wall forms which represented a different philosophy (to be discussed below). Löf argued that the engineering requirements should not determine the architectural expression:

> You wouldn't build your house around the conventional furnace. So you won't build it in the future around the solar-heat equipment. The latter has to fit into the house.[8]

Indeed, the flat-roof scheme can be seen as an implicit criticism of other solar buildings where the collectors dominated the image. A *Popular Science* writer remarked that prior solar houses were "all odd looking, because they were primarily outsize collectors of solar energy with the living quarters attached to them" and praised Hunter and Löf's design as being "the first American house to have a solar-heating unit as optional equipment that didn't dictate and distort the design of the house to suit its needs."[9] Likewise, Farrington Daniels later remarked that collectors could be "ugly" and that flat-roofed houses were better for solar collectors.[10]

Opposite, top left: System diagram of George Löf's "Denver House," 1955. *Proceedings of the World Symposium on Applied Solar Energy* (Phoenix: Association for Applied Solar Energy, 1956)

Opposite, top right: George Löf's "Denver House" by James Hunter, 1956. Photograph by author

Opposite, bottom: George Löf's "Denver House" by James Hunter, 1956. John I. Yellott Collection, American Heritage Center, University of Wyoming

Left: George Löf's "Denver House" by James Hunter, 1956. Historic Denver

Löf said the flat roof would allow for "complete freedom of choice" for the engineer in terms of positioning equipment.[11] In fact, the true beneficiary of this independence was the architect, because the organization of space within the house could be disengaged from the solar path. Any given plan could be rotated to a particular orientation, while the rooftop collectors could face south, allowing Hunter to design a relatively deep, squarish floor plan. In principle this would make narrow suburban lots suitable for solar houses.

Löf decided to build the house for his own family in Denver in 1956. Hunter produced a seven-page set of construction drawings in May, and the house was built later that year for a cost of $40,000—not including the $10,000 price for the collector equipment, which was financed by the American Window Glass Company. The collectors, 600 square feet in total, were organized in two rows atop the roof and set at a 45-degree tilt angle. Then, perhaps paradoxically, Hunter added a plywood screen to (partially) shield the collectors from view. (Late in his life Löf said that Tician Papachristou, who worked in Hunter's office at this time and later partnered with Marcel Breuer, had performed considerable design work, but all other evidence points to Hunter as the designer.[12]) Hunter credited Keck's early solar houses as influences, although the Löf House's deep floor plan did not follow Keck's usual strategies.[13]

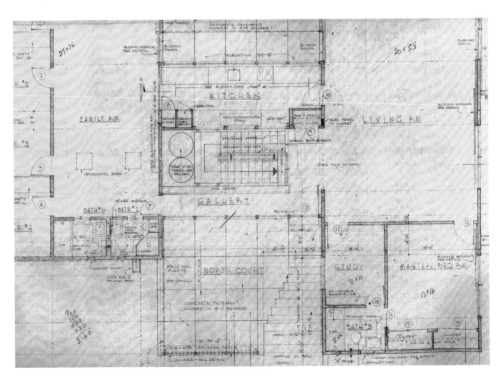

For the solar heating system, Löf again employed overlapped-plate collectors, hot-air distribution, and gravel storage. But he changed the nature of the storage bins, and this proved to be an opportunity for the architect. Löf wanted the gravel bins to be thin and vertical because stratification was desirable. Then he decided to locate the storage inside the house, rather than in a basement, so that ambient losses would remain in the living space.[14] Twelve tons of rock would be needed. Hunter realized that the vertical bins could be treated as a major expressive feature. He specified two large cardboard tubes and located them in the staircase in the center of the house, visible from the entrance. After being painted bright red, the tubes became "unique totems to today's solar technology."[15] It marked the first time an engineering feature was prominently expressed inside a solar house.

Löf undersized his system to provide only 25 percent of the heating load with solar energy. This reflected the low price of natural gas and Löf's detailed attention to economics—particularly first costs. In fact, Löf argued that a "hand-made, one-of-a-kind collector" was so expensive compared to the cost of heating by fuel that the "economic optimum" choice was not to use solar heating at all.[16] As a result, he only used 600 square feet of collectors for the 3,200-square-foot house. The collectors at the Dover Sun House, by comparison, were three and a half times larger. When comparing the collector size, floor area, and solar heat contribution, Austin Whillier concluded that Löf's system was "in the range of optimum economic performance," and that increasing the collector area "would not have improved the overall economic gain."[17] To make this point especially clear, Löf created a "design adequacy index" to compare collector area to house heating load and other variables. His own house scored very low, meaning it could not supply a large portion of the house's needs.[18]

The system was extensively monitored, and its performance varied. During a nineteen-day period in November and December 1958, the sun supplied about 16 percent of the heating load, but there were "no net savings" due to the large amount of electrical power required to push the air through the gravel tubes. Additionally, the collectors suffered considerable leakage, pointing yet again to the broad theme that solar gains are easily defeated by convection losses.[19] By the 1959–60 winter season, after additional sealing, 25 percent of the heating load was carried by solar energy. But, while he had saved $80 in natural gas, he spent $60 more in electricity; for a $10,000 first cost, he saved about $20 per year. Still, Löf reported: ". . . the economic aspects of this application are encouraging,"[20] in large part because he believed the collectors could be improved and made considerably cheaper if mass produced. Löf later patented a vertical gravel storage system where auxiliary gas or electric heat could be used in off-peak times to heat the rock bed.[21]

The system did prove durable. In 1974, Löf decided to reassess its performance to see if it had degraded over time. No maintenance had been needed in the intervening period. He discovered that the system operated at 72 percent of its original capability, a decline of about 2 percent per year, due to broken glass inside the collectors and increased air leakage due to degradation of caulking.[22] A few years later, Löf admitted the system "cannot yet compete with

Top: George Löf on the roof of his "Denver House," c. 1975. Photograph by Jon Naar

Above: Hoyt Hottel at MIT Solar House IV, c. 1957. Courtesy MIT Museum

Opposite: George Löf's "Denver House" by James Hunter, 1956. Author's collection

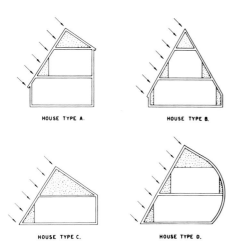

HOUSE TYPE A. HOUSE TYPE B.

HOUSE TYPE C. HOUSE TYPE D.

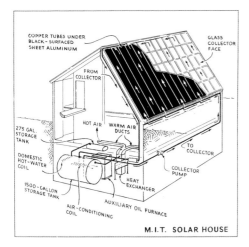

COPPER TUBES UNDER
BLACK-SURFACED
SHEET ALUMINUM

GLASS
COLLECTOR
FACE

FROM
COLLECTOR

HOT AIR WARM AIR
DUCTS

275 GAL.
STORAGE
TANK

DOMESTIC
HOT-WATER
COIL

TO
COLLECTOR

1500-GALLON
STORAGE TANK

COLLECTOR
PUMP

HEAT
EXCHANGER

AIR-CONDITIONING
COIL

AUXILIARY OIL FURNACE

M.I.T. SOLAR HOUSE

Top: Shape studies for MIT Solar House IV by Austin
Whillier and Robert Pelletier, 1955. *Proceedings of the
World Symposium on Applied Solar Energy* (Phoenix:
Association for Applied Solar Energy, 1956)

Above: MIT Solar House IV, Lexington, Massachusetts,
1957. Courtesy MIT Museum

Opposite: MIT Solar House IV, Lexington, Massachusetts,
1957. Courtesy MIT Museum

Denver's cheap natural gas." But, he emphasized, "if the alternate source of heat in our house were electricity, we would have paid for the collectors long ago."[23] It was frequently hailed in the 1970s as the oldest continuously operating solar heating system in the world, and Löf lived in the home until his death in October 2009.

In the same time frame, Löf's mentor Hoyt Hottel and his team at MIT created house IV after deciding: ". . . we would go into solar housing in a big way. We would build the best house we knew how to build."[24] Internally, Hottel had received a major vote of confidence in the form of a thirty-one-page report from the MIT's dean of science, and the dismissal of Maria Telkes, whose "rather radical opinions . . . affected the color of public opinion regarding the M.I.T. solar energy project."[25] In 1954, he and Lawrence Anderson returned to the vision that had been outlined in 1945: to build a house which would be sold on the open market. They envisioned a serial effort to build additional houses "using what we learned on the first one, and slowly we would get better at building solar houses."[26] The solar house movement had never seen such a sweeping vision for iterative refinement in both technology and design.

The design process for MIT IV was highly integrated among disciplines, led by architects in sustained collaboration with chemical, civil, and mechanical engineers. This required the architects to relinquish a degree of creative control. For example, the house's shape—normally the domain of the architect alone—was determined after scientific "building shape studies" by engineers Austin Whillier and Robert Pelletier, who sought to find the "optimum form" considering heat loss, solar collection, and construction costs.[27] The engineers prescribed the collector area (640 square feet) and the tilt angle (60 degrees), but they offered flexibility in the shape of the floor plan and the amount of south-facing windows, though Whillier warned about overheating. The architects covered the lower south wall with an earth berm and used no south-facing windows at all. Anderson, probably the principal architectural designer, called the effort "a successful marriage."[28]

In November 1955, the MIT team announced the project and unveiled drawings at the World Symposium on Applied Solar Energy in Phoenix.[29] After delays, construction was substantially completed by November 1957, and the house was advertised for sale in March 1958. The press, as usual, reacted enthusiastically, with *Look* magazine claiming: "The town that struck America's first blow for liberty now boasts the world's most revolutionary house."[30] This is the type of reporting that caused Hottel later to complain: "There is no field in which it is easier for a researcher to draw media attention than solar energy."[31] Having been featured in Kate Ellen Rogers's *The Modern House U.S.A.*, it remains the only house with flat-plate collection that has ever even merited consideration in the canon of modern architecture.

MIT IV introduced the sloped facade, a powerful symbol of integration in the sense that the architectural expression worked in concert with an engineering requirement, and a theme which

Popular Mechanics (October 1957)

Opposite: Bridgers and Paxton, "Solar Building," Albuquerque, New Mexico, 1956. Bridgers & Paxton Consulting Engineers, Inc.

later became common in solar houses. At the time it endured criticism on aesthetic and technical grounds. After seeing an architectural rendering of MIT IV, the *Boston Globe* warned readers:

> What will the "solar home" look like? Not much like your present house, say those who know . . . The entire structure—from, the south, at least—may look something like a cross between a large greenhouse, and an artist's studio.[32]

In reality, site planning mitigated MIT IV's appearance. From the street, the panels could not be seen, and the north face looked unremarkable. Also, the house's eccentric geometry was somewhat occluded by earth berms.

For heat collection, the tilted surface was "rather questionable," according to engineer Maria Telkes and architect Aladar Olgyay. They argued that a 60-degree tilt would (beneficially) collect 10 percent more solar radiation than a vertical wall in winter, but it would (undesirably) collect 235 percent more in summer. (Most collectors were designed to expel unwanted summer heat, although the passive gains from collectors could be significant, even when dormant.) Moreover, Telkes and Olgyay warned that a tilted wall "limits freedom in planning."[33] And MIT IV did indeed produce an unusable and awkward "wedge" of space underneath the sloped wall in the living room. For many of these reasons, particularly summer overheating, a tilted-glass design is generally not recommended (for direct-gain) by the leading "how-to" solar house book today.[34]

As a system, MIT IV was considerably more complex than its predecessors but less ambitious. Again Hottel used flat-plate collectors with water circulation, but the storage and distribution system exhibited a new level of complexity, with three separate tanks feeding a forced-air system. Automated controls—described as the house's "electronic brain"—would awaken the solar collectors only when justified against the cost of pumping.[35] By design, the sun would provide only 75–80 percent of the house's heat. Why did they lower the bar? In a word, economics. Butti and Perlin have noted "the high cost of aluminum, copper and glass" at this time, a strong motive for minimizing collector area.[36] MIT IV would provide 640 square feet of collectors for 1,450 square feet of living space, a much lower ratio than previous structures except Löf's. Anything higher "just doesn't make sense," the official news release said.[37]

When complete, the system failed to meet the engineers' criteria. In the winter of 1959–60 the solar collectors provided only 45 percent of the space heating demand. This was explained by temperatures "more severe than predicted" and unusual cloudiness. The next season, the solar contribution rose to 64 percent, still significantly lower than expectations.[38] The experiment failed in another respect: it did not sell. The structure had cost $38,000 *plus* about $6,500 for the heating system.[39] But, as a journalist noted after visiting the area, it looked "like a uniquely conceived modern home in the $18,000 to $20,000 price class."[40] (An MIT engineer ended up living in the house.) In terms of energy economics, the MIT engineers calculated that the cost of the solar heating system would have to be one-fifth the price in order to pay for itself

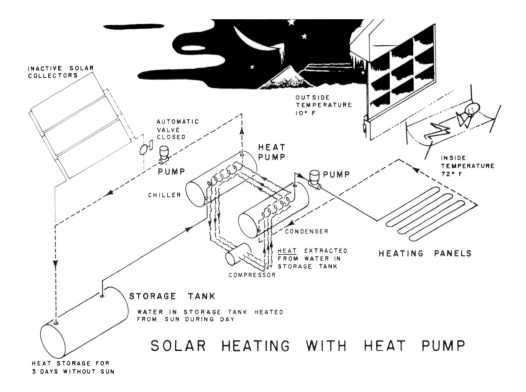

INACTIVE SOLAR
COLLECTORS

OUTSIDE
TEMPERATURE
10° F

AUTOMATIC
VALVE
CLOSED

HEAT
PUMP

PUMP

PUMP

CHILLER

INSIDE
TEMPERATURE
72° F

CONDENSER

HEATING PANELS

HEAT EXTRACTED
FROM WATER IN
STORAGE TANK

COMPRESSOR

STORAGE TANK

WATER IN STORAGE TANK HEATED
FROM SUN DURING DAY

SOLAR HEATING WITH HEAT PUMP

HEAT STORAGE FOR
3 DAYS WITHOUT SUN

in ten years.[41] In short, you might describe MIT IV as a public relations success, a noteworthy aesthetic effort, an inefficient machine, and an economic tragedy.

An important lesson of MIT IV, and the reason for its ultimate demise, was that a unique and complex custom-built system required a great deal of specialized maintenance. "We woke up to the fact that any little thing that went wrong would require consulting and correction by a member of the MIT faculty," Hottel recalled. To dispose of the house in late 1961, staffers began "ripping out all its solar parts and refitting it with a conventional heating system." The south-facing collectors were replaced by standard roofing shingles, and the house was sold. Hottel remembered with disappointment that the larger effort toward marketability "sounded like a good idea, but it was not."[42] He and Anderson shut down MIT's solar house program and it remained dormant through the 1960s and early '70s.

About the same time as MIT IV, a pair of mechanical engineers in Albuquerque, New Mexico, added a third major example of integration to the solar architecture canon—an office building rather than a house. When completed in 1956, the Bridgers and Paxton "Solar Building" became the country's first commercial structure powered (partially) by the sun, and it included the first example of a new technology, the solar-assisted heat pump.[43] In retrospect the Bridgers and Paxton Building appears to have been both a major technical advance and an aesthetic success.

Frank Bridgers had learned about solar energy as a graduate student at Purdue University, where he participated in the 1945 Hutchinson experiment for Libbey-Owens-Ford. (Bridgers's solar career can be seen as a legacy effect of the glass company's support, in the same way that George Löf's contribution came from Godfrey Lowell Cabot's gift.) As professional engineers, Bridgers and Don Paxton conceived the solar-assisted heat pump in 1954 after designing the heating and cooling systems for an Albuquerque building with both north- and south-facing glass walls. Bridgers recalled that on winter days the south zones would need cooling (due to solar gains) while the north side would require heat. Using a ground-source heat-pump system with two wells, they extracted enough energy from the south side to heat the north. "We decided then that if you could accidentally solar-heat a building, even when the architect provided drapes and heat-absorbing glass, think what you could do if you did it on purpose."[44]

Bridgers and Paxton had no benefactor for this "research," no academic affiliation, no government grant, and no corporate sponsor. They were practicing engineers who needed an office building and sought to explore a new idea. In fact, when they looked for construction financing, "banks balked and the men used personal loans."[45] Yet in some sense the engineers acted like scholars when they published the results, and in general the popular press did not treat the sponsored research projects differently from the private projects. Solar architecture, as a movement, consisted of discrete initiatives, each with its own questions, its own techniques, and its own mechanism of support.

The introduction of the heat pump was a major technical advance. A heat pump creates hot and cold coils by compressing and expanding a fluid in a closed-loop circulation. In a typical application—a refrigerator or air conditioner—the coils heat or cool the air passing over them, but the device operates even more efficiently when the coils are submerged in water. (As more heat can be "expelled" on the hot side, more cold can be produced, and vice versa.) The transformative insight of Bridgers and Paxton was to use solar-heated water to assist this process, with a 6,000-gallon underground water tank for heat storage (sized to provide for three winter days without sun). Therefore they could collect much more solar energy per collector area than ever before, and the building included only 800 square feet of collector area for 4,300 square feet of space. Bridgers said this was "the most economical" type of solar heating, although the building's mechanical systems cost $17,400—30 percent of the $58,500 project total. For the flat-plate collectors, the engineers found no need to innovate, using a variant Hottel-type design. They noted that the panels were "the only unconventional equipment . . . All other items are of standard manufacture."[46]

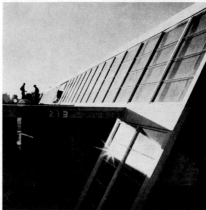

SOUTH WALL OF SOLAR OFFICE BUILDING TILTS BACK 30°

750 SQUARE-FOOT GLASS WALL LETS IN HEAT BUT NO LIGHT. LIGHT ENTERS THROUGH WINDOWS AND SKYLIGHTS

An Albuquerque office building is heated entirely by the sun

An odd-looking new office building in Albuquerque, N. Mex. has one wall sheathed in glass and tilted to face the sun. The glass wall is a solar heating unit and the building, designed by engineers to house their offices, is the first commercial structure in the country to be heated entirely by the sun.

The building uses water in its heating system. Its glass wall is backed by hollow metal panels through which water circulates. The sun's rays pierce the glass, strike the panels and warm the water, which flows through a conventional heating system. The glass traps the heat. An insulated storage tank of sunheated water tides the building through sunless days, when a special device extracts the last bit of heat from the circulating water. The designers believe the sun will keep their office at 72° even in the chilliest winter weather.

SOLAR DESIGNERS, consulting engineers Frank H. Bridgers (left), Donald Paxton, study plans in new $58,000 quarters.

Life, December 17, 1956

Opposite: Bridgers and Paxton, "Solar Building," Albuquerque, New Mexico, 1956. Bridgers & Paxton Consulting Engineers, Inc.

The heat pump also offered the ability to produce cooling in summer. In this mode, the heat pump could extract heat from the water in the storage tank in order to produce chilled water, which was sent to a radiant panel system. Bridgers and Paxton also gave the system an evaporative water cooler and multiple switching permutations, which produced five different possible operational modes to address different environmental needs. In the swing seasons, for example, the system could cool the building in the afternoon while collecting and storing heat for the morning.

As architecture, the Bridgers and Paxton project expressed the engineering requirements of a large sloped collector in the very shape of the building, like MIT IV. The architects, Stanley & Wright,[47] seem to have accepted that the given collector tilt (60 degrees above horizontal) should determine the building form. This alone would not constitute "integrated design," but the architects enhanced its identity as a solar building with every refinement. Instead of "hiding" its unusual shape from public view like MIT IV did, the architects emphasized the major angular form by pairing it with a low rectilinear sibling, which created a delightful compositional interplay. Visitors would interact with the collector—surely feeling its heat—due to the location of the entrance. Furthermore, the exterior detailing expressed a high level of aesthetic integration, particularly where the brick infill revealed the steel structure. There were conflicting interpretations of the overall effect: *Life* magazine called it "an odd-looking new office building," but *Architectural Record* said it "combines good architectural and mechanical design."[48] In *Progressive Architecture*, Stanley & Wright were credited with "integrating structure and environmental control," the first time integration was explicitly mentioned in the discourse around solar architecture.[49]

After the first winter, Bridgers and Paxton reported they had saved 53 percent in energy costs, including the added electrical costs for running the heat pump and other pumps. Plus the weather conditions had been much cloudier than normal. These savings would not necessarily justify the initial cost, but they argued: "The trend of fuel cost increasing at a faster rate than electrical energy cost will probably continue, particularly in view of the possibility of atomic-generated electrical energy. This could make a heat-pump solar-heated system economically attractive in a relatively short time."[50] Once again we find the logic for solar architecture, even before 1973, formed by notions of scarcity and thrift.

Bridgers and Paxton deactivated the solar heat-pump system in 1962 because "fossil fuels were so plentiful and at such low cost that the system was not economically viable." Then, after the energy crisis of 1973, Bridgers reactivated the system and found significant renewed interest in its performance. In 1974, the National Science Foundation funded a study to gather accurate data over two winter heating seasons. The solar-assisted heat pump supplied 54 percent and 62 percent of the building's heat needs. The study's director, Pennsylvania State University professor Stanley Gilman, concluded that the combination of a water-type solar collector, a water storage tank, and a water-source heat pump unit "has excellent potential in regards to energy conservation."[51] In this later period, Bridgers and Paxton completed a number of much larger solar projects, showing that the technology could be scaled. These included the New Mexico

Department of Agriculture Building (1973–75) and the Community College of Denver North Campus (1973–77).[52] Each was the largest project of its kind at the time of completion.

The National Register of Historic Places admitted the Bridgers and Paxton Building in 1989 as "an exceptionally significant structure," despite its being less than fifty years old. It was acknowledged that the building's "developmental or design value" had been "quickly recognized as historically significant by the architectural profession," and that early solar buildings were "very scarce."[53]

Ultimately all three examples of integration completed in 1956–57 resulted in disappointment of one type or another: the Löf House showed barely any savings; MIT IV could not be sold on the open market; and Bridgers and Paxton put their system to sleep. But these issues do not diminish the larger search for a compelling expressive language to integrate the concerns of architecture and engineering. To overemphasize the economic contingencies would be to miss the importance of innovation, both as process and product, in the three buildings. In general, architectural history (for better or worse) almost never considers economy as a criterion when judging a building's importance, and in fact excess is often interpreted as a virtue because it indicates cultural needs transcending everyday concerns. Here, the appearance of novel features such as sloped facades and cardboard tubes of gravel represented answers to the historical problem of Giedion's schism.

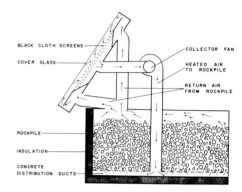

Above: Desert Grassland Station by Donavan and Bliss, Amado, Arizona, 1954. *Proceedings of the World Symposium on Applied Solar Energy* (Phoenix: Association for Applied Solar Energy, 1956)

Left: Desert Grassland Station by Donavan and Bliss, Amado, Arizona, 1954. University of Arizona, Special Collections

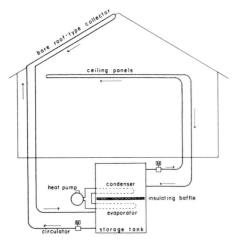

FIG. 1 — Winter heating flow scheme.

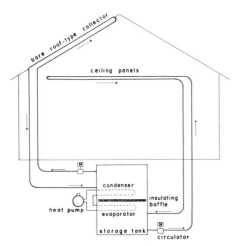

FIG. 2 — Summer cooling flow scheme.

University of Arizona Solar Energy Laboratory by Donavan and Bliss (Tempe, 1958). John I. Yellott Collection, American Heritage Center, University of Wyoming

At least one engineering team resisted the trend toward integration and earned a new level of technical success while ignoring architectural problems. In 1954, Mary Donovan and Raymond W. Bliss, Jr., built an idiosyncratic solar heater for a "dilapidated" bungalow in a remote location near Amado, Arizona. (The building was owned by the U.S. Forest Service, and the project is alternatively called "Desert Grassland Station" or "Bliss House.") Donovan and Bliss designed a bulky apparatus to sit outside the house and deliver air through "a 'Rube Goldberg' arrangement of ducts."[54] Bliss acknowledged:

> It is not a properly integrated structure of house and collector, circumstances having dictated the very awkward expedient of "bolting on" the system to an existing small house not at all adapted to the purpose. Architecturally and aesthetically the result is best described as a monstrosity.[55]

Yet after one winter, the monstrosity supplied 100 percent of the building's heat from the sun, and Bliss could confidently describe the project as "the Nation's Only Fully Solar-Heated House." In essence Bliss perpetuated the schism to realize an engineering achievement, and he seems to have recognized this as a Faustian bargain.

The system used George Löf's general strategy of hot-air collection and gravel storage, with some new techniques. The flat-plate collectors at Amado incorporated four layers of black cotton cloth behind the cover glass to absorb heat. The cloth was economical but "probably not too permanent," Bliss said, and he suggested black metal screening as a more durable substitute. Fans moved air thorough the screens and delivered heat to an underground rock bed which was sized to store about two days' heat. In a mild climate, with 315 square feet of collector for 672 square feet of interior space, the system was "probably greatly overdesigned," according to Hoyt Hottel.[56] It cost $4,000, but Bliss believed the next one would be considerably cheaper, comparable to a conventional furnace when considering operating and amortizing costs. Donovan and Bliss (a husband-and-wife team) built the system themselves, with their own funding, and lived in the house. Löf visited in 1954 and sent a report to Hottel: ". . . considering the severe limitations on his activities in this field, Bliss has done some of the most remarkable work I have seen in the field of solar energy."[57] The system was demolished by the Forest Service in 1956.

Donovan and Bliss subsequently built an experimental structure at the University of Arizona in 1958 which abandoned air-and-gravel in favor of a water system with a heat pump. To collect heat, they covered the entire roof in copper tube-in-plate, without any glass cover. Leaving it exposed to the sky would reduce its efficiency but allow cooling of water by "nocturnal radiation" at night. A large water storage tank consisted of hot and cold chambers, with the coils of the heat pump submerged, one in each. The same tube-in-strip material formed radiant panels in the ceilings, for both heating and cooling. This system was practically identical, in every respect, to a contemporaneous system in Tokyo by Masanosuke Yanagimachi, to be discussed in chapter 9. Regarding the Yanagimachi and Arizona projects, an MIT engineer remarked: "It would be interesting to know which one was invented first."[58]

After eighteen months of operation, the system performed very well, using about 53 percent as much energy (measured in dollars) as a conventional heating and cooling system. Bliss described the system as expensive, and said: ". . . it is probably not a prototype of any economically practicable solar-heating system which may appear in the future."[59] The building design was credited to architect William Wilde, who created some visual interest by treating the 4,500-gallon water storage tank as a freestanding cylindrical element. At the same time as the laboratory building was constructed, Bliss published a theoretical paper on flat-plate collection which refined earlier work at MIT.[60] The formula for determining collector efficiency is known to this day as the Hottel-Whillier-Bliss equation.

When the solar house became a mass movement with plenty of do-it-yourself "Rube Goldberg" experiments in the 1970s, Bliss used his experience, surprisingly, to preach integration:

> An engineer with a narrow specialty (this writer is an engineer with the narrow specialty of heat transfer) must constantly remind himself that any fuel-saving design improvements he may conceive of for a house must do more than merely fit his own ingrained desire for "cost-effective efficiency": more importantly, those design improvements must contribute to a house that most people would consider pleasant to live in, comfortable and beautiful.[61]

Bliss's essential realization, that the solar house required the participation of architects, surely failed to resonate at this late date, decades after a generation of engineers not only made this point but acted upon it. Apparently the schism remained so powerful that it needed to be resolved again and again.

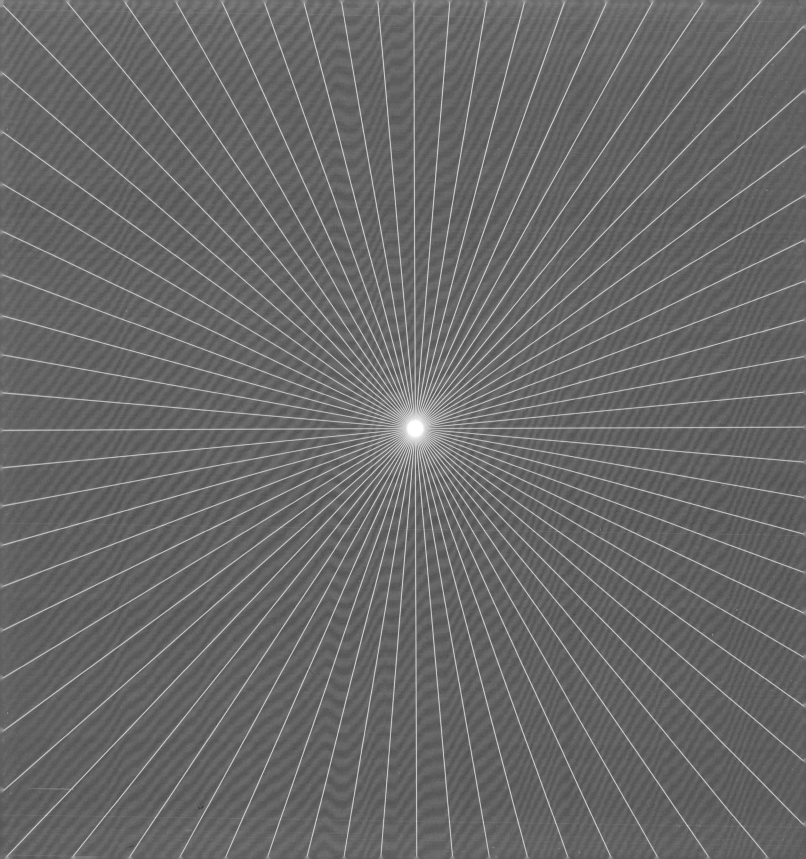

CHAPTER 8

TOO CHEAP TO METER: THE ECONOMIC CONTEXT

The eventual depletion of fossil fuel will not be disastrous. On the contrary, for our children's children the dream of our architects and engineers will come true—communities of people who live in comfort without combustion, free from atmospheric pollution, with no dark corners, with windows everywhere.

—Eugene Ayres (1951)[1]

We are coming to realize that our fossil fuels will not always be abundant. In the long run they will be exhausted . . .

—Farrington Daniels in the *New York Times* (1956)[2]

Throughout the 1950s, the solar house movement gained momentum from a perception of impending scarcity. As indicated by the quotations above, the future depletion of energy sources was routinely discussed and widely accepted. Early in the decade, the Korean War caused shortages, steep inflation, and rationing of some materials. This "evoked great public concern about scarcities."[3] Amidst these shortages, in 1951, President Truman created the Materials Policy Commission to examine "the broader and longer range aspects" of the problem and suggest solutions. William Paley, the founder of CBS, chaired the group, and it became known as the Paley Commission. They completed a five-volume report entitled *Resources for Freedom* in 1952, which predicted future oil shortages, warned against dependence on imports, and recommended a national energy agency. *Life* magazine called it a "monumental report" which detailed "our gargantuan appetite" for energy.[4]

The solar house movement, past and future, figured prominently in the Paley Commission report. It included a section called "The Possibilities of Solar Energy," written by Palmer Putnam, a consultant to the Atomic Energy Commission. Putnam discussed—in the most positive terms—the projects by MIT, Maria Telkes at Dover, and George Löf at Boulder (although these were listed under the heading "Methods Not Yet Economical"). Somehow Putnam determined, after mentioning the Duncan House and Purdue studies, that total fuel savings could be "as high as 30 percent" in these types of houses. Rosy optimism, indeed. He complained correctly that an "infinitesimal" amount had been spent on solar energy research, and he concluded: "It is time for aggressive research in the whole field of solar energy." The most startling in retrospect is Putnam's projection of a market for 13 million solar heated houses in the U.S. by 1975.[5]

After the Paley Commission report, fossil fuel scarcity and the solar future occupied a central position in the energy discourse, at least for a short time. Putnam's book *Energy in the Future* (1953) again painted a rosy picture of solar house experiments and urged more support for research. Likewise, California Institute of Technology geochemist Harrison Brown echoed many of the Paley Commission's warnings in his book *The Challenge of Man's Future* (1954), where he predicted fuel shortages to come in twenty to thirty years. Finally, in 1954, the government's own Office of Defense Mobilization proposed a "World Solar Energy Project," to be administered by the United Nations and to include an international solar energy laboratory.[6] This idea did not gain traction. Meanwhile, President Eisenhower "ignored" Paley's recommendations and "torpedoed" legislation that would have expanded funding for solar energy research from $100,000 to $1,000,000 per year.[7]

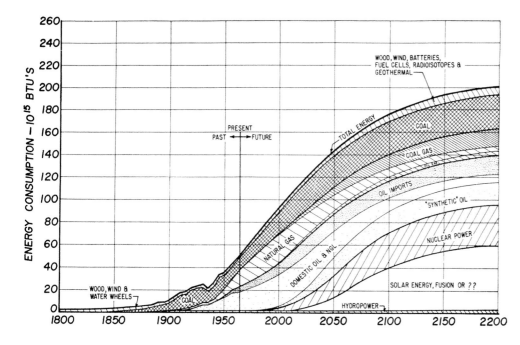

A projection of future energy sources in 1965. *Solar Energy* (July–September 1965)

After the Paley Commission, the idea that "current trends in energy use and urban growth were unsustainable" became a "familiar narrative."[8] More warning signs emerged. In 1956 came the first decline in new oil drilling in the U.S. after decades of consistent growth. The same year, geologist M. King Hubbert predicted that oil production in the U.S. would peak as soon as 1965 and no later than 1970.[9] His argument, illustrated by the "Hubbert curve," is now famous for its prescience. Even to disinterested observers, the solar house appeared to be an inevitable solution in the late 1950s:

> Whether we like solar houses or not is beside the point. As our supply of fuels grows slimmer we shall be forced to design and live in houses that put the energy of the sun to work. Perhaps you will be designing and building such houses in the future . . . chances are, someday you will be living in one of your own.[10]

Statements such as these reflected the Paley Commission's influence and showed a larger historical mood stimulating the vigorous solar house activity of the mid-1950s. The broader theme, seen time and again through the twentieth century, is that architecture's attention to energy use has responded quickly to the state of energy economics and, in particular, to the perception of crisis. In the 1950s, then, the dark forecasts about oil helped sustain what Jeffrey Cook has called a "golden age of solar explorations and applications."[11]

In the middle of this "golden age," in November 1955, came the World Symposium on Applied Solar Energy—solar architecture's defining moment prior to the 1970s. This event included a two-day technical conference in Tucson, attended by more than five hundred professionals (mostly engineers), and a five-day symposium in Phoenix. A photo of the black-tie grand banquet shows over a thousand people dining on pheasant. It seemed that a movement had come of age, and the World Symposium "set the stage for a new era of solar energy."[12] In his keynote address, Farrington Daniels asked: ". . . why this *new* and almost explosive interest in utilizing solar energy?" He acknowledged that "there are many reasons," but the centerpiece of his answer was long-term economic necessity:

> Dollar-wise, competition with cheap fossil fuels has been unattractive, and "social-conscious-wise" there has been no demand . . . But these conditions

are changing . . . We realize, as never before, that our fossil fuels—coal, oil, and gas—will not last forever.[13]

Likewise, J. E. Hobson told the attendees: "In the not too distant future we will be confronted by an imminent, ominous shortage. Men of our generation in countries the world over must prepare today for this coming crisis."[14] Surely the solar house movement would have followed a different trajectory if scarcity had not dominated the discourse in 1955.

The architects and engineers at the 1955 symposium generally adopted a pragmatic and modest position, and limited their scope to descriptions of individual projects. George Löf and James Hunter discussed the evolution of the design that would become the Löf House. Hoyt Hottel revealed the plans for MIT IV. There were no fantastic proposals involving houses on turntables or space-age forms. Aside from James Hunter's reflections on the solar ranch house, aesthetic issues were not discussed at all. And the "passive"-type solar house was not represented; it is not clear that any new work in that area existed. According to Alexis Madrigal: "The elegant and simple solar home, as conceived by Keck . . . had been forgotten."[15]

The World Symposium included a large outdoor exhibit called "The Sun at Work," which featured a number of collector-types, solar cooking ovens, solar stills, and so on. "No one paid for the privilege of exhibiting in those days," organizer John Yellott recalled, because "there was no solar energy industry."[16] Two new products were most noteworthy. First, Harry Tabor of Israel demonstrated a selective black surface which would absorb more longwave radiation from the sun and emit fewer losses in the form of shortwave radiation, doubling the efficiency of Hottel-type collectors. Second, Bell Telephone Laboratories introduced silicon photovoltaic cells to the public for the first time. These cells, invented just two years earlier, "provided the first real proof that electricity could be generated directly from the rays of the sun."[17] The exhibits "made quite an impression and were widely publicized," according to Tabor and John Duffie. "They must be regarded as the jumping-off point for solar R&D on a world scale."[18] About 30,000 people visited.

The World Symposium was sponsored by a new organization called the Association for Applied Solar Energy (AFASE). The symposium's success became "a catalyst for the nascent society."[19] Initially the AFASE consisted of a group of businessmen, lawyers, financiers, and educators, indicating a new level of interest from institutional sources.[20] (Similarly, the World Symposium was underwritten by a variety of agencies and foundations, including the National Academy of Sciences and the United Nations.) With establishment support, and the success of the 1955 event, AFASE charted an ambitious and optimistic course forward. In 1956, the group created a technical journal, *Solar Energy*, and the quarterly magazine *Sun at Work*, intended for a more general audience. And they began to conceive a worldwide open competition for a demonstration solar house.

Hoyt Hottel and George Löf at the *World Symposium*, Phoenix, Arizona, 1955. SRI International.

Opposite: Grand banquet of the 1955 World Symposium on Applied Solar Energy, Phoenix, Arizona, 1955. SRI International

In reality, the anticipated fossil fuel crisis did not materialize in this period; energy remained plentiful and cheap, and consumption soared.[21] Mainstream building practices not only ignored leading-edge solar techniques, but they also rejected traditional ones in the pursuit of heating and cooling methods that relied on "conventional" energy sources. Adam Rome has adroitly proposed that the solar house was eclipsed by the "all-electric house" in the 1950s and that air-conditioning, not solar heat, constituted the environmental revolution that truly reshaped the twentieth-century American home. For Rome, the dramatic increase in American energy use during the postwar period can be attributed in large part to the homebuilding industry and its aggressive promotion of air-conditioning:

> The ever-increasing amount of energy used for cooling was partly a sign that Americans could afford a higher level of comfort, but the air-conditioning load was also a consequence of decisions builders made in order to hold down the cost of new construction: To install air conditioning on a budget, builders eliminated traditional ways of providing shade and ventilation.[22]

Features such as breezeways, screened sleeping porches, and awnings disappeared in the 1950s, and "the typical tract house was a hotbox" with higher standards for comfort. "The nation's consumers," Rome concluded, "were either unwilling or unable to conserve energy."[23] The same assertion would remain valid if you substituted "architects" or "engineers" for "consumers."

This culture of consumption was accompanied by the lack of a large-scale visionary research program for solar. As early as 1951—before the Paley Commission—solar researchers such as Maria Telkes complained about the limited support: "The total research and development expenditures made thus far in solar energy utilization are infinitesimal when compared with the expenditures made in the development of other natural resources. Sunlight will be used as a source of energy sooner or later anyway. Why wait?"[24] To justify waiting, energy officials developed a powerful counter-narrative to the dark forecasts about fossil fuel depletion: "Our children will enjoy in their homes electrical energy too cheap to meter."[25]

How could electricity become "too cheap to meter"? By a massive investiture in nuclear power. From 1953 to 1973, as Tracy Kidder noted, the U.S. government spent five billion dollars on nuclear energy research but less than a million on solar.[26] "Alongside the glamorous and upcoming atom," D. S. Halacy quipped, "solar energy was a drab country cousin."[27] It is difficult to imagine how the solar house could succeed as a mass phenomenon in the face of such an imbalance; the support of a Cabot, a Peabody, and a couple of glass companies appears insignificant. Solar energy faced what Roger Pielke, Jr., has called a catch-22: it could not attract substantial public investments because its economic feasibility had not been proven, yet it needed research funding to compete in the marketplace. Here, one wonders if Hottel and Löf in particular may have overemphasized the economic obstacles to solar house heating. In 2002, Pielke provocatively asked: "If research and development investments between solar and nuclear had been reversed, would the United States today be flush with energy too cheap too meter?"[28]

Despite the lack of large-scale government support, the solar house attracted some interest from industry after the high-profile success of the 1955 symposium. The Curtiss-Wright Corporation began courting Maria Telkes at about the time of the symposium because they were interested in producing a solar cooking oven. By 1958, the aviation company decided to "move rapidly and decisively in all fields of solar energy," and hired Telkes to direct a new solar energy laboratory in Princeton, New Jersey.[29] Telkes wrote to her old client "Amy" Peabody: ". . . really good news! the Dover house is finally accepted by Industry."[30] Apart from Libbey-Owens-Ford's promotional efforts in the 1940s, this would mark the first instance where a private enterprise saw the solar house as a worthy investment. Even pessimists considered solar house heating to be "on the border of feasibility" at this time, Telkes argued, and she anticipated that design improvements would decrease costs "by about one-half," leading to a "break-through."[31]

For Curtiss-Wright at Princeton, Telkes initially proposed an ambitious program for "a group of prototype solar houses [to] be built as soon as feasible." She envisioned "at least 4–8 houses" and said they should be built "in pairs—one using solely solar energy, the other off-peak electric energy with heat storage."[32] The effort would include solar cooking ovens, water heaters, and stills, as well as solar power plants and a high-temperature furnace. "This program," Telkes wrote, "represents the first major and comprehensive Industrial activity in this field ever attempted anywhere in the World."[33] She was given a staff of six engineers, and internal documents clearly show that the company expected marketable products to be developed quickly. Soon Telkes scaled back her vision to a "Sun-Court," to include a single solar house and several smaller-scale demonstrations. She promised the house would heat and cool itself with solar energy alone and would not cost more than a conventional dwelling.

To design the solar house, Telkes called upon fellow Hungarian émigré Aladar Olgyay, an architect in Princeton. (He was also professor of architecture at Princeton University, but there was no connection between the university and this project. Telkes remained in her position as professor of engineering at New York University while working for Curtiss-Wright.) In fact, Telkes and Olgyay had already worked together on a project called "Solar Estates," where Olgyay created several schemes that maximized the amount of south-facing area to accommodate a combined collector-and-storage "solar wall" unit. The "Solar Estates" project was not realized but probably strongly informed the Curtiss-Wright project.[34]

Olgyay's architectural design for the Princeton Sun House was disappointingly simple and unrefined, contributing nothing to the aesthetic development of solar architecture. Olgyay described it as "an experimental solar laboratory . . . with the characteristics of a house."[35] Since it was not meant to function as a house, a generic spatial conception apparently could not stimu-

Maria Telkes in 1956. Library of Congress

late a critical or creative architecture. He faced the same essential problems that Eleanor Raymond had encountered at Dover: the need for a shallow, linear plan, and the recognition that the south facade would be dominated by collectors. Olgyay created a four-walled structure with a flat roof, practically devoid of articulation or detail, and did nothing to alleviate the monotony of a south face consisting only of black-glass collectors. No views to the south were possible, and the method of dividing the glass lacked any grace in its proportions. Overall the structure paled in comparison to the refined contemporary work of Olgyay and Olgyay.

Telkes designed a heating system for the Princeton Sun House which was remarkably similar to the Peabody house at Dover. Little had changed, in terms of technology, in eleven years. With 600 square feet of collector area for 1,200 square feet of interior space, the system would be slightly more efficient than Dover's. This was because the collectors consisted of two glass panes in front of the black metal plate, and because the back of the collectors were inside the building, so that "any heat leakage from the back surface is a net gain in the heating of the house."[36] Air moved either between the glass and the plate, or in a duct behind the plate, and then the heated air was pushed to bins of Glauber's salt immediately behind the wall. A conventional system of ducts heated the building by moving air over the bins and into the rooms. Telkes had no breakthrough method of preventing the stratification of the salt, but she planned to test different types of containers. She told Amy Peabody: ". . . the Dover house had a great deal to do with our present projects."[37]

The actual performance of the Princeton Sun House was never reported. Daniel Barber, in the only independent review of the project, concluded: ". . . the solar system at the Princeton house never worked very well." He continued:

> The list of shortcomings was extensive: the collector/storage units performed at half of their anticipated storage capacity, leading to design discussions regarding significant increase in the collector area; the chemical storage cans corroded and leaked; the heat distribution system was inadequate and heat did not reach the north side of the lab.[38]

Barber also noted the storage bins only transmitted 10 percent of the amount of heat expected. Curiously, the architect Olgyay had claimed that the building was operated "through two heating seasons and has performed with sufficient success" without auxiliary heating, but he did not include any data.[39] (George Löf complained about this: "There is consequently no way of appraising the effectiveness of the heat storage agent or of learning whether the attempt to prevent stratification was successful."[40]) Telkes never published a technical paper about the Princeton Sun House.

Frustrated with these problems, Curtiss-Wright officials demanded "a product with appreciable sales potential in a reasonable time." Telkes responded by proposing "a Solar House 'KIT'" that she imagined would be retailed for use on existing houses. It would provide heating and cooling, and she claimed it could be produced at a cost achieving a "borderline balance" for the consumer when compared to a typical heating and cooling bill.[41] She never developed this idea any further. Curtiss-Wright terminated Telkes in July 1960, just two years after she was hired. This and other speculative ventures caused great damage to the aviation company. Curtiss-Wright could be added to a list of disappointed solar patrons such as Godfrey Lowell Cabot, Amelia Peabody, and Libbey-Owens-Ford.

Aladar Olgyay's contribution to the Princeton Sun House should be understood within the context of his partnership with his twin brother, Victor, and their larger effort toward a "bioclimatic" architecture which had begun at MIT in 1950. Now, through their positions at Princeton University and through their private architectural practice, Olgyay and Olgyay brought a new level of scientific rigor to solar geometry and shading. They created a device called the thermoheliodon, contained within a glass dome, which attempted to improve upon the traditional heliodon. The brothers' book *Solar Control and Shading Devices* (1957) represented another product of this inquiry. They built several passive solar houses in the city of Princeton, including the Bernstein House (1958) and Frank House (1959), leading historian Jeffrey Cook to find that the Olgyays' work "should underline a much larger bioclimatic patrimony from the 1950s than is usually recognized."[42]

The failure of Curtiss-Wright's program indicated a larger structural problem for the "active"-type solar house. Due to economies of scale, flat-plate collectors for house heating could not be mass-produced by industry. It was "a chicken or egg situation," according to Robert Pelletier, an engineer from Hoyt Hottel's team:

> . . . a manufacturer hesitates to produce anything in quantity without having a demonstrably large market, while the high cost of limited production prevents the large market from appearing.[43]

In retrospect it appears the solar house faced a disastrous confluence of economic conditions in the late 1950s: the lack of federal support for research and development, the absence of a commercial market to stimulate mass production, and the general mood swing from scarcity to abundance. Mass interest in the solar house would virtually disappear in the 1960s, and so too did the major figures in solar house engineering—Hottel, Löf, and Telkes. By 1964, the movement's godfather, Farrington Daniels, wondered what had happened: "An optimistic report to President Truman a decade ago suggested that by 1975 there would be a market for 13 million solar heated houses in the United States . . . but practical progress toward such a situation has been almost negligible."[44]

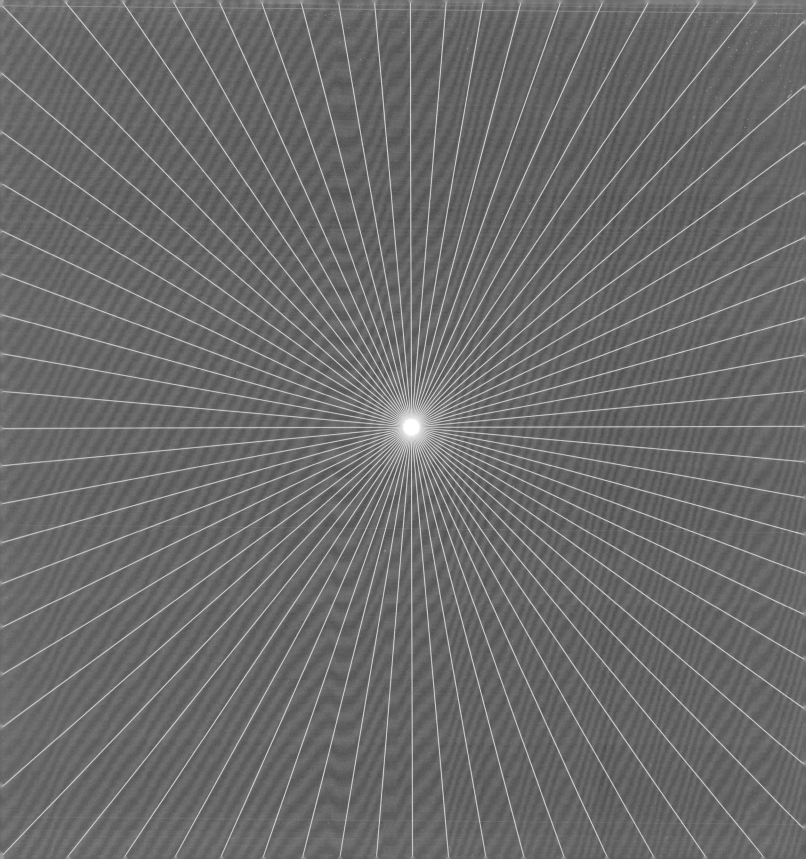

CHAPTER 9

LIVING WITH THE SUN: A GLOBAL MOVEMENT

Top: Solar house by Charles M. Shaw and Associates and John Yellott, Casablanca, Morocco, 1958. John I. Yellott Papers, Arizona State University Libraries, Special Collections

Above: Solar house by Charles M. Shaw and Associates and John Yellott, Casablanca, Morocco, 1958. John I. Yellott Collection, American Heritage Center, University of Wyoming

Opposite: Solar Energy exhibition organized by John Yellott and AFASE, Thessaloniki, Greece, 1957. John I. Yellott Collection, American Heritage Center, University of Wyoming

In addition to the emphases on integration and energy scarcity/abundance, a third major theme that characterized the "golden age" of the 1950s was globalization. By the middle of the decade, the solar house had become a worldwide movement. The 1955 World Symposium included 130 international delegates representing 31 nations. Additionally, the AFASE's *World Directory on Applied Solar Energy Research* included approximately 4,000 publications relevant to 27 countries, and it found: "Applied solar energy research is scattered thinly throughout most of the world with occasional foci of specialized interest."[1] A witty observer remarked: ". . . the list of solar activities internationally read like the alphabet."[2]

The AFASE, led by John Yellott, took a global outlook on its activities. Yellott, a mechanical engineer who had participated in the Manhattan Project, had recently come to the field of solar energy "more as a novice than as a cardinal."[3] In 1957, Yellott worked with U.S. Department of Commerce to create a solar energy exhibit which would travel around the world. At the first stop in Thessaloniki, Greece (also called Salonika), Yellott proudly announced: "Solar science returned to the land of Archimedes."[4] A thirty-five-foot tall solar water heater, bearing the AFASE logo, became known as "The Colossus of Thessaloniki." As in Phoenix, numerous solar-powered devices were demonstrated: flat-plate collectors, stills, furnaces, stoves, and electronic devices. Attendance at Thessaloniki topped 1.5 million. Yellott then took the exhibits to Casablanca, Tunis, Madras, and New Delhi in 1958.

When the trade fair arrived in Casablanca, Yellott decided to include a solar house suitable for the Mediterranean region. The house, "for demonstration rather than actual living purposes," was designed by Charles M. Shaw and Associates (architects and contractors for the Casablanca fair).[5] It employed the sloped wall strategy but did not resemble any previous solar house due to its irregular shape—a bit like a reclined lounge chair. Yellott apparently designed the heating system, a modification of George Löf's Denver system. It used flat-plate air collectors, with finned aluminum plate substituted for overlapping glass, and vertical tubes of gravel. Little is known about its performance. It would be especially interesting to learn how the locals reacted (in the summer). At the next stop, Tunis, the house was described as having "the features of a southwestern ranch house with such typically Arabic details as an open interior court with a pool and fountain."[6]

At same time, the AFASE launched an ambitious competition to design and build a demonstration solar house in the Phoenix suburbs. The 1957 *Living with the Sun* competition can be seen in retrospect as a pivotal episode in the history of the modern solar house movement.[7] Yellott expected the contest "to stimulate public interest in the utilization of the sun's energy for man's benefit in his living environment," and he intended to demonstrate that solar energy was immediately feasible for use at a domestic scale.[8] Again, the issue of resource scarcity loomed because "fossil fuels . . . are already approaching exhaustion in areas of the world."[9] Since Yellott had no

specific experience with architecture at this time, he selected James Hunter to be *Living with the Sun*'s architectural adviser. Due to his prominent role at the 1955 World Symposium, and the just-completed Löf house, Hunter figured as the leading solar architect in the country at this time.

Hunter and Yellott wrote a sixteen-page program which effectively defined the solar house in 1957 as a machine rather than an organism: "It is expected that the competitor will thoroughly familiarize himself with the experimentation which has been accomplished so far in this field, and commit the design of the house to a particular system," involving flat-plate collectors and storage.[10] Because of these conditions, the solar house in 1957 looked considerably different from its conception ten years earlier with *Your Solar House*. In 1947, the architects took an exclusively "passive" position. Now, the imperative for flat-plate collectors meant that the solar house would be a technological creature, and it forced the participants to shape the house while integrating unfamiliar equipment and finding an authentic expressive language.

Moreover, *Living with the Sun* demanded of architects a new level of technical virtuosity in its requirement to estimate gains and losses (using the method prescribed by the 1956 ASHRAE guide). Surely almost none of the participants had even the slightest bit of experience in this regard. To assist the designers, the program included detailed climate data for Phoenix, and a technical primer on current methods for solar energy heating. According to Daniel Barber, in this brief "we can glimpse a moment where the lifestyle project of modern design proposes to produce a new relationship to technology."[11]

On the issue of site specificity, Yellott and Hunter must have faced difficult conceptual questions. If the house were designed for a colder climate and built in Phoenix, its value as a scientific experiment would be compromised, and culturally it might appear as a "misplaced" object like so many museum houses. But if the house were designed specifically for Phoenix, its value as a model would be weakened for a nationwide audience. They risked the latter pitfall, and in the end (for this reason and others) the winning design attracted little national publicity and had little influence.

Soon after the competition was announced, applications for participation poured in. The competition drew strong interest from around the world—about 1,600 competitors from 36 nations enrolled. Hunter proudly emphasized the international profile:

> It is encouraging to know that so many architects from nations in all parts of the world have turned their talents toward the solution of the common problem of how to live with the sun. Despite the barriers of language and distance, nearly 5 per cent of the world's architects are now studying ways to use solar energy.[12]

Living with the Sun jury, 1957. *Living with the* Sun (Phoenix: Association for Applied Solar Energy, 1958)

The solar house clearly remained a familiar and attractive concept for architects in 1957. But soon Hunter and Yellott would discover that only 126 of the 1,600 interested participants were able to submit an entry, probably because of the quantitative work required. Estimating the heat gains, in particular, would have been extremely difficult, requiring the designers to find and interpret data from obscure technical papers by Hottel, Löf, or Telkes, adjusting for Phoenix. For instance, none of the *Your Solar House* participants entered the 1957 competition. AFASE later attributed the poor participation to the "exacting" requirements.[13] In retrospect, it seems the competition expected too much "engineering" for an open competition among architects. Among the jurors, only Pietro Belluschi had explored the solar house problem, having participated in the 1947 *Your Solar House* program. With no engineers, it is not clear that the jurors were qualified to assess the entries according to the technical requirements. The schism remained significant.

Peter R. Lee, an undergraduate student at the University of Minnesota, won the competition (and earned a $2,500 prize). MIT students earned third and fifth place. Surely the organizers hoped for more prestigious honorees, and the student-winners gave the contest a too-hypothetical character. Among the sixty entries that were later published, virtually none came from prominent solar architects, and none gained significant success later. (Victor Olgyay, the notable exception, contributed an immensely interesting passive design with a hollow floor.[14])

Lee's winning scheme featured a deep plan with shaded courtyards and a flat roof. (Daniel Barber has suggested that Lee's scheme was influenced by Ralph Rapson's Case Study House

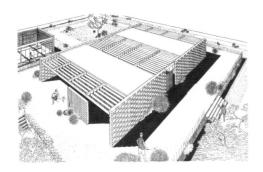

Living with the Sun house by Peter R. Lee, 1957–58. *Living with the Sun* (Phoenix: Association for Applied Solar Energy, 1958)

Opposite: *Living with the Sun* house by Peter R. Lee, Scottsdale, Arizona, 1957–58. Photograph by Charles R. Conley. John I. Yellott Collection, American Heritage Center, University of Wyoming

#4, or "Greenbelt House," of 1945.[15] Rapson was the dean of architecture at Minnesota at the time.) In general, *Living with the Sun* effectively endorsed the notion that flat-roofed architecture was most appropriate for the solar house. Of the sixty most notable entries, thirty-four used a flat roof—perhaps a new aesthetic consensus. Very few *Living with the Sun* architects adopted the sloped-wall strategy of MIT IV and Bridgers and Paxton.

Essentially a minimalist pavilion, Lee's modernist design featured a repetitive structural expressionism that underscored qualities of lightness and transparency. (Hunter told competitors the solar house should "express itself in terms of this era's techniques, materials, and concepts," rather than referring to the region's Spanish architectural history.) Most significantly, the design celebrated the flat-plate collectors rather than hiding them. Lee emphasized this idea by presenting an aerial view. He avoided the engineering issues by including generic "solar panels" without specifying how the system would work, and it is unknown to what extent he satisfied the competition's requirement to compute gains and losses. Still, he creatively used the flat-plate collectors to provide shade on the south and to act as daylight reflectors for the north. The jury praised its "directness and sense of unity; the logic of its solar equipment, which acts in a double capacity of shade louvers in summer and heat collectors in winter; the way in which the mechanical devices are integrated into the design; its feasibility as to cost; its livability; and, finally, the direct organization of the plan."[16]

The fact that Yellott designed the mechanical system himself (with assistance from Bridgers and Paxton) raises two intriguing possibilities. He may have been compelled to intervene because of Lee's generic scheme and overall lack of technical knowledge among the entries; or, possibly, he intended from the beginning that the exhibition house would ultimately feature "his" system. (Archival sources do not clarify this question.) Yellott's design was, essentially, a close cousin to the Bridgers and Paxton system in Albuquerque, but surely the most complex and expensive solar heating system to date. Private industry helped: DuPont donated Mylar film and Dacron insulation for the flat-plate collectors, and Revere Copper and Brass created a new "tube-in-strip" collector plate. "Complete instrumentation" was funded by a $13,000 grant from the John B. Pierce Foundation. Overall the house included more than 1,600 square feet of collector area for about 2,000 square feet of interior space—the highest ratio ever, even considering the mild climate and high insolation.[17]

The house was built beginning in December 1957 and finished by the following April. At the ceremonial opening Yellott performed a solar ribbon-cutting using a Fresnel lens. The house was celebrated briefly (and dubiously) as "America's first house designed to receive all its heat requirements from the sun."[18] But neighbors rebelled and it became a failure rather than a triumph. For a variety of zoning reasons, local officials closed the exhibition after one month; it is unknown how many people actually visited. Less than five months after the dedication, the house was sold to a private owner.[19] *Living with the Sun's* failure essentially bankrupted the AFASE.[20] Yellott was terminated in 1958, and the organization offered no major initiatives in the following years.[21]

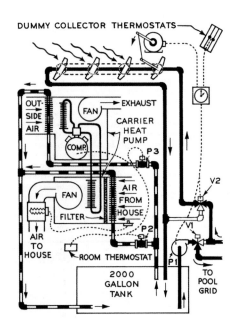

Living with the Sun house system by John Yellott and
Bridgers and Paxton, 1957. John I. Yellott Collection,
American Heritage Center, University of Wyoming

Opposite: Yanagimachi Solar House II by Masanosuke
Yanagimachi, Tokyo, Japan, 1958. John I. Yellott Collection,
American Heritage Center, University of Wyoming

Finally, the *Living with the Sun* episode showed, again, a pronounced difference in perception between the architect and engineer. In anticipation of the house's grand opening, Yellott claimed: "We are now definitely past the experimental stage in solar heating."[22] By contrast, when jury chairman Pietro Belluschi reflected on the contest, he came to the opposite conclusion: "Utilization of solar energy is still in its infancy." Architects, he argued, should play a central role in the development of the solar house: "The way in which architects will succeed in . . . giving it aesthetic appeal will have a great affect on the rapidity with which it will receive general acceptance."[23] As the engineering issues were declared solved, the architectural problems had barely been explored.

To document in full the solar houses built worldwide after 1955 would be impossible, but a few examples stand out for their novel contributions. With diverse innovative experiments in Japan, France, and England in the late 1950s, the solar house evolved a new richness as the movement grew and ideas moved across borders.

In Japan, all of the solar house activity before the 1970s can be credited to a single person: engineer Masanosuke Yanagimachi, who said he pursued solar heating "to promote the public welfare."[24] He completed his first solar heating project, an "experimental installation" in his own home, in late 1956, but it was destroyed by fire a few months later. Then he embarked on the project that would bring significant international attention: Yanagimachi Solar House II (Tokyo, 1958). This project included flat-plate collectors in conjunction with three heat pumps, two storage tanks, and radiant ceiling panels for both heating and cooling.

For Yanagimachi II, the engineer began by transforming the traditional flat-plate collector. He covered the roof of his project with black-painted aluminum tube-in-strip collectors, with a startling omission: no glass cover. (As noted earlier, in Arizona, Bliss and Donovan also designed an unglazed collector at approximately the same time.) Yanagimachi acknowledged that the collectors would be extremely inefficient without a cover if he were trying to collect heat at a high temperature. Instead, he said, this issue would be minimized by operating the collectors at about 90–100°F and "upgrading the collected heat" with a water-to-water heat pump. The "upgraded" hot water was then moved to radiant ceiling panels made of the same aluminum tube-in-strip as the roof.

Yanagimachi used the flat-plate collectors in a wholly original method for summer cooling. Although the greatest cooling needs occurred during the daytime, Yanagimachi recognized that water could be cooled in the panels at night, a process he called "nocturnal radiational cooling." He then determined he could produce ice in the storage tank by running the heat pump at night. During the heat of the day, water for the radiant panels would be cooled by the stored ice. The combined effects of these techniques improved the efficiency of the heat pump, while "avoiding the daytime peak load of electricity."[25] Both techniques—night sky radiant cooling and off-peak ice storage—remain effective green building methods.

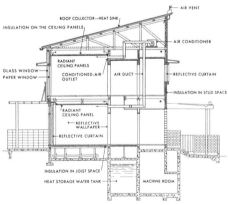

Top: Yanagimachi Solar House II by Masanosuke Yanagimachi, Tokyo, Japan, 1958. John I. Yellott Collection, American Heritage Center, University of Wyoming

Above: Yanagimachi Solar House II by Masanosuke Yanagimachi, Tokyo, Japan, 1958. *Western Architect and Engineer* (March 1960)

Yanagimachi II achieved a beautifully integrated appearance, though the architect is unknown. (Yanagimachi himself? A standard house type?) Its single-slope roof was set low, about 15 degrees above horizontal, for night sky radiation and winter solar collection. Because the bare tube-in-strip collectors were used as the roofing material, rather than attached above an existing roof, the solar "equipment" achieved a logical and understated appearance. (The full-roof strategy, of course, maximized the collector area for a two-story structure; it accommodated 1,078 square feet of panels for 2,460 square feet of interior space.) The interiors offered more pleasures of aesthetic integration, largely because the tube-in-strip radiant ceiling panels worked brilliantly with the traditional Japanese elements such as shoji screens and tatami mats. Yanagimachi also treated the interiors with reflective curtains and wall surfaces in addition to the radiant heating and cooling panels. He said these techniques in combination "bring a refreshing coolness to the rooms by virtue of their attractive appearance and special thermal characteristics."[26]

The theme of international interchange figured heavily in Yanagimachi's pursuits, indicating again that the solar house had become a global movement. Before he had ever built a solar heating system, Yanagimachi attended the 1955 World Symposium. (His presentation proposed the theory of combining solar heat and night sky cooling before its first application.[27]) John Yellott visited Japan in 1959 and subsequently introduced Yanagimachi II to American audiences in a variety of publications.[28] He also found more than 200,000 solar water heaters in use throughout central and southern Japan.[29] Similarly, George Löf was "much impressed" when he went to Japan and met Yanagimachi in 1960.

After two heating and cooling seasons, the house "showed quite satisfactory results and provided comfort for its residents." Yanagimachi estimated that he saved about 50 percent on space heating costs compared to an oil-fired boiler. For a Western audience he adopted a conservative position: "At the present stage, it is premature to appeal to the public with this solar system" for economic reasons. Here the influence of Hottel and Löf is palpable. But due to its postwar reconstruction, and because the country had little fossil-fuel production of its own, Japan confronted more authentic issues of resource scarcity than most other industrialized nations. Therefore Yanagimachi anticipated that "in the very near future . . . it may become economically feasible to have such a solar system in every residence."[30] In the early 1960s, Yanagimachi built three similar projects in a mountain resort area, but for unknown reasons little else occurred. After Yanagimachi II "no technical progress was made" in Japan until 1973, when the solar house entered a period of vigorous growth; more than a dozen experiments appeared in the following few years.[31]

A seminal achievement in the evolution of solar architecture occurred in England, with the 1961–62 St. George's School addition in Wallasey. Here, architect Emslie Morgan created a building which operated for decades without any mechanical heating, despite its poor location (at a latitude matching Edmonton, with about one hour of "median direct sunlight" per day in

St. George's School by Emslie Morgan, Wallasey, Merseyside, U.K., 1961–62. Photograph by Geoffrey Court. English Heritage National Monuments Record

winter). The achievement is all the more impressive because Morgan was a mid-level public servant with no known prior experience in solar heating, and he apparently required no engineering assistance. Morgan conceived a novel "solar wall," a "double-skin facade," covering practically the entire south face of the building. Unlike earlier "direct-gain" architects who emphasized the importance of shading, Morgan provided no protection for the south-facing glass. For the inner layer of the solar wall, the architect specified "figured glass," which scattered the radiation across the interior and restricted views out. Morgan patented the solar wall at the time he designed St. George's.[32]

Additionally, Morgan gave unprecedented creative thought to the concepts of thermal mass and insulation. The two-story structure included a 10-inch concrete floor at the ground, a 9-inch concrete floor at the upper level, and a 7-inch concrete ceiling. (With refracting glass, even the ceiling would function as a significant heat store.) Small portions of the solar wall had black-painted concrete wall sections behind the glass, and brick formed the north wall and interior partitions. There were no separate collectors or storage systems. Then Morgan specified 5 inches of expanded polystyrene insulation outside the mass walls and roof. This was considered a "remarkable thickness" at the time, and decades before the combined effects of insulated concrete were understood. "The earliest reaction," it was reported, "was that the architect had somehow harnessed a new physical principle."[33]

For at least fifteen years St. George's was the largest passive solar heated structure in the world. In fact, the auxiliary heating system which Morgan installed was subsequently removed. Then, a team of engineers from the University of Liverpool conducted extensive studies to determine how the building actually worked. With echoes of Hoyt Hottel, the lead researcher complained: "With its prospect of free heat, the school has been the subject of many press and technical articles . . . often expressing an optimism unsupported by fact or analysis."[34] They recognized that the solar wall would incur "very large losses of heat" at night. After two years of study beginning in 1968, the team found that the solar wall produced a net-gain on an annual basis, although heat losses outweighed gains from November through March. The researchers determined that the sun accounted for about 70 percent of the building's heat, while a considerable 22 percent came from electric lighting (which Morgan anticipated), and the remaining 8 percent from the occupants' body heat.[35] A separate lighting study found the solar wall produced some relatively minor glare problems but praised Morgan for providing good-to-excellent lighting conditions at most student desks.[36]

Reyner Banham understood the St. George's School as a triumphal resolution to the "schism" between architects and engineers, but not due to collaboration. Indeed, Banham used the project to condemn the entire engineering discipline. "Those who have the knowledge," he claimed, "are rarely (as some of them will admit) also equipped with the necessary imagination." He presented Morgan's "professional courage" as a new and transformative paradigm:

> We have a right to look for this kind of self-confidence on the part of the architect, the self-confidence to reject the obvious mechanical solution because they know a better way—and not for the usual reason that they don't know enough about the mechanical methods available to choose the right one, or that they can't find one that fits in with their prefigured ideas of how the architecture should look. And architects will need this kind of self-confidence if they are to make sense of the range of choice in environmental method now open to them.[37]

Another British critic complained that architects had played little part in solar heating, and urged the profession to cease thinking of the subject "as some kind of miracle" and instead "apply themselves to the understanding of the basic energy balances involved."[38] There is no indication that the St. George's School created a subsequent movement in Britain, and the design apparently was not adopted elsewhere.

In France, the great contribution to the solar house movement came from scientist Félix Trombe, who developed and refined the *mur accumulateur* (storage wall), which eventually became known as the Trombe wall. The basic idea that Trombe pursued, placing a mass wall behind south-facing glass to collect and store heat, was not new. John Yellott liked to note that Edward Sylvester Morse patented this concept in 1881, but actually Morse's device, an air heater, would be more accurately characterized as an early flat-plate collector than a storage wall.[39] Nevertheless, several projects discussed earlier employed the general concept of a "storage wall" behind glass, though none used the specific technique Trombe developed. When

Félix Trombe built his first prototype "house" with storage wall in 1956, he launched an experimental and analytical program that would continue for decades and culminate in a new scientific understanding of heat transfer processes. In the end, to argue that Trombe did not technically "invent" the Trombe wall is akin to pointing out that Henry Ford did not invent the automobile. Ironically, the Trombe wall occupied a distinctly minor place in the larger sweep of Trombe's life and work—a side-project. He gave most of his attention to building and operating industrial-scale solar power plants.

Trombe's 1956 project was little more than a shed, whose south wall was built of concrete, approximately one foot thick, painted black and covered with single-pane glass. "Aesthetically, it resembled an overgrown lean-to, its entire south wall blanked out by the solar collector," Daniel Behrman said.[40] He worked in the sunny village of Odeillo, where he led a team of researchers for the French National Center for Scientific Research (CNRS). The timing, in 1956, was significant. Trombe later recalled "passing enthusiasm" for this experiment because France experienced temporary oil rationing due to the Suez crisis at this time.[41] Again, interest in the solar house ebbed and flowed depending on world events and the perception of scarcity. When compared to the major American solar house experiments being built at the same time, Trombe's pursuit reflected a wholly different sensibility. Methods using flat-plate collection were complicated and expensive. "Trombe struck out on a different line," according to Behrman. "Instead of turning on the heat, he acted like a peasant, getting all that he could from the everyday world at the lowest possible cost. That was how the peasants lived during his childhood in the Pyrenees."[42]

The storage wall concept that Trombe built in 1956 included both air heating and thermal mass effects. Solar radiation would rapidly heat the air behind the glass and then this heat was moved by convection into the interior. The concrete wall included vents at the top and bottom to promote this process without fan power. Additionally, the sun would slowly heat the storage wall, which would later heat the interior by radiation. The house remained an uninhabited laboratory, while Trombe and his scientists tested different vent sizes and placements over time. The freethinking environment that Trombe fostered in Odeillo is suggestively indicated by a 1962 experiment—probably a whole new structure—where black-painted containers of water replaced the concrete storage wall. These early experiments were not widely published and little else is known about them.[43]

Trombe began collaborating with architect Jacques Michel in 1966. Michel had worked for Le Corbusier at Chandigarh and Ahmedabad, beginning in 1952, and credited that experience for his interest in "climatic architecture." He also studied at Harvard's Graduate School of Design, earning a master's degree in 1958.[44] Together they built two identical houses for CNRS workers in Odeillo in 1967. This design received considerable publicity and is known as the canonical "Trombe-wall House." Architecturally, Michel treated the 1967 houses in a straightforward manner—four walls and a shed roof, accommodating Trombe's concern for a large south-wall-to-volume ratio. Michel seems to have recognized and accepted that the glass-and-black concrete

collector would dominate the expression. He placed a large door and balcony dead center in the collecting wall, emphasizing its monumentality. On the east and west, rough-cut log siding provided a peculiar contrast, but helped the houses fit their rustic surroundings.

The storage wall generally provided one day of heat. "What happens when the sun doesn't shine?" Daniel Behrman asked. "Trombe decided to solve the problem of long-term heat storage by ignoring it," and relied on electric heaters.[45] Based on personal correspondence with Trombe, William Shurcliff reported some other qualitative results: "Rooms are too cold on some midwinter nights and mornings (unless auxiliary heat is used) and are too warm on some sunny autumn afternoons (unless certain simple ventilation schemes are used), but are entirely comfortable throughout most of the year."[46] Trombe and his team collected data for years, and found very good results. (When Trombe reported these results in technical papers, he referred to the 1967 houses as the "prototypes" and "experimental models," and did not discuss the earlier work.) Over a two-year period, from 1973 to 1975, with interior temperatures maintained at 68°F, solar energy contributed 70 percent of the total heat required. Over eight years, the results were similar. Trombe found about 30 percent of the energy was contributed by air heating and 70 percent by the storage wall. The wall's outer surface would reach 150°F at the afternoon peak, but its internal temperature remained a "fairly uniform" 85°F. In terms of overall efficiency, the collector converted about 36 percent of incident solar energy to space heating, a figure comparable to the best "active" systems. Trombe then developed a sophisticated set of calculations to describe the wall's heat transfer characteristics.[47]

In his experiments, Trombe paid careful attention to the thermal lag time, which he called "time of transmission." The 1956 experiment used a poured-in-place concrete wall approximately 12 inches thick, resulting in an insufficient lag time of 6–8 hours. In the 1967 houses, he used solid concrete blocks and increased the thickness to 60 centimeters (about 24 inches). This extended the "time of transmission" to 14–16 hours, which Trombe said was "too long." Then in the 1974 Odeillo complex, he specified a thinner storage wall—37 centimeters, or about 14.5 inches. This resulted in a lag time of 9–10 hours, "too short." He finally determined that the ideal thickness would be 40–45 centimeters, aiming for about 12 hours of lag.[48]

Michel and Trombe then completed a number of other projects using the same storage wall system. For a private developer in the northeastern location of Chauvency-le-Château, they completed three attached solar houses in 1969–72. This project included several innovations to address the commercial market and the new (less ideal) location. To promote more heating and cooling, the architect and engineer created a "vertical greenhouse" by building the houses into a slope and extending the wall below the floor level.[49] The Chauvency-le-Château project also featured modular steel construction and a more refined aesthetic expression. This led to a prototype prefabricated solar house exhibited at the Paris Fair in 1973, about which little else is known. Back in Odeillo, Trombe and Michel planned a solar village in 1973–74, to consist of thirty-four units in two- and four-story blocks. Here, the architect treated the building as a three-dimensional cubic sculpture, with elements that projected and receded, varying rooflines,

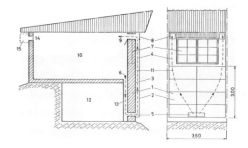

Solar houses by Félix Trombe and Jacques Michel, Chauvency-le-Château, France, 1969–72. Redfield Allen, ed., *Proceedings of the Solar Heating and Cooling for Buildings Workshop* (Washington, D.C.: U.S. Government Printing Office, 1973)

Opposite: Solar house by Félix Trombe and Jacques Michel, Odeillo, France, 1967. Maria Telkes Papers, Arizona State University Libraries, Special Collections

Kelbaugh House by Douglas Kelbaugh, Princeton, New Jersey, 1975. Douglas Kelbaugh

and different glass sections in conflicting sizes and proportions, like patchwork or collage. The effect suggested a medieval hill town with Trombe's solar technology. (Only three units were built.) Michel continued to innovate with storage walls in the 1980s and '90s.[50]

How did the Trombe wall get its name? On the surface this seems an absurd question, but Félix Trombe never used the label, even when he patented the details of its operation. He simply used the term *mur accumulateur* (storage wall). The British magazine *Architectural Design* coined the term "Trombe-Michel wall" in 1973. New Jersey architect Douglas Kelbaugh read that article, "fell in love with the Trombe wall," and brought the technique to America in the design of his own house (Princeton, 1975). Kelbaugh used the term "Trombe wall" when the project was published in 1977, and widespread adoption followed.[51] From an American perspective, the exotic name is appropriate because it marked the first time a solar technology had been "imported," the theme of global interchange now coming full circle. Trombe, a modest man by all accounts, was said to be "embarrassed" that the strategy was named for him.[52]

The Trombe wall appealed to Kelbaugh in part because he and his wife enjoyed the "thermal and architectural presence" of the thick stone walls in their eighteenth-century farmhouse.[53] More importantly, Kelbaugh liked the Trombe wall's "low-tech" nature:

> The easy understandability of the system is very important. Many people like to understand and maintain the mechanical systems in their houses. One of the more alienating aspects of modern home appliances has been that they are rendered useless when one part breaks, and are too complicated to understand or fix. The Trombe system is refreshingly simple and not dependent on 100 percent of its parts working. It is easily understood by most people that I have explained it to, which is an eminently important aspect in the public acceptance of it or any other solar heating system.[54]

The Kelbaugh House was not only the first Trombe wall project in the U.S., but the first two-story application anywhere: "a big risk," according to the architect, due to the possibility of unforeseen effects.[55] (A bit of air stratification occurred, as in any two-story house.) The arrangement made the Princeton house quite "efficient," with 600 square feet of storage wall serving 2,100 square feet of floor space. Kelbaugh punctured his storage wall with a large doorway and six "window" apertures—again, a big risk.

Though Kelbaugh was an architect, Reyner Banham would have admired his "professional courage" in learning to calculate heat balances. His storage wall was 18 inches thick, but later he determined the optimum to be 12 inches for this location. He set it 6 inches behind the insulated glass facade, and on each floor he included upper and lower vents to promote natural

convection, as Trombe did. Kelbaugh also understood, at an early date, the benefits of what would later be called superinsulation, as he created R-20 walls and an R-40 roof. For additional solar heating, he added a prefabricated greenhouse to the all-glass south facade. The greenhouse included a thick floor for storage and retractable shades to prevent summer overheating. Aesthetically, Kelbaugh wanted the house "to be modest, an example of post-industrial, yankee economy." The four exhaust fans at the top of the glass wall delightfully expressed an engineering function, summer cooling.

In terms of energy savings and economics, Kelbaugh's system was remarkably successful— much more so than many notable "active" systems. The architect said the storage wall satisfied 72 percent of the heating load in its first winter, although interior temperatures were a bit low: 63°F downstairs and 67°F upstairs, on average. A few problems were easily solved. At night the house initially experienced "reverse thermosiphoning" (warm air falling down the glass wall and being cooled), which Kelbaugh prevented with some simple plastic dampers. Also, the greenhouse suffered wide temperature swings in the first winter. The architect solved this problem with some water storage tanks. In the end, Kelbaugh figured the payback period to be seventeen years, and he emphasized that its long lifespan would be the critical economic factor. As of late 2011, the house is still occupied and works well.

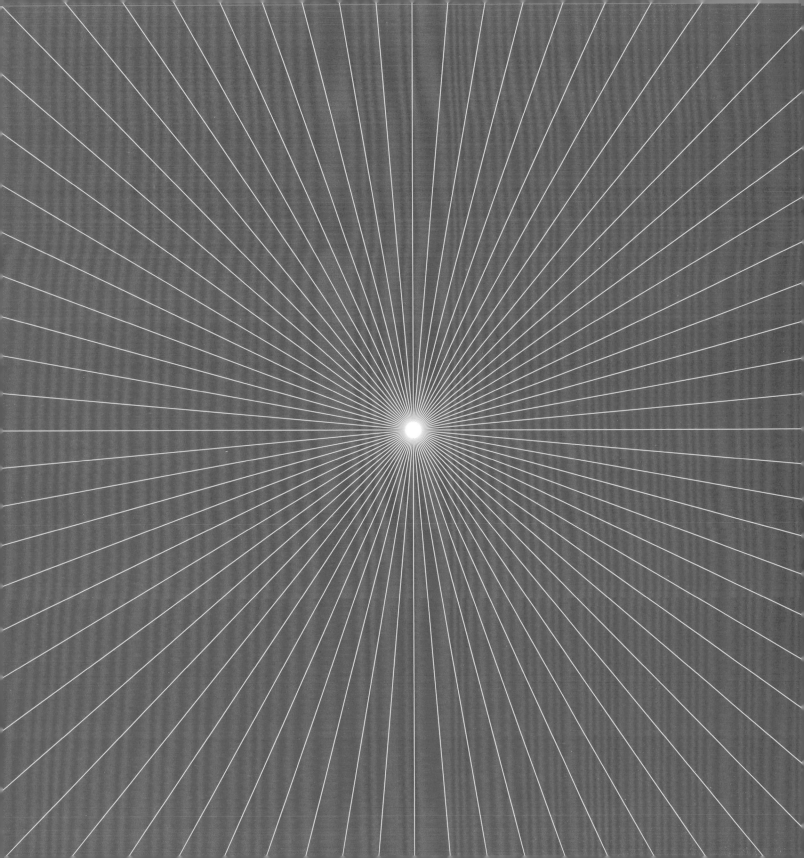

CHAPTER 10

THE 1960S: CREATIVE ACTIVISTS

This whole business of Ph.D.'s and other fancy titles and bureaucratic credentials of all kinds is vastly overrated. The whole field of research has become institutionalized . . . This is one of the big problems in the field of solar energy. Certain people have come to dominate "the club."

. . . There are others. People such as Steve Baer and Harry Thomason. People who've taken their own time and their own money and worked with their own hands to develop a solar energy system that works . . . I call them "creative activists."

—Harold Hay (1976)[1]

While the 1950s represented a "golden age" for solar house experiments in America, it is commonly believed that the movement regressed in the 1960s. Just a few years into the decade, Dan Halacy concluded that "the solar bubble" had "burst" about 1958, in part because the public was disillusioned by "fanciful" and expensive schemes.[2] And from the perspective of the mid-1970s, Daniel Behrman found solar heating had been "an intellectual backwater, almost a forgotten subject," in the 1960s. "Most of its leading practitioners had busied themselves with other things."[3] Indeed, when old friends Hoyt Hottel and George Löf corresponded in summer 1964, Hottel said, "I have got pretty much out of the solar energy field," and Löf replied that his own efforts were "dormant at the present time."[4] The mood of the time is also captured by the fact that there were no solar house presentations—not one—at the Solar Energy Society's 1966 and 1967 meetings.

But in fact experimental zeal moved from university laboratories to backyards and workshops in the 1960s (a "long decade," running from about 1958 to 1973). A new generation of

Peter van Dresser House, Santa Fe, New Mexico, remodeled 1958. Photograph by Richard Register

"creative activists," including mad-scientist types, hippies, and dropouts, effectively created a solar counterculture with a strong antiestablishment streak (as the quotation above indicated). Their work proved to be inventive and successful without external support—a collection of major contributions. The theme of disciplinary integration receded in favor of concerns such as indigenous traditions and technological simplicity. Indeed, in retrospect it is clear that the 1960s constituted a different type of golden age.

Peter van Dresser, who called himself a "drop-out from the Eastern megalopolis," moved to rural New Mexico to work with folk traditions and "natural energy" after studying architecture and engineering at Cornell.[5] In 1949, he designed what he called "an early biotechnic house" using native materials, solar heating, and wind energy. "I put a *great* deal of effort into that pioneering house," he recalled, "and inevitably, I guess, made some basic mistakes in the design."[6] As a proto-hippie, van Dresser brought a countercultural flavor to the solar house movement, a theme which will fully emerge in the 1970s. Looking backward, he participated in the 1930s decentralist movement and thus embodies another historical link between the Great Depression and the solar house.

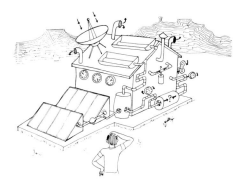

Must a Solar House be so Complicated?

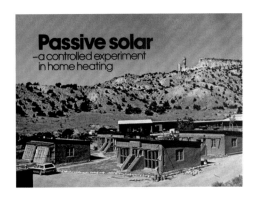

Top: Illustration from *Homegrown Sundwellings* by Peter van Dresser, 1977

Above: Sundwellings by Peter van Dresser et al., Abiquiu, New Mexico, 1974. *Popular Science* (April 1978)

Opposite: David Wright House, Santa Fe, New Mexico, 1974. John I. Yellott Papers, Arizona State University Libraries, Special Collections

In a more influential 1958 project, he found a 1930s adobe building in Santa Fe and extensively remodeled it for solar heating. Besides learning from his earlier mistakes, van Dresser "studied all the literature that was available" and "all the newest ideas from other experimenters" before he began to build (undermining his image as a true outsider). He even visited Maria Telkes at the Dover house. He decided to use a Löf-type air-and-rock system, with steel absorber plates rather than overlapping glass. Because the existing house was oriented north-south, he created two banks of flat-plate collectors and two separate storage beds beneath the floor. He used 230 square feet of collectors for about 500 square feet of floor space. The system functioned well, providing about 60 percent of the heating required. Architecturally, van Dresser built tall slanting attics to accommodate the panels, which gave the structure a unique shape and exploited adobe's sculptural quality. It produced an unusual combination of high- and low-tech imagery. In 1981 it was placed on the New Mexico State Register as a historic site.

Although van Dresser's 1958 project used collectors and storage, he later criticized the tendency to rely on mechanical solutions:

> Solar homes are viewed as engineered products and we naturally apply to their design and fabrication the well-tried techniques of the heating and air conditioning industry, of hydronic engineering and assembly-line metal fabrication . . . these systems, of course, tend to be complex and costly.[7]

Indeed, the rejection of complexity became a common theme among the "creative activists" in the long decade of the 1960s. Many believed that failed schemes like the *Living with the Sun* house had actually harmed the solar movement: "Fanciful drawings of homes roofed with solar batteries . . . were taken too literally, and when people learned that such a roof would cost hundreds of thousands of dollars . . . interest understandably waned."[8]

Van Dresser later assembled a team to complete an unprecedented experiment called "Sundwellings." This project, built at the Ghost Ranch Conference Center in Abiquiu, New Mexico, in 1974, consisted of four small adobe buildings: a control unit with "ordinary windows," a direct-gain unit, a Trombe wall unit, and a greenhouse unit. "There's nothing spectacular about these designs," van Dresser said.[9] On a characteristic February day, the greenhouse type worked best, supplying 77 percent of heat needs. The direct-gain method supplied 68 percent, and the (vented) Trombe wall contributed 57 percent.[10] The attached "sunspace" subsequently became a popular strategy nationwide. In general, van Dresser advocated for adobe as a "low-energy material," showing an early interest in what is now called embodied energy.[11] Jeffrey Cook argued that the attention to both solar energy and indigenous building practices made Sundwellings a "model of ecological and human integrity."[12]

Van Dresser became recognized as "one of the granddaddies of environmental and natural-energy activists"[13] in New Mexico, which became a center of solar house activity. Sundwellings veteran David Wright built a direct-gain adobe house for himself in Santa Fe in 1974. "I began to

look around," Wright said, "and think about how the native peoples there in New Mexico had survived and kept themselves comfortable."[14] He recognized the importance of thermal mass—with modern transformations. Wright designed what he called "the traditional Southwest floor," brick over 24 inches of adobe, but then he added a layer of insulation beneath the adobe. Similarly, in the adobe walls, he realized that the insulation should be placed *outside* the thermal mass (as at the St George's School). The house could store enough heat for three sunless days.[15]

The David Wright House (sometimes called "Sunscoop") surely reflected the influence of an earlier "Wright" house—the Jacobs Hemicycle. (There is no familial relation.) Though David Wright's all-glass south facade was not curved, its rear wall was both circular and earth-bermed. And its interior essentially consisted of a single room with a sleeping loft. As in Frank Lloyd Wright's hemicycle, occupants of the Santa Fe house would experience profound contrasts between heavy and light, front and back. In terms of aesthetics, David Wright treated the double-height glass in a plain, repetitive manner, and simply enframed it with the adobe structure and four-foot timber roof overhang. He determined the depth of the house by the solar angle at the winter solstice.

Wright, like Fred Keck, studied the integrative but uncommon field of architectural engineering, and therefore was predisposed to tackle technical as well as aesthetic issues. He eventually planned to add a small active system to supplement the passive gains, making the house a "hybrid"-type. After studying and admiring Löf's system, he "began playing around with air collectors." (Like van Dresser, he embraced both ancient/vernacular techniques and the modern history of the solar house.) He preferred Löf's technology because "it just wasn't nearly

as costly to build and seal a system that pumped air around as it was to build and seal a system that pumped water or some other fluid around."[16] An early photo shows tubes sticking out of the floor slab; these were meant to deliver hot air from the external collectors (mounted to the ground) to air chambers in the adobe sub-floor.

And Wright's Santa Fe house, more than thirty years later, recapitulated an issue that Keck experienced in the 1940s: overheating and wide temperature swings. During a two-week evaluation in January 1976, temperatures fluctuated between 58°F and 80°F, with considerable stratification. Wright added fifteen water drums behind the glass wall to help reduce temperature swings. He also designed interior folding Styrofoam panels for night insulation, but these did "not fit snugly enough against the glass" to prevent cold drafts. Still, Bruce Anderson marveled that Wright "achieves more than 90 percent solar heating in a 6200 degree day climate."[17] It was claimed that Wright designed over eighty "sun tempered" and "passively solar conditioned" homes in the mid-1970s, including "Sundown" in Sea Ranch, California (1976). He also published *Natural Solar Architecture* (1978).

Another member of van Dresser's team, architect William Lumpkins, designed a solar adobe house which took the most effective strategy from Sundwellings, the greenhouse, and made it an integral feature in a larger dwelling. The Balcomb House (Santa Fe, 1976) demonstrated the concept of *isolated gain* or the *sunspace* (first used by Arthur Brown in 1946). A sunspace is defined as a room that is deliberately allowed to overheat (and overcool) in order to heat the occupied spaces behind it. The Balcomb House—so known for its owner, solar researcher J. Douglas Balcomb—earned a place in the HUD Solar Demonstration Program and was probably the first passive solar house to receive federal funding as a research project.[18]

Lumpkins gave the Balcomb House a unique form, much more compact than Keck-type linear plans. He created a two-story elbow-shaped structure with the void space facing south, then bridged across the two wings diagonally to enclose the sunspace with 400 square feet of glass. Because it was integral to the structure, the Balcomb sunspace avoided some the typical drawbacks of attached greenhouses: nighttime losses through east- and west-facing walls and the tendency to superheat in late afternoons. Adobe interior walls between the sunspace and living areas stored heat for night. Balcomb found the sunspace suitable for growing plants, which also helped humidify the air. Yet again the adobe was given a soft sculptural appearance; the exterior resembled a well-worn catcher's mitt.

The Balcomb system included ducts and fans to send hot air from the top of the sunspace to two rock beds beneath the ground-floor interior rooms. This boosted the amount of heat storage and mitigated overheating.[19] Its performance was recorded in detail. The results showed the house was 80-percent solar heated (with a 65°F set-point). The 14-inch storage wall between the sunspace and living room behaved "like a Trombe wall but with less pronounced response." Moreover, the house's interior spaces showed "amazing thermal stability."[20] After the Balcomb House, the popularity of the sunspace would become "the most significant trend in passive solar design" by 1980.[21]

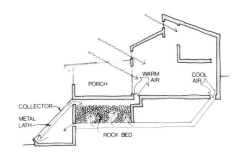

Paul Davis House by Steve Baer, Corrales, New Mexico, 1972. Martin McPhillips, *The Solar Age Resource Book* (Houston: Everest, 1979)

Opposite: "Zome" House by Steve Baer, Corrales, New Mexico, 1971–72. Photograph by Boyd Norton. National Archives and Records Administration

Van Dresser's "outsider" influence in New Mexico strongly affected the work of Steve Baer, a self-described "crackpot" who contributed several techniques to the history of the solar house based on a low-tech homemade approach. "Solar heating just seemed like the obvious thing to do around here," Baer remembered.[22] After visiting van Dresser's Santa Fe house in the late 1960s, he began to experiment with solar air heaters. His house for Paul Davis (Corrales, New Mexico, 1972) used adobe walls, flat-plate air heaters, and rock storage, but improved upon van Dresser's system in a pair of important ways. Inside the collectors, Baer used multiple layers of expanded metal lath as the "collector plate." And, more importantly, Baer placed the collector *below* the storage bed (which remained below the house), allowing the system to work by natural convection. With no fans, the system operated silently and provided 75 percent of the house's heat needs.[23]

Baer was one of the few major figures in the solar house movement educated neither as architect or engineer (though he did calculate heat gains and losses and storage capacities). Indeed, Baer developed a healthy skepticism of the professional engineers:

> Paul Davis and I were told by engineers at the Los Alamos Lab, who had been studying fan-driven air loop rock storage systems, that convective systems were "way down in the mud," with little to recommend them . . . After talking to the Los Alamos group we found that they had never actually experimented with any rocks, but instead were using only computer simulations.
>
> I can't help dwelling on these petty slights at the hands of the engineers, probably because there is an element of truth in what they say. Designing a convective air loop system is a somewhat tricky and difficult task. If you aren't very respectful of the will of the air, the system won't work.[24]

Baer offered fifteen design tips for what he called "Air Loop Rock Storage Systems," all of which remain generally applicable.

In his own "Zome" House (Corrales, 1971–72), Baer created a solar house that was absolutely original, both in terms of architecture and engineering. Baer created the "zome" (from zonohedron and dome) after initial inspiration from German children's toys and then further study of crystals and Buckminster Fuller's geodesic structures. He sometimes called the zomes "exploded rhombic dodecahedra"; they consisted of a network of 120-degree angles.[25] Before building his own house, Baer experimented with these geometries at the hippie commune Drop City (Trinidad, Colorado) where he used salvaged auto body parts. (He also built his first air collectors at Drop City.) At the Corrales house, the walls were made of insulated aluminum panels, similar to those used in trailers and airplanes, giving the exterior a completely different character than the adobe-and-glass tradition. Architectural historian Jeffrey Cook called the aesthetic effect "a whole other trip."[26]

"Zome" House by Steve Baer, Corrales, New Mexico, 1971–72. Photograph by Boyd Norton. National Archives and Records Administration

To collect solar heat, Baer reintroduced the water wall concept that MIT scientists had tried and abandoned in 1946–48. He claimed he only learned about MIT II *after* he built the Corrales house. When Baer did examine the project, he criticized Hoyt Hottel and again invoked a larger critique of the engineering mindset:

> He decided it didn't work. But that was because he didn't do it the right way. And he didn't keep on. If he'd been some crackpot, he might have . . . The crackpot is ready to explore new territory without government funding. There's gotta be room for crackpots in any society.[27]

Baer's "drumwall"—a collection of 55-gallon drums of water—absorbed solar heat all day and slowly radiated it at night and warmed the air by convection. Like a Trombe wall, it worked without ducts, fans, or plumbing, and therefore required no operating energy and little maintenance. Bruce Anderson found the drumwall "an aesthetically pleasing contribution to interior living spaces," and it became a widespread technique in the 1970s.[28]

To address the losses outward at night, Baer devised a series of large insulated wall panels, outside the glass, which were hinged at the bottom and could be operated from inside with winches. In their "open" position, the shiny aluminum panels would act as reflectors. Edge leaks remained a significant problem, as they were in Cambridge a generation earlier. The zome geometry and the drum wall with movable insulation were essentially independent concepts, and Baer acknowledged that the design created a large amount of surface area and extra heat loss. Still, because of the excellent thermal properties of water, the design only required 400 square feet of collection area for 2,000 square feet of interior space: ". . . about half the conventional ratio of collector to floor area," Baer boasted. The house's performance was not rigorously recorded, but Baer reported using one cord of wood per winter as auxiliary heat, with solar heat fulfilling about 90 percent of the total need.[29] (Reyner Banham derisively referred to "Wood-burning Baer" and criticized the house's technology as "far from radical . . . individualistic, property-oriented, conservative and defensive."[30] Again, Banham was practically unique among architectural historians in his attention to such issues.) Baer also invented the "Skylid," a skylight with automated ventilators and insulated shutters, and the "bead wall," which consisted of two layers of glass and a method for filling the cavity with beads of Styrofoam at night.

When Baer's zome house attracted media attention for the Santa Fe school, a new discourse emerged around larger cultural/political issues. Baer discussed the power companies' desire for "predictable consumers," and van Dresser, as the Santa Fe school's elder statesman, voiced a sweeping critique:

> So much of our thinking about energy—about everything—is based on false assumptions. In America we assume we need all the energy we use. But for the most part we just fabricate amusements and distractions.[31]

Now the solar house moved beyond its professional and academic roots to align with the counterculture and the emerging environmental movement. Van Dresser and Baer, the dropout and the Drop City crackpot, clearly transformed both the art and science of the solar house through a rich mix of scientific exploration, sensitivity to history, cultural critique, and disciplinary independence.

Harry Thomason agitated against the solar house "establishment" in the 1960s from a different angle than van Dresser and his allies. A patent attorney for the Pentagon, Thomason was not a hippie but he relished his role as an outsider. He always took pains to mention that he worked "individually and without institutional support."[32] Eventually he could claim to hold more patents in the field of solar energy than anyone else in the world—nearly three dozen—and more than a thousand people had purchased his house plans. At least twenty were in operation in the mid-1970s.

Thomason's major contribution was his development of an "open-flow" or "trickle-type" collector where water ran down the surface of the absorber plate rather than being pushed

through pipes. Like Fred Keck and Arthur Brown before him, Thomason attributed his interest in solar heating to a happy accident. As quoted by Tracy Kidder, Thomason stood near a barn on a sunny day, when a storm rolled in:

> Down came the rain. I ran under the overhang on the barn roof and I thought to myself, "Gosh, that's nice warm water." I looked up to see where it was comin' from. Right off the old barn roof. Instantly—of course, it's what we call a flash of genius—I realized what was goin' on. "That's a solar collector there." I just dashed under the overhang. Cold water had been fallin' on my head. Now here came warm water on my head off the barn roof. That was the original inspiration.[33]

Thomason built his first house solar house in 1959 in District Heights, Maryland, and the trickle system he devised was barely any more complicated than the barn roof.

The basic concept was familiar: to heat water with a flat-plate collector, store the water in a tank inside the structure, and use that water to heat the air inside the house. What made Thomason's system different and successful was its low-tech nature and its effectiveness. Thomason constantly asked: "How can the cost be lowered?" His answer was to use conventional materials and construction methods that were simple and easy for semi-skilled workmen.[34] The Thomason collector basically consisted of black-painted corrugated aluminum and a glass cover. Water was pumped to the ridge and flowed freely down the metal valleys where it collected in a horizontal gutter and then flowed to the storage tanks. Compared to the Hottel-type collector, much more surface area of water would be exposed to heat. And the system was said to be fail-safe, because there was no threat of pipes freezing and bursting and the collector was easy to drain.[35] One observer called it a "seat-of-the-pants design," and another said this was "about as simple and cheap as an active solar collector can get."[36] Thomason's 1959 prototype ("Solaris") included a storage and distribution system practically identical to the very first active solar house—MIT I— with a basement storage tank (surrounded by stone rather than insulation) and air heated by being moved over the surface of the tank.[37]

Aesthetically, Thomason's 1959 house did not make any pretense to the art of architecture; even one of his promoters called it a "gawky, odd-looking structure."[38] Thomason designed the house himself, probably from a standard builder's plan, and he picked a north-facing lot so that the sloped collector wall could not be seen from the street. The roof folded down over the eave line in the rear to become a sloped wall, increasing its area but blocking views to the south. The

Left: "Solaris" House III by Harry Thomason, District Heights, Maryland, 1959. *Popular Mechanics* (June 1973)

Opposite: "Solaris" House I by Harry Thomason, District Heights, Maryland, 1962. Author's collection

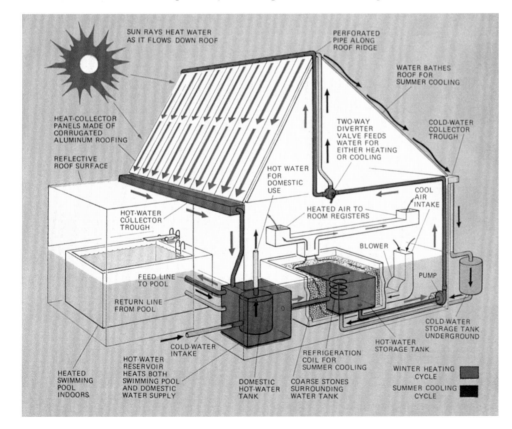

overall effect recalled a dull tract house with a strangely shaped, oversized greenhouse on the back. Thomason conceded that the house had "a few bizarre flourishes," but he argued: "Regardless of how it looks, it works."[39]

The prototype proved to be both economical and very effective—certainly the most successful solar house to date on the basis of performance. With a total construction cost of $13,000, Thomason figured the solar heating system accounted for less than $2,500, and it included a conventional furnace and water heater. (Recall MIT IV had cost $38,000 plus about $6,500 for the heating system two years earlier.) In the first winter, the trickle system provided an astonishing 95–98 percent of the heat requirements, despite the location, which offered about 42 percent sunshine. His heating bill totaled $4.65 for the entire winter.[40] The storage system provided enough carry-through for five successive overcast days. Thomason constantly measured water temperatures and flow rates, and he was most surprised to find that, even on a cloudy day, the trickle collector heated the water by 10 degrees.[41] (Hottel- and Löf-type collectors were not effective without direct sun.)

Immediately, in 1960, Thomason built a second Solaris house next door to the first. He made minor improvements to simplify the system and reduce its cost, but otherwise it was a twin and performed similarly well.[42] In Solaris III (for client Omer Henry, 1962), Thomason reconfigured the roof to create a taller attic section in back, again an awkward look. He then created room on the south with a flat roof and an indoor pool, where the roof would reflect additional radiation up to the collectors. By 1965 he had built four houses. The fourth house introduced a new method for heat storage: a "pancake" water tank 12–15 inches deep beneath the entire floor. Later, in the "Sunny South Model," he added a shallow roof pond to the south room after learning about work by John Yellott and Harold Hay (discussed later in this chapter).[43]

William Shurcliff, a retired Harvard physicist who became a solar house champion in his retirement, found Solaris installations to be sound and economical: ". . . they avoid about a dozen complexities and pitfalls." He wrote a list of fifteen reasons to prefer the trickle collectors to conventional types.[44] Another scientist remarked that the Solaris system "makes real good engineers climb the walls. It's a Pinto, not a Cadillac. It's like a Model A, it'll rattle around some, but the data coming in looks good. He's a little guy with a widget that works."[45] In fact, Thomason enjoyed contrasting his successes with "past failures" by engineers. He expressed astonishment that MIT abandoned their $6,500 system after three years, while his own $2,500 system still worked well after fifteen years.[46] He also argued against what he called "solar welfare"—federal funding of academic projects.

By the 1970s, Thomason was recognized as "the leading folk figure in solar energy, a pole of attraction for all those who want to believe that ingenuity in a home workshop can achieve results faster than Ph.D.'s on government grants."[47] The antagonism between Thomason and the engineering community culminated in Congressional testimony in 1973. George Löf, now planning a series of federally funded solar houses at Colorado State University, told a subcommittee on energy:

Harry Thomason with trickle collector, 1974.
Author's collection

Opposite: "Solaris" House I by Harry Thomason, District Heights, Maryland, 1959. John I. Yellott Collection, American Heritage Center, University of Wyoming

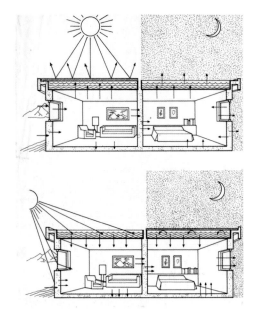

Skytherm "operating principles." John I. Yellott Papers, Arizona State University Libraries, Special Collections

Opposite: Skytherm prototype by Harold Hay and John Yellott, Phoenix, Arizona, 1967. D. S. Halacy, *The Coming Age of Solar Energy* (New York: Harper & Row, 1963)

> Virtually all of our knowledge of solar heating and cooling has resulted from the work of a few forward looking, persistent university faculty members; ample support of their continuing research should receive high priority in order that the data needed by potential manufacturers can be available.[48]

Thomason called Löf's statement "baloney" and "poppycock." He complained: "All of that 'knowledge' of the university faculty members *has not produced one single solar heating and cooling system for public use.*"[49] Thomason even asked the *Congressional Record* to remove Löf's Denver house from a list of solar-heated houses, because it did not receive a majority of its heat from the sun.[50]

Harold Hay, like Thomason, provided Congressional testimony in 1973 and used the opportunity to draw clear distinctions between the "creative activists" and the establishment.

> About 25 solar-heated buildings have been built in the U.S. Practically all those built with government (state or federal) funds have been failures and are now abandoned. In the main they were academic, impractical ventures . . . [Thomason and Baer] have built more solar houses without government support than any other individuals who have such support.[51]

Hay could speak from authority, having developed the "Skytherm" system, a novel method of using roof ponds and moveable insulation for 100-percent passive heating and cooling. Hay was a chemist and building-materials expert, described by a friend as "a caricature of the mad inventor."[52] He studied vernacular building traditions, and could discuss at length how indigenous people around the world achieved comfort in hot climates.[53] When traveling to India in 1954, Hay saw people living in tin houses which were too hot by day and too cold at night. He recalled: "I realized that even if such houses had insulation, it would be in the wrong place half of the time. What was really needed was insulation on wheels."[54]

Back in America, Hay began to explore and then demonstrate the principle that would become the "Skytherm" system. Steve Baer recalled:

> I would count Harold Hay's experiment with a styrofoam ice chest as among the most exciting and illuminating ever done. In Phoenix, Hay filled one of the insulated chests one sees in the supermarkets with water. During the summer he put the lid on during the day and took it off during the night. The water stayed cool, for it was protected from the sun during the day and at night heat radiated to the night sky. During the cool months of winter, Hay

reversed it—he opened the lid during the day and closed it during the night. The water stayed warm.[55]

(In fact, Hay's experiment convinced Baer to use water storage and movable insulation in his "Zome" House, discussed above.) Hay's idea also aroused the interest of John Yellott, and the two of them began to collaborate. They might have constituted an "odd couple," with Hay being "contemptuous" of "the 'aerospace approach' of engineers who experiment with complex systems of pumps, pipes, valves, fans and airducts"—a fair characterization of Yellott's *Living with the Sun* system.[56]

Hay and Yellott built a one-room prototype structure in Phoenix in 1966, with a roof-pond and sliding insulation panels. The initial test dwelling was built "without as much as an advance sketch," and details "often followed ideas conceived the night before."[57] Due to the need for receptacle positions for the insulation panels, the design included a carport on the west and an open porch on the east. The roof-pond (enclosed within plastic bags) rested upon a metal ceiling which would directly heat or cool the interior. No ducts or pumps were required. Hay, who was aware of Fred Keck's water-cooled roofs, always emphasized the simple physics involved: "When black pavement gets so hot that you can't walk on it, that's solar heating. The next morning, it's too cold to walk on barefoot and it wasn't air conditioning that cooled it but the heat going off to the night sky. That's what happens on my roof."[58] When Hay was asked how people would know when to move the panels, Baer recalled: "His answer was that people learn when to put on and when to take off their coats."[59] Here, Hay could be accused of oversimplifying. In more scientific terms, they found the insulation should be moved within a half-hour of the "optimum time," but did not explain how to determine that time.[60]

After an eighteen-month trial in 1967–68, Hay and Yellott could boast that interior comfort levels (68–82°F) had been maintained without supplementary heating or cooling.[61] In winter, when the water reached 85°F, it provided enough heat to carry over for five cloudy days. Nighttime losses proved to be significant because better methods of sealing were needed. In summer they removed the plastic bags and used an open pond to promote evaporation. (Subsequently they recommended covering the bags with a thin layer of water.) The dew point temperature, they found, was "the most important factor in determining the cooling capability of the night sky."[62] Hay explained the Skytherm concept was not only scalable for larger footprints, it would work even better because wall effects would be minimized.

Then, after searching in vain for research funding for years, Hay finally used his own money to build a full-scale house—the Skytherm House, completed in 1972–73, in Atascadero, California. The lack of support may be difficult to understand, given the prototype's success and Yellott's connections, but this only serves to illuminate the political context that had developed by the late 1960s. Support for solar energy research was essentially nonexistent at this time.[63] "Why this widespread lack of concern?" William Shurcliff asked. "Because fuel was so cheap. The prevailing attitude was: if the house loses heat rapidly, let the furnace run harder and longer!"[64] Between 1948 and 1972, oil prices dropped 30 percent.[65]

Harold Hay with SkyTherm House, Atascadero, California, 1972–73. Norma Skurka and Jon Naar, *Design for a Limited Planet: Living with Natural Energy* (New York: Ballantine Books, 1976

For the Atascadero house, Hay worked with a group of faculty members at the California Polytechnic State University at San Luis Obispo to design the house; Kenneth Haggard was the principal architect. For both thermal mass and structural strength, the team used concrete block construction, expressed as a series of north-south walls. The thick roof plane, to conceal 8.5 inches of water and three layers of insulated panels, extended to shade the south wall. This gave the overall image a pronounced visual heaviness, a solar fortress. Both Hay and Yellott considered it an aesthetic asset that the system would not be visible from the street. Haggard believed he could build the next Skytherm house at "no greater first cost than a typical custom designed home."[66]

The Atascadero house remained comfortable for a year with the water bags providing 100 percent of the heating and cooling needs. In post-1973 parlance, it saved forty-two barrels of oil per year.[67] The occupants judged the heating to be "distinctly superior" to a furnace, and they found the cooling "far superior" to air-conditioning.[68] With no fans or pumps, the system was quiet and required little maintenance. Hay said: "I think I have a cheaper way of storing solar heat than anyone."[69] Yellott (and others) later developed a system he called the "Energy Roof," which moved the water rather than the insulation, using pumps and plastic containers. This system was demonstrated at Arizona State University in 1976–77.[70] Hay built "Skytherm North,"

a two-story house, near St. Paul, Minnesota, in 1979. It included a sloped glass cover above the usual roof to deflect snow. The system was "not advantageous for heating" in such a cold climate.[71] Later studies found the Skytherm method could produce comfortable interior temperatures during all hours of a typical summer in all American climates.[72]

In the Boston area, electrical engineer Norman Saunders reconsidered the idea of a solar house from first principles. Saunders, like Thomason, was more a mad scientist than a hippie or dropout. A friend called him "an inventor of the lone-wolf type" who succeeded by "ignoring the popular trends in solar design."[73] Like many of the other "creative activists," Saunders considered simplicity a virtue. "The best way to collect the sun's heat energy at the place you want to use it is through windows," he said.[74] His interest in "passive" strategies challenged the major assumptions of the engineering establishment in the 1950s and '60s.

Beginning in 1959, Saunders built "Experimental Manor," in Weston, Massachusetts, which served both as his home and solar laboratory for decades. He began by contracting a "stock architectural design" from The Architects Collaborative (TAC), Walter Gropius's firm. He wanted to see if such a house "could be modified to incorporate solar heating to produce a situation that was comfortable to live in and experiment with."[75] The extent of TAC's involvement in the project is unknown. The TAC design, a two-story box, came with a distinct disadvantage for direct solar gains: a deep plan with a low ratio of south facade to total area (900 square feet to 2,625 square feet). However the design did treat the south wall in an intelligent manner, with large glass panes protected by a six-foot-deep overhang and wing walls.

"Sun shining directly upon concrete at an oblique angle," Saunders said, "can be stored quite satisfactorily right there in the concrete," and so he gave unprecedented attention to thermal mass.[76] He may have been the first to calculate the total storage capacity of a solar house. (Experimental Manor held 75,000 Btu/°F.) He also experimented with wall and roof constructions to achieve high R-values.[77] Sometime after original construction, Saunders moved the lower-level glass wall out to the edge of the balcony, in effect creating a low-mass sunspace, or air heater. Fans sent hot air from the south-facing rooms to the north and helped minimize overheating. A hollow-mass floor (concrete blocks under a poured concrete slab) could also store heat when the direct gain was "exceptionally large."[78] (The cavities were originally intended to contain Glauber's salt, but he "await[ed] Telkes' perfected change of phase stores" for sixteen years.[79]) Overall, Saunders estimated one-third of the solar gains went to direct space heating, one-third to the northern rooms, and one-third to storage.

On the flat roof, Saunders deployed a variety of collectors over time, mostly flat-plate air heaters. In total, he tried eleven different collectors, including a parabolic-trough, but none apparently showed enough promise for broader application.[80] "Each development at Experimental Manor," he said, "was only undertaken when it seemed likely that the investment would be quickly

SAUNDERS SHREWSBURY HOUSE

100% SOLAR HEATED   FULLY AUTOMATIC   TRULY LOW COST

BY

W.A. SHURCLIFF

NO FURNACE, NO WOODSTOVE • WEEK-LONG CARRYTHROUGH
NOTHING TO ADJUST EACH DAY • NO THERMAL SHADES
HUGE SOUTH WINDOWS • 12 NON-SOUTH WINDOWS
FRESH AIR INPUT AT ALL TIMES
COOL ALL SUMMER • INTEGRAL GREENHOUSE
COST SAME AS FOR CONVENTIONAL HOUSE

Saunders Shrewsbury House by William A. Shurcliff, 1982. Author's collection

Opposite: "Experimental Manor" by Norman Saunders and The Architects' Collaborative, Weston, Massachusetts, 1959. Dean Carriere, *Solar Houses for a Cold Climate* (New York: Scribner, 1980)

returned," underlining the pragmatic basis of his experiments and the contrast with his academic neighbors.[81] After its completion in 1961, Experimental Manor's performance varied as new ideas were tested, but finally stabilized years later at a 65 percent solar contribution. Jeanne Saunders said the house only overheated three times in twenty years.[82] The engineer freely admitted that Experimental Manor was a poor prototype for future work, in part because of the limitations of the architectural plan. He believed: "I've made more mistakes than anyone else in the field."[83] (It is difficult to imagine such a statement from "establishment" figures like Hottel or Löf.) Still, by 1976, he had accumulated enough wisdom to issue some "important guidelines" for solar heating:

> 1) Insulate as much as you can.
> 2) Collect as much heat as you can.
> 3) Store as much heat as you can afford.
> 4) Avoid moving the heat.[84]

By giving top priority to a non-solar strategy, Saunders anticipated the concerns of the superinsulation movement of the 1980s. Similarly, he complained about TAC's insistence on metal-framed windows, because he recognized "metal is a thermal short circuit."[85] Here he recognized a concept—the *thermal bridge*—years before it was formally established.

Next, Saunders developed the "Solar Staircase," a completely original method of construction for creating controlled direct-gain in a south-facing roof slope. This design was essentially a large skylight with an interior structure quite literally like a staircase, with a series of vertical "risers" and horizontal "treads." The risers were glass or plastic and the treads were mirrors on both sides. The whole assembly was then encased in sloped glass on both sides. With the proper geometric design, the heat would be reflected away in summer and admitted in winter. In fact, because of the mirroring effects, Saunders's design would effectively add one-third to the total vertical height of the risers. A one-room prototype, built in 1976, achieved near-100-percent solar heating with water storage containers at ceiling level (and some temperature swings).[86] Then, in 1976–77, he built a large-scale version at the Cambridge School in Weston. It provided 40 percent of the building's heat, excellent daylighting, and a payback period of six years.[87] Saunders built five such systems by 1978, and patented the concept.[88]

In 1981–82, Saunders achieved 100 percent solar heating in the Boston area "at no operating cost and at no greater construction cost than the conventional fully insulated buildings."[89] The Shrewsbury House used a variation on the Solar Staircase, where he placed glass bottles of water in an attic directly beneath the glass-roofed staircase. The entire concept was novel; you might call it an "attic-driven house." Additionally, Saunders treated the entire south side of the house as an integral greenhouse, and devised special "thermosiphoning" windows to place between this sunspace and the living spaces. All of this hot air was sent to the attic. Then, on the superinsulated north side, a series of fans and ducts pushed "residual" hot air from the attic to a rock bed beneath the lower floor slab. The living spaces were "sandwiched" between upper and lower heat storage, with three walls superinsulated (R-30) and one solar heated. Through the first winter, owner Robert Bushey was able to keep the house at about 70°F with no backup heat.[90] Harvard physicist William Shurcliff admired the structure so much he published a book about it. "Each [strategy], although simple and unimpressive, contributes significantly. Together, they provide a full, but low-cost, solution."[91] In 1973, George Löf and economist Richard Tybout had warned against attempting to achieve 100-percent solar heating in cold climates, because the costs would be too high.[92] This became a rallying point for Shurcliff, who called Löf's position "the classic rule" and enjoyed announcing: "The performance of Shrewsbury House, and its low cost, permit us now to declare the classic rule is dead."[93]

Ultimately, the creative activists exhibited the same fundamental weakness in the long decade of the 1960s that the establishment had experienced in the 1950s: limited influence. Thomason may have sold a thousand plans, but a legacy of importance never materialized. Likewise, Harold Hay reflected with frustration that the Skytherm system was "DOE's best kept-secret buried under hundreds of reports," and was forced to admit "it's gone nowhere."[94] In fact Fred Keck, who was essentially retired in the 1960s, remained the most successful solar house builder in terms of sheer numbers, and those numbers were small. By 1971, Farrington Daniels was forced to conclude:

> Solar house heating has not been successful. In a report to President Truman in 1952, it was stated that by 1975 there would be a market for 2 million solar heated houses in the United States, mostly in the southern half. As of 1971, there are only a few solar heated houses, with storage of heat, in the whole world.[95]

However noble and prescient it may have been, the solar house remained a fringe movement rather than a mainstream concern of architecture, engineering, or the building industry. When the context changed dramatically, in 1973, the solar house possessed a robust record of experimental successes and failures, but not a coherent identity.

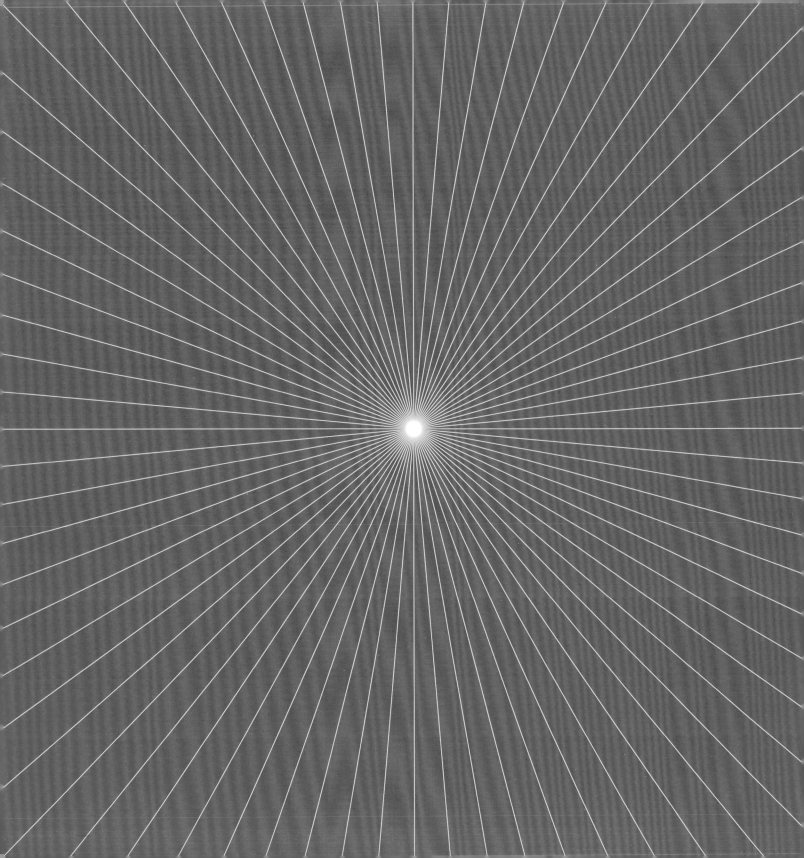

CHAPTER 11

AFTER THE CRISIS

No one can ever embargo the sun or interrupt its delivery to us.

—President Jimmy Carter (1979)[1]

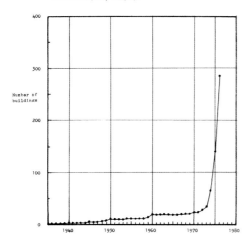

From *Solar Heated Buildings: A Brief Survey* by William A. Shurcliff (13th ed., 1977)

Saudi Arabia's oil embargo beginning in October 1973 gave new momentum to the solar house movement in America. Oil prices jumped 600 percent within months, and lines at gasoline stations were common. President Nixon responded with "Project Independence," which aimed to achieve energy self-sufficiency for the country by 1980.[2] Although the embargo was sudden and unexpected, concerns about energy had been mounting for a few years. For example, Nixon established an Energy Policy Office and sent a message to Congress in 1971 which promised "greater attention to solar energy."[3] The oil crisis intersected with another key factor in the solar house's renaissance—the environmental movement—which also emerged before 1973, as Witold Rybczynski recently noted in a review of the exhibition *Sorry, Out of Gas.*[4] The first Earth Day, in 1970, was the largest demonstration in American history.

In his epic series *Solar Heated Buildings: A Brief Survey*, William Shurcliff documented solar architecture's remarkable success after 1973. After thirteen editions he terminated the project in 1977 because: "(a) the number of solar heated buildings is increasing so fast . . . and (b) duplicate designs are becoming increasingly common."[5] The final edition comprised 319 discrete examples (not including direct-gain buildings). In a sense, the solar house movement was "ready" for this explosive growth due to the decades of exploratory work described above. If you set out to build a solar house in 1973, no invention would be needed—plenty of techniques were available and the results could be reasonably well predicted.

Still it was widely recognized that the solar house had not reached a mature stage in its development, either technologically or aesthetically. For architects the lack of a stable historical form and the emergence of postmodernism gave tremendous expressive freedom:

> The years immediately following the 1973 energy crisis seemed full of potential for architects. There was an opportunity to be at the forefront of solving one of society's major problems. Moreover, in solving that problem, architects had the opportunity to develop new kinds of expression that would allow them to escape the tired conventions of modernism.[6]

In a similar vein, historian Jeffrey Cook noted in 1975: ". . . solar architecture can look like anything. It can seem like a log cabin, a salt box, a planar composition, a ski lodge, a greenhouse, or a high technology crystal from the 21st Century."[7] If you browse any solar house book that features work of the 1970s, the most striking characteristic is variety. There was no dogma. For an engineer, the possibilities must have appeared equally limitless. Shurcliff, the most informed observer, remarked in 1976: "There are thousands of ways of building a solar heated house . . . We are still in the romantic, wide open, inventing stage."[8]

After 1973, the "passive vs. active" debate, which had been simmering for decades without a nomenclature, finally became explicit and vigorously discussed. The term "passive" was coined in 1972 by Benjamin T. "Buck" Rogers, a mechanical engineer and member of Peter van Dresser's Sundwellings team.[9] Rogers wanted a special label to commend those systems which did not rely on a significant amount of mechanical energy for pumps, fans, etc. (Others, like Harold Hay, preferred the word "natural.") Newspapers and architectural journals adopted the word passive to describe the Kelbaugh House, in 1975, and used it more broadly in about 1978.[10] The finer semantic meaning of "passive" endured much discussion.[11]

The appeal of passive methods resided in their low-tech simplicity. For Steve Baer, the issue of technological complexity carried political implications:

> I just don't think we can depend on General Motors or the Pentagon or NASA to produce the things that we really want and need . . . At one time an individual could pretty much fix everything in his life with his thumbnail or his teeth. But now the big corporations and organizations have so much to do with everyday life . . . and I really don't think it's necessary.[12]

Attitudes about passive technology reflected some antagonism between countercultural practitioners and the academic establishment. "The basics of passive solar design can be understood by anyone (even a cat or dog)," David Bainbridge claimed. "You don't need to have a Ph.D. in Engineering and an Architectural degree to be successful. (In fact, not having one sometimes seems to help!)"[13]

But most advocates recognized that passive methods needed scientific rigor. Douglas Balcomb and his team at the federally funded Los Alamos National Laboratory provided answers. They developed the solar savings fraction (SSF) to "measure" a passive solar building (compared with an equivalent nonsolar building).[14] More importantly, Balcomb and his team developed dozens of rules of thumb, published in the *Passive Solar Design Handbook* (1980) for the Department of Energy and *Passive Solar Heating Analysis: A Design Manual* (1984) for ASHRAE. Of the latter, William Shurcliff wrote: "Architects familiar with the book can design almost any kind of passive solar house with the assurance that it will perform well and provide at least 50-70% of the wintertime heat need."[15] There was great demand for such information. *The Solar Home Book*, by Bruce Anderson and Michael Riordan (1976), which included active and passive examples, sold in excess of 125,000 copies, and sales of Edward Mazria's *The Passive Solar Energy Book* (1979) totaled 500,000. If any doubt remained about passive methods, the Solar Energy Research Institute (SERI), a federal agency established in 1974, monitored seventy passive solar homes and reported an average 70 percent savings.[16]

As passive methods gained popularity in the 1970s, proponents of active systems counterattacked. George Löf, now a legendary figure, wrote "A Problem with Passive," which appeared in *Solar Age* in 1978 and was used by a Congressional subcommittee allocating research funds.[17] Löf argued that passive houses were "impractical" for "people who require reasonably uniform house temperatures" because they tended to be cold in the morning and hot in the afternoon. Storage devices such as Trombe walls could help, but still Löf emphasized that thermal mass operates "out of phase" with the envelope. (Even champions of passive admitted that temperature fluctuations were difficult to manage.) A few bravely campaigned for the middle ground. John Yellott respected both traditions. And Shurcliff commented: "It is hard to see why [anyone] would specify *just* an active system. Nearly always the use of combination passive-and-active seems preferable."[18]

Löf preached from a position of unparalleled authority in the 1970s. He assembled a team of engineers and built a "Solar Village" at Colorado State University (CSU) in Fort Collins in 1974–75. It consisted of three houses—identical as architecture—each containing its own method of solar heating, so that their performance could be directly compared. Additionally, House I was touted as the first in the world engineered to be both heated *and cooled* with solar energy. For active systems, exploration at the leading edge remained an expensive proposition, reserved for universities and government research labs. With support from the National Science Foundation and other sources, the CSU project probably represents the most ambitious research program ever in solar architecture. Löf's Solar Energy Applications Laboratory (SEAL) had a staff of eighteen.[19]

Löf engaged Denver architect Richard Crowther to design the CSU structures. Crowther had been using passive strategies since the 1940s. At 3,000 square feet, the design was considerably larger than any previous "laboratory" house, indicating a pragmatic aspiration to appeal to the marketplace. Likewise, Löf told Crowther he wanted a house with a "typical" rather than "extreme" or "unusual" appearance."[20] Crowther gave the CSU design a number of other energy conservation features, including partial earth-berming, airlock entries, and "vertical exterior fins," which Crowther said would reduce convective losses.[21] The engineers specified a 45-degree roof slope, a compromise between summer and winter needs, and the architect detailed the structure so that the equipment appeared well-integrated. The diagonal cedar siding and plain geometric forms showed, again, an aesthetic influence from Sea Ranch that would become popular in 1970s solar houses.

The first CSU house used a Hottel-type system of flat-plate collectors and water circulation and storage, plus an absorption air conditioner assisted by solar heat. The engineers tested a variety of new types of glass in the collectors, including one specially treated to reduce reflection losses and another with infrared reflective coating facing in. With 768 square feet of collector area for 3,000 square feet of space, the system provided 86 percent of the space heating plus 68 percent of the hot water needs, and 40 percent of the cooling load.[22] House II used a variation of the air-and-gravel system that Löf had invented thirty years earlier.[23] The researchers found the performance differences between House I and II were "not great," and Löf concluded:

The question is: Can you pay for it? And the final answer is Btus per buck. We have no doubt that with present technology in flat plate collectors you get more Btus per buck with the air system than you do with a liquid system. And maintenance, and the cost of repair and replacement, are far less for an air system.[24]

Additionally, the liquid system used "considerably more electricity" than the air system.[25] But House II's cooling system—circulating night air over the gravel storage, and then using the pebbles to cool the indoor air during the day—did not prove to be effective. Löf-type air-and-gravel systems became quite popular in the late 1970s and '80s, both in America and Europe.[26]

For House III at CSU, Löf and his team used a new system of evacuated tube collectors. This technology, developed in the 1960s and used today, places a narrow tube-in-plate absorber within a vacuum-filled glass tube; the vacuum reduces heat losses and therefore creates hot water very efficiently. With 384 tubes, six pumps, and at least six separate tanks, House III was probably the most mechanically elaborate solar house to date. Like House I it could use the hot water reservoir to create cooling in summer.[27] It worked well, and the engineers concluded that this type of system could supply "up to twice the space heating and several times the cooling obtainable from an equal occupied area of good quality flat-plate collectors."[28] In fact, the system worked so well that the team retrofitted House I with evacuated tubes of a different design. The costs were not discussed.

Another legendary figure from the history of the solar house remained active in the 1970s. Maria Telkes joined the University of Delaware, where she and physicist Karl Böer created "Solar One," the first building to generate both heat and electricity from the sun. It featured thin film photovoltaic (PV) cells encased within flat-plate collectors, and three types of phase-change salts in the basement for storing heat and cold. After completion in 1973, the Delaware house was celebrated as "the most technologically advanced solar home now in existence"[29]

Chicago architect Harry Weese gave Delaware's Solar One a distinctive image: not traditional, but not quite modernist or futurist either. With its 45-degree roof pointing to the sky, it reflected a preoccupation with wedge-shaped geometries characteristic of the period, as in Sea Ranch and Charles Gwathmey's early work. It looked, according to one writer, as if it had been "sliced neatly along the ridge of its roof with the northern half thrown away." Böer described it as "a silhouette . . . designed by the architect for maximum solar harvesting." If it aroused some debate, Böer said, "a little controversy isn't a bad thing."[30] The shallow linear floor plan may have represented a subtle homage to Fred Keck, whom Weese admired greatly.[31]

Twenty-five years after the Dover Sun House, Telkes believed she had finally solved the fundamental problem with Glauber's salt, using thickening agents and storing the salt in sausage-like tubes to reduce stratification. Böer reported that the salts "work satisfactorily" with "no degradation of performance" after two years.[32] The Delaware team later worked with the DuPont company to develop tubes of the salt for commercial sale.[33]

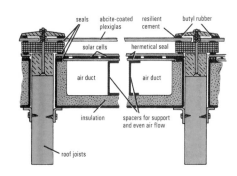

Top: Karl Böer at "Solar One," 1973. Author's collection

Above: "Solar One" collectors. *ChemTech* (July 1973)

Opposite: "Solar One" by Harry Weese, Karl Böer, and Maria Telkes, Newark, Delaware, 1973. Maria Telkes Papers, Arizona State University Libraries, Special Collections

Yet when Böer designed a PV-and-heat system for his own house at the same time, he used a Hottel-type water system rather Telkes's method of air and salts. Solar One received about 60 percent of its heat from the sun in its first winter, and that figure improved to 80 percent by 1979 with improved collector design.[34]

Delaware's Solar One envisioned new economic relationships between consumers and utility companies and introduced the concepts *peak shaving* and *load leveling* to the discourse. Böer envisioned that this type of house, when replicated in mass, could significantly reduce a utility company's peak demand, because they could be switched to battery power at critical times, and in summer air conditioners could be run at night, storing "coolness" in the salts.[35] He wanted utility companies to subsidize or even own and service these systems: ". . . the peak shaving and load leveling potential of solar energy conversion may provide sufficient incentives for power utilities to . . . create a major new market."[36] The project cost $125,000, and PV cells remained prohibitively expensive through the 1970s, but Böer said the method of producing heat and electricity was "expected to be economically very attractive" when the first costs of the cells dropped.[37] Solar One did not immediately generate followers, but in the longer term Böer correctly anticipated that the future of the solar house would be defined by PV.

After Telkes and Löf, a third icon from the solar house's history joined the revival. MIT, the institution that pioneered active systems beginning in 1939, built a fifth house, notable for its departure from the tradition of Hoyt Hottel. MIT's solar research program in the 1970s resided within the department of architecture, independent of its historical roots in the engineering disciplines (though still funded by Godfrey Lowell Cabot's endowment). And "MIT Solar Building 5," completed in February 1978, was based on a passive concept. It also represented a grand irony: the use of Glauber's salt, which had caused such agony among MIT engineers in the 1940s.

The new concept, devised by MIT architect Timothy Johnson, involved south-facing windows and blinds to reflect solar radiation to storage panels in the ceiling. "The ceiling is the least used area of a room and storage located there does not interfere with wall hangings or floor coverings."[38] The architects, working with industrial partners, created a proprietary ceiling panel made of polyester concrete and a thin pillow of Glauber's salt formulated to melt and freeze at 73°F.[39] They were subsequently commercially produced under the brand name Sol-Ar-Tile. Likewise, the mirrored-surface venetian blinds and low emissivity "Heat Mirror" glass indicated close relationships with industry. Johnson took pains to emphasize: "Passive heating differs from non-passive systems in that it requires no special equipment, such as solar collectors, pumps and fans."[40] Still, the project's "high-tech" and commercially oriented character deviated from the general trend toward low-tech passive houses.

Like its predecessors in Cambridge, MIT 5 was a modest structure, 880 square feet. It was used as a classroom. The sawtooth configuration of the south facade, a product of site constraints and the need for directly south-facing windows, gave the building its distinctive architectural form. The designers created a flat roof to demonstrate that this method could be applied to apartment buildings as well as to single-family homes—in essence the same insight that Fred Keck realized

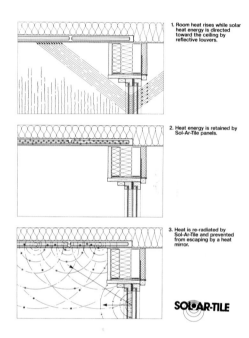

MIT Solar Building 5, Timothy Johnson et al., 1978.
Courtesy MIT Museum

Opposite: MIT Solar Building 5, Timothy Johnson et al., 1978.
Courtesy MIT Museum

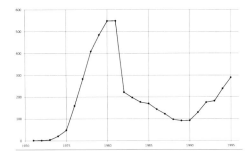

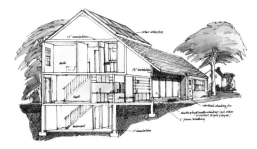

Top: U.S. Federal Funding for Solar Research (millions; unadjusted). Data from DOE in Donald A. Beattie, ed., *History and Overview of Solar Heat Technologies* (Cambridge, Mass.: MIT Press, 1997)

Above: Solar house for Exxon Corporation by Ehrenkrantz Group, Largo, Maryland, c. 1979. Illustration by Victor Lazzaro. *The Lamp* (Fall 1979)

Opposite: President Carter at the dedication of the White House solar hot-water system (June 20, 1979). Courtesy: Jimmy Carter Library

in his 1950 Prairie Avenue Courts. MIT 5 performed well, with 70 percent of its heating needs from solar. (Eighteen percent came from internal gains and the remaining 12 percent from conventional heating.) Johnson figured the payback period for the additional costs would be five to seven years. A few larger projects in New England—the Society for the Preservation of New Hampshire Forests building and the New Canaan Nature Center—subsequently used similar methods of upper-level salt storage. Johnson published *Solar Architecture: The Direct Gain Approach* (1981).

Hoyt Hottel, the father of MIT's solar house program, was now retired and did not participate in MIT 5. But he retained his skepticism about the economics of solar heating, even during the 1970s energy crisis. In 1977, he wrote an article entitled "Cloudy Forecast" for *Skeptic* magazine, where he argued that the costs of flat-plate collectors had increased just as much as oil prices. He opposed federal subsidies for solar houses. Finally, in 1989, the fiftieth anniversary of MIT I, Hottel offered his final opinion on the subject: "Solar energy is almost certain to be important in the distant future. When that time comes, it is my belief that the harness for Apollo's horses will be based on a design about which we know almost nothing today."[41]

Through the 1970s, the U.S. federal government increased funding for solar energy, supporting research projects like those mentioned above (and many more) plus a new commercial market. In 1974, Congress passed and President Ford signed four measures which created a National Solar Energy Program and an agency to administer it: the Energy Research and Development Administration (ERDA). The Solar Energy Research Institute (SERI) was established, and federal spending for solar research jumped from $100,000 annually in 1970 to $410 million in 1978.[42]

But the most promising methods of solar house heating barely benefitted. The numbers are deceiving, first because "solar" was defined to include a host of other alternative energy sources such as wind, biomass, and tidal energy. ERDA had "a pro-nuclear and anti-solar energy bias" and it commissioned studies "looking for unfavorable conclusions about solar energy," and when ERDA was absorbed by the newly created Department of Energy (DOE) in 1977 solar energy remained a minor concern. Many in the agency saw solar supporters as "radical anti-nuclear activists."[43] Actual solar research represented only 4 percent of the DOE's budget in 1978, while 38 percent went to petroleum buying. And much of that 4 percent went to utility-scale power generation; very little was left for house heating. Douglas Balcomb remembered that "minimal funding was devoted to passive system research."[44] And William Shurcliff complained that the support went to "big name universities and corporations" rather than small-scale experiments: "To give a grant to a lone-wolf inventor with nothing in his favor (except perhaps a truly successful solar heated house!) takes more courage than government agencies can muster."[45]

Apart from research, and perhaps more importantly, a variety of government initiatives created a commercial market for solar heating systems. Some states began to offer incentives for homeowners in the mid-1970s. In Denver, George Löf founded a private company, Solaron,

whose flat-plate air collector was known as "the Cadillac of the solar heating business." It was also expensive, with a payback period reaching seventy years.[46] Delaware's Karl Böer established Solar Energy Systems in partnership with Shell Oil. "Hardly a week goes by without the formation of a new company eager to sell collectors or associated equipment," Shurcliff observed in 1976.[47] Then, in 1978, came the truly transformative event: a federal tax credit for residential solar systems, which reached 40 percent. Politics mattered; with large-scale incentives, major corporations entered the field. Libbey-Owens-Ford, Honeywell, PPG, and Grumman Aerospace (to name a few) manufactured flat-plate collectors. Exxon built three solar houses designed by the Ehrenkrantz Group, in Boston, Washington, and Philadelphia. The "fly-by-night" operations flourished too. Steve Bliss, an editor of *Solar Age*, recalled: "I wrote a lot of articles about what wasn't working. There was a new perpetual motion machine every six months. Proprietary things, magic things."[48] Over 1.1 million people used the credits between 1978 and 1984—loosely speaking, more than a million American homes became solar houses.[49] Many attached an engineering solution to a preexisting architectural form without regard for aesthetic integration. There were many absurd-looking results.

NASA Technology Utilization House by Forrest Coile and Associates and Charles W. Moore Associates, Langley, Virginia, 1976. NASA Langley Research Center

At the same time, President Carter raised the profile for solar energy through some high-profile symbolic measures. On "Sun Day," May 3, 1978, President Carter traveled to SERI's future home in Golden, Colorado, and confirmed he would add another $100 million to the federal solar research program. He also announced his intention to install solar collectors on the roof of the White House.[50] This project, completed the following year, gave extraordinary spark to the solar house movement, although it cannot be claimed that the White House became a solar house. The collectors did not produce space heating, but domestic hot water for the West Wing, and they were placed to minimize their effect on the historic views of the White House. In terms of economics, the project's value was purely symbolic because the White House was already served by inexpensive steam heat from a central plant. The system cost more than $41,000 and saved about $1,000 per year.[51]

As solar panels were being placed on the roof of the White House, the energy crisis worsened, with a "Second Oil Shock" in early 1979; prices tripled, and again Americans waited in line for gas. Carter decided another grand gesture was needed. At the dedication of the White House solar heating system in June 1979, he announced a new goal: by the year 2000, 20 percent of America's energy needs would be met by solar energy.[52] (Again, solar energy was broadly defined to include alternatives such as wind. The current level in 1979 was about 6 percent.) Despite this initiative, and the symbolic power of solar panels on the White House roof, the Solar Lobby's chairman Denis Hayes scolded Carter for making "only a rhetorical commitment to solar energy."[53] Carter subsequently appointed Hayes to head SERI. It is indicative of its technical orientation that SERI never built a solar house. Instead they created a "Validation Test House" in 1980. This structure— an existing tract house originally built in the early 1950s and retrofitted with direct-gain windows and a brick floor—was meant to collect data that could be used to evaluate computation and simulation methods. Its agenda was exclusively scientific and not architectural. SERI was later renamed the National Renewable Energy Laboratory (NREL), and its development of whole building energy simulation software (EnergyPlus) remains a major legacy for architecture.

The only federal solar house to embody an architectural proposition was NASA's "Tech House," designed by Charles W. Moore Associates, and built in 1976 at the Langley Research Center. Moore was, of course, a leading architect of postmodernism, and his Sea Ranch project had a profound influence on 1970s solar architecture, as discussed previously. (It is not known to what extent Moore himself participated in the NASA project, but about this time he said energy "is the most important quality in the world, and understanding it, using it and saving it are the most important human acts."[54]) Moore's firm initially designed an east-west linear plan with flat-plate collectors integrated at the attic level—aesthetically similar to Crowther's design for CSU. But the architects argued that such a plan "should not be considered a prototype . . . suitable for all locations" because energy-conserving architecture was necessarily site-specific.[55] The final design addressed this problem by creating a series of square modules which could be rearranged. With its clustered asymmetrical roof forms, the house took on the character of a small village. Because the house included some PV cells, NASA officials said it represented "the many benefits [of] space-age technology."[56] But its heating system resembled the Bridgers and Paxton design of

1956. The Tech House achieved 41-percent solar heating, and a NASA researcher concluded: "Whether the Tech House is the shape of things to come is not clear at this time."[57]

By the end of the 1970s, a significant discourse emerged about the solar house's aesthetic problems and potentials. In numerous cases, solar architecture was treated as a historically emergent type with a secure and inevitable future. One example from 1978:

> The first steam powered vessels to cross the Atlantic looked like awkward sailing ships not steamships (just as the first automobiles looked like awkward carriages, not Model T's). They carried a full complement of sails because their reliability was well below 100%. It was not long before they achieved the reliability necessary to evolve their own form and their own structure, vastly different from the form of its progenitors.
>
> Solar building is beginning to embark on this same sort of evolution—awkward, not able to do the job alone, working with adaptations of unsuitable existing forms. The turning point will be when we change our commitment from an add-on, booster mentality to a 100% solar sensibility. At that point evolution will be swift and irreversible. Solar devices, solar buildings and solar villages will rapidly develop appropriate forms and structures.[58]

Such an evolution did not mature in the 1970s. Paul Goldberger concluded: ". . . architecture based on the requirements of solar energy, whether passive or active, is bringing us some very disappointing buildings . . . To be blunt about it, most solar houses are just plain ugly."[59]

When President Reagan was elected in 1980, it foreshadowed the end of an era for solar energy. He immediately slashed the budgets for solar energy by two-thirds. At SERI, Hayes was fired and the staff was cut from 950 to 350. In 1985, Congress allowed the solar tax credits to lapse and companies like Solaron folded. Löf recalled: "When they removed the subsidies the market disappeared."[60] Some of these companies and their technologies, Thomas Friedman has noted, "ended up being bought by Japanese and European firms—helping to propel those countries' renewable industries."[61] Finally, the Reagan staff removed the solar panels from the White House roof in 1986, even though the system was performing well.

In the midst of the late-1970s solar renaissance, a small number of experimental houses began to redirect the basic priorities of the movement by emphasizing "superinsulation" over solar heating. After the success of a few key prototypes, the superinsulated house became a legitimate challenger to the solar house. By the mid-1980s, it could be claimed that "several tens of thousands of superinsulated houses were in routine use."[62] "Solar vs. superinsulation" became

"Illinois Lo-Cal House" by University of Illinois Small Homes Council-Building Research Council, 1976. University of Illinois Small Homes Council-Building Research Council

a serious question for those interested in passive methods of reducing building energy use, and it remains so today (though the concepts are not mutually exclusive).[63] Light-and-tight vs. mass-and-glass is another way of expressing this philosophical debate.[64]

The history of superinsulated houses in North America began in 1976 with the Lo-Cal house at the University of Illinois. ("Lo-Cal" signified low-calorie, a clever bit of marketing which tapped into dieting fads popular at the time. Of course, a calorie is also a unit of heat.) The Illinois team, comprised of architects and engineers, departed from the tradition of demonstration houses; they used early computer simulation techniques to create a series of prototype designs generally applicable to cold climates, and built a "test house" in Champaign in 1977. With an outwardly unremarkable appearance, the Lo-Cal house kept its innovative features hidden: R-40 insulation in the ceiling, R-28 in the double-layer 2 x 4 walls, and R-20 in the floor.[65] Wayne Schick, leader of the Lo-Cal project, is sometimes credited with coining the term superinsulation.

The Lo-Cal design was much more opaque than the passive tradition, and the designers spoke of "sun tempering" rather than solar heating. Windows were triple-glazed, and 85 percent of the glass faced south. The design "corrects the deficiencies of the early solar houses," the researchers argued, by reducing the heat losses and eliminating the problem of summer overheating.[66] Ninety percent of the energy savings would come from insulation and very tight construction; 10 percent from solar gains. Ventilation was provided by an air-to-air heat exchanger. Schick called it "a totally integrated thermal-solar home."[67] Though the researchers never built their design, as many as a hundred houses across the U.S. were built using Lo-Cal characteristics.

The most convincing and consequential demonstration of superinsulation occurred in Canada, where a group of engineers built the Saskatchewan Conservation House in the provincial capital of Regina in 1977. Building science expert Joseph Lstiburek remembers that the

Right: Saskatchewan Conservation House by Saskatchewan Research Council, Regina, Saskatchewan, Canada, 1977. *Solar Age* (May 1979)

Opposite: Saskatchewan Conservation House by Saskatchewan Research Council, Regina, Saskatchewan, Canada, 1977. Saskatchewan Archives Board

Saskatchewan Conservation House challenged the conventional wisdom of the time:

> There wasn't a bunch of thermal mass and lots of south-facing glass in the house—no Trombe Wall, no tubes of water in the living room, no phase-change salts, no dark ceramic tile floors. It was just a house with boring technology—lots of insulation, airtight construction, controlled ventilation and not a lot of windows.[68]

The walls measured R-40 and the ceilings R-60, levels approximately three times greater than the Canadian standard. Following the Lo-Cal principles, the structure included only a modest amount of triple-glazed windows—only 6.4 percent of the floor area—and R-30 shutters reduced nighttime heat loss. The project also achieved an unprecedented level of "tight" construction. In combination, all of these measures gave the house a heating requirement 1/28 of the average Regina house.[69]

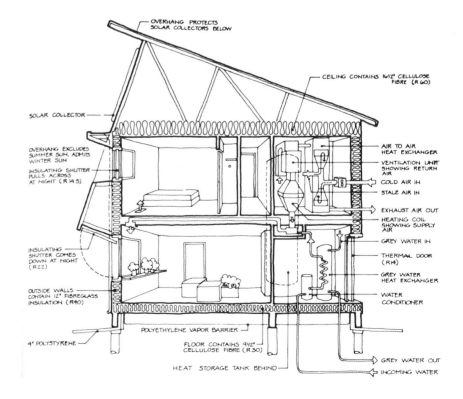

First Passivhaus project by Wolfgang Feist et al.,
Darmstadt-Kranichstein, Germany, 1991. Passive House
Institute, Darmstadt

After a year, the Saskatchewan Conservation House did not need any auxiliary heat—never before had a building achieved "net-zero" heating in a truly cold climate. Despite the limited window area, direct gain provided 44 percent of the heat. The remainder came from internal gains, an air-to-air heat exchanger, and heat recovery from gray water. Evacuated tube solar collectors, to produce domestic hot water, were not needed for space heating, and the researchers later recommended omitting them. The Saskatchewan Conservation House was probably the most successful demonstration house ever, anywhere, in terms of influencing a large-scale reduction in energy use. When it was opened to the public in January 1978, approximately 30,000 people visited. As a result of the positive reception, the Canadian government launched the R-2000 program in 1984. This program offered $100,000,000 in performance-based incentives to promote superinsulation. The first group of R-2000 houses consumed about 57 percent less energy than baseline standards, and the program (with refinements) remains active today.

The "boring technology" of superinsulation did not require years of scientific research, as demonstrated by Eugene Leger's 1978–79 house in Pepperell, Massachusetts. As a part-time homebuilder, Leger chose superinsulation after he studied many alternatives and concluded an active solar house would cost $15,000 more than a conventional house. He basically followed the Lo-Cal principles: double-wall construction, small amounts of triple-glazed windows, tight construction with vestibules, and an air-to-air heat exchanger. He argued:

> Any house that has to be fitted with solar collectors or huge amounts of south glass or that requires more than pocket change for heating fuel, simply wasn't designed properly in the first place.[70]

During the winter of 1978–79 (a particularly cold season in the northeast), Leger's house used only $38 of heating, while his neighbors paid around $800. When it became clear that these superinsulated houses used "extraordinarily low amounts of energy," Martin Holladay recalls, "progressive builders and energy researchers throughout North America sat up and paid attention."[71] An early champion for superinsulation was William Shurcliff, the Harvard physicist who catalogued solar houses. After Shurcliff studied the Lo-Cal, Saskatchewan, and Leger houses, he issued a press release in mid-1979 which argued for superinsulation as a "new category" with "a big future." He exclaimed: "Down with Trombe walls! Down with water-filled drums and thick concrete floors!"[72]

Beyond performance, the superinsulated house stimulated a new aesthetic approach. Again, the solar house and the superinsulated house were not mutually exclusive categories, with some overlap in strategies, but in terms of architectural expression there were clear differences. Shurcliff admired that superinsulation required "no weird shape of house, no weird architecture."[73] The Lo-Cal prototype design resembled a more refined suburban ranch house, with some prairie-style influences. Although the Lo-Cal methods did not have a prescriptive appearance, it was characteristic of the type that it "doesn't look spectacular."[74] Likewise, Leger said: "I designed this house to fit into the neighborhood and not to jar anyone's sensibilities."[75] At the time, this attitude seemed refreshing to some. Lstiburek marveled: "The Leger House wasn't weird looking. It was normal looking. It looked just like your neighbor's house."[76] The Saskatchewan house was an exception and perpetuated the association between energy-saving architecture and aesthetic eccentricity.

Even though superinsulation is technologically simple, economically proven, and aesthetically "normal," its influence in the United States has been limited. After a flurry of activity in the early 1980s, interest waned. These methods "hardly spread beyond a small band of dedicated custom-home builders," and even Canada's R-2000 program has been called "a boutique program that was pretty much ignored by mainstream builders."[77] There was not a dynamic public champion after Shurcliff. Although superinsulation remains an excellent energy-saving technique today, the most recent book on the subject was published in 1985. Meanwhile, according to Holladay, "American builders completed tens of millions of leaky new homes, most with 2 x 4 walls haphazardly filled with fiberglass batts." To be fair, the superinsulated house probably had a greater effect on energy codes and the housing industry than the solar house. In any case,

Solar Decathlon, 2009. Photograph by Stefano Paltera.
U.S. Department of Energy Solar Decathlon

Lstiburek recently observed: "In the United States . . . we're not building a lot of efficient houses…. We all know what to do, but we can't seem to do it."[78]

Today, the influence of the superinsulated house persists most significantly in the Passivhaus movement. German physicist Wolfgang Feist and Swedish professor Bo Adamson conceived the Passivhaus standard in 1988 after studying Shurcliff's accounts of the Saskatchewan and Leger houses. "The basic idea of the Passivhaus concept," Feist wrote, "is to improve the thermal performance of the envelope to a level that the heating system can be kept very simple."[79] In other words, the standard promotes high insulation values and supertight construction. (The term Passivhaus is problematic, as Martin Holladay notes, because the houses are not passive; they require active space heating and ventilation systems.[80]) Feist built the first Passivhaus, a four-family housing block, in Darmstadt-Kranichstein in 1991. It expressed a Bauhaus-like rationalism, with large south windows and virtually opaque east and west walls. (The north side included an unheated greenhouse buffer zone.) It used 85 percent less heating than an equivalent building meeting German national code. Then in 1996 he founded the Passivhaus Institut, which administers the voluntary standard. Feist and his team evaluated 221 Passivhaus units in five European countries in 2005 and found a total energy savings of 80 percent.[81] As of early 2012, there were over 1,700 projects registered in the Passivhaus database, the vast majority located in Germany.[82]

German practitioners also revived the experimental solar house tradition. In 1992, in Freiburg, a group at the Fraunhofer Institute for Solar Energy Systems built the "Self Sufficient Solar House." It included a Trombe wall with transparent insulation, an active water-type system with flat-plate collectors, a PV system, and a hydrogen fuel cell.[83] Freiburg became a center for vigorous solar research and practice. Architect Rolf Disch's "Heliotrope" (1994) was claimed to be the first home in the world that produced more energy than it consumed: "emission-free, CO2-neutral and 100% regenerative."[84] It resembled a spacecraft, and revolved about a central column to face the sun. Disch also designed an office complex called the Sonnenschiff (Sun Ship) in 2004. He has built as many as sixty "PlusEnergy" houses in and around Freiburg.

Currently solar house experimentation is largely identified with the Solar Decathlon, a large-scale student competition organized by DOE and NREL. Selected university teams design and build small solar houses then transport them to a common location for competition and public display. (The term Decathlon signifies that there are ten contests.) The program began in 2002 and has been scheduled biennially since 2005. Each house is intended to be "a living demonstration laboratory" for homeowners and builders.[85] The event became a true public spectacle; as many as 250,000 people visited the Decathlon when it occupied the National Mall in Washington, D.C. As a result of this success, the Solar Decathlon has expanded to include contests in Europe and China.

The Decathlon has effectively encouraged stylistic pluralism by providing vague aesthetic criteria and a diverse jury. Although NREL acknowledged "the art of architecture cannot be quantified," they created aesthetic "events" judged subjectively but scored numerically.[86] (In other events performance is measured objectively.) Given the pluralistic nature of architectural culture at large, it is especially interesting to examine how the projects are evaluated, and how the process has been refined over time. In 2002, for example, the jurors of the aesthetic event were curiously directed to use the classical standards of firmness, commodity, and delight. Participants found this process frustratingly opaque,[87] and juror Glenn Murcutt affirmed the difficulty in his statement: "The design of solar homes must be as poetic as it is rational."[88]

The Solar Decathlon has endured criticism on a number of points. The need to build the houses at various "home" locations and then transport them to the competition site requires "an inordinate amount of time, energy and cost" for the teams.[89] It also gives the competition itself a large carbon footprint.[90] Narrow boxy shapes have predominated due to the rigors of transportation, but more problematically this requirement compels lightweight construction materials and effectively deters students from exploring thermal mass strategies. "The average home owner will never move their home anywhere, much less thousands of miles," Colorado student Jeffrey Lyng stated in Congressional testimony. "There is an inherent contradiction here. The mainstream home buyer is not interested in a product that is driven architecturally by the need for mobility."[91] Another problematic issue, independent from transportation but exacerbated by it, has been the high cost of the homes. The 2007 winner from the Technische Universität Darmstadt cost $1.4 million, including $250,000 for transoceanic shipping. To address this problem, in 2011 the Decathlon introduced an "affordability" contest. Still, the projects ranged from $230,000 to $470,000 (for an 800-square-foot house without land), and these figures reflected estimates, not actual project costs. For alternative examples of student design-build programs which achieve affordability in a green building context, one might look to the University of Virginia's ecoMOD program and Studio 804 at the University of Kansas.

More positively, the Decathlon has addressed the historic schism between architects and engineers by requiring interdisciplinary collaboration and demanding that the projects "integrate" architectural design and engineering systems.[92] Before the inaugural event, the Decathlon's organizers explained:

> Possibly the most significant technical barrier to the widespread adoption of [solar] zero-energy buildings is the need to coordinate among many participants early in the building design and throughout the construction process. These participants, such as architects, engineers, and building tradespeople, traditionally do not communicate extensively (or at all) during the design and construction of a typical new building.[93]

Virtually every piece of the (vast) Solar Decathlon literature—scholarly papers, news reports, blogs—is suffused with the notion that interdisciplinary collaboration is difficult but rewarding. In some cases, faculty advisers discovered conflicting teaching styles which needed to be resolved.[94]

In terms of government policy and its relationship to the history of the solar house, the Decathlon marks a major shift from the DOE and NREL's former emphasis on fundamental scientific research to a new recognition that the most pressing challenge in the early twenty-first century is "public acceptance" of solar houses.[95] Although the student-participants do indeed solve innumerable technical problems, they are not specifically encouraged to develop new methods of solar heating nor are they expressly rewarded for doing so. A number of projects, to their credit, have pursued innovation anyway. Still, many teams in the 2007 competition, for example, "employed similar if not identical equipment into their designs," as if all the important technical questions had been answered.[96]

More to the point, the Decathlon's organizers have nakedly admitted from the beginning that the objective is to "have an immediate effect on consumers" and "to achieve the projected market penetration" for photovoltaic systems.[97] The influence of industry is an enduring theme—think of Fred Keck's close ties with Libbey-Owens-Ford or Maria Telkes's affiliation with Curtiss-Wright. Nevertheless, questions must be raised about the promotion of commercial products over fundamental green building principles. John Quale, University of Virginia professor whose team won the architecture contest in the 2002 Decathlon, has argued:

> One of the hardest things to believe about the Solar Decathlon is that an event meant to promote highly energy-efficient housing has no specific rewards for teams that use passive design . . .
>
> The heavy emphasis on photovoltaics puts the focus of the event very much on the side of technology—at the expense of low- or no-tech design solutions. In fact, the event perpetuates the falsehood that photovoltaics are the primary solution to energy-efficient housing. In my opinion, expensive and complex technologies like photovoltaics, while an important strategy, should be the last choice—after designers have exhausted all the other commonsense strategies.[98]

Quale's position, which is uncannily similar to the views of Harold Hay and Peter van Dresser in the 1970s, points to an alternative future. With long-term energy costs still climbing, passive strategies are more relevant than ever. And with accumulated historical knowledge, plus improvements in building technology and major advances in simulation software, full solar heating is more feasible than ever.

Although most Solar Decathlon teams appear to have proceeded from a historical vacuum, in some instances the contest has provided direct references or oblique allusions to the history of the solar house. A number of teams have quickly discovered solar control to be a paramount concern, just as Fred Keck did in the 1930s. Some even pursued Keck's initial solution—exterior blinds. Practically every team has acknowledged the age-old questions associated with

Purdue University's entry in the 2011 Solar Decathlon. Photograph by Jim Tetro. U.S. Department of Energy Solar Decathlon

SCI-Arc/Caltech's entry in the 2011 Solar Decathlon. Photograph by Jim Tetro. U.S. Department of Energy Solar Decathlon

roof form: whether to place collectors on an apparatus on a flat roof (as in the Löf Denver house), or whether to "integrate" the collectors in an asymmetrical form (as in MIT IV). More broadly, some participants have commented on the solar house's mixed legacy of aesthetics. After the 2005 competition, faculty advisers from Virginia Tech concluded:

> Solar technology is burdened with a stigma that contradicts a sense of proportion and beauty in building. Arbitrarily attached to new or existing construction, the technology is often associated with a small clique of individuals disenfranchised from the mainstream.[99]

And notably, when MIT entered the Solar Decathlon in 2007, the student team rewrote history by calling their house "Solar 7." In this revisionist view, the Dover Sun House by Telkes and Raymond was labeled "Solar 6," disturbing the chronology but presumably honoring Telkes's contribution to the MIT program.[100]

Although the Decathlon's historical importance remains to be seen, it seems clear that the program has defined a new era for the solar house characterized by high-tech and expensive solutions. The event also seems symptomatic of a larger trend in green building that Ted Shelton has described: ". . . the superficial attachment of 'green' items . . . become signs announcing the building's good intentions."[101] (Significantly, there is no superinsulation decathlon.) Future historians will determine whether the Decathlon houses will be interpreted as peculiar vanity projects or whether a more profound meaning will emerge. The most likely legacy will be found in the future work of Decathlon participants. "You don't go back to crawling after you've learned to walk," said Colorado student Matthew Henry.[102] And despite his critique above, John Quale sees in the Solar Decathlon "powerful evidence that we should expect a lot of great things from the next generation of architects and engineers."[103]

As of early 2012, there have been 109 solar houses built for the Decathlons, all of them unique. In terms of aesthetics, the program has reiterated a central theme of solar house history by promoting variety rather than consensus. In 2005, for example, the University of Michigan's project resembled a futuristic machine, while the Missouri-Rolla team built a craftsman-style solar house, arguing that "people might shy away from something more modern."[104] Likewise, in 2011, the design from SCI-Arc and Caltech—a folded shape with a quilted fabric skin—was meant "to challenge every architectural and engineering preconception regarding the net-zero-energy home," while Purdue's design—oriented to "Midwestern styling" and "functional aesthetics"—looked quite ordinary.[105] How should a solar house look and feel? Should it "fit in" with its neighbors or express difference? Is the solar house a machine or organism? For better or worse, virtually all of these essential questions remain open to debate, more than eight decades on.

Notes

Abbreviations
ASES. American Solar Energy Society
AF. Architectural Forum
AR. Architectural Record
BG. Boston Globe
CSM. Christian Science Monitor
CT. Chicago Tribune
HB. House Beautiful
H&V. Heating and Ventilating
ISES. International Solar Energy Society
NYT. New York Times
PA. Progressive Architecture
PopSci. Popular Science

Frequently Cited Sources

2nd Passive Proceedings. Don Prowler, ed., *Proceedings of the 2nd National Passive Solar Conference* (Philadelphia: Mid-Atlantic Solar Energy Association, 1978).

3rd Passive Proceedings. Harry Miller et. al., eds., *Proceedings of the 3rd National Passive Solar Conference* (Newark: American Section of the ISES, 1979).

Allen 1973. Redfield Allen, ed., *Proceedings of the Solar Heating and Cooling for Buildings Workshop* (Washington, D.C.: U.S. Government Printing Office, 1973).

Albuquerque 1976. *Passive Solar Heating and Cooling Conference and Workshop Proceedings, May 18–19, 1976* (Washington, D.C.: ERDA, 1977).

Anderson 1976. Bruce Anderson and Michael Riordan, *The Solar Home Book* (Harrisville, New Hampshire: Cheshire Books, 1976).

ATB. Arthur T. Brown and Kathryn M. Wayne, *Arthur T. Brown, FAIA: Architect, Artist, Inventor* (Tucson: University of Arizona, 1985).

Ayres 1951. Eugene Ayres, "Windows," *Scientific American* 184, no. 2 (February 1951): 60–65.

Barber dissertation. Daniel A. Barber, "The Modern Solar House: Architecture, Energy, and the Emergence of Environmentalism, 1938–1959," Ph.D. dissertation, Columbia University, 2010.

Behrman. Daniel Behrman, *Solar Energy, The Awakening Science* (Boston: Little Brown and Company, 1976).

Bernick thesis. Christine A. Bernick, "Preservation of Keck & Keck's Passive-Solar Subdivisions of the 1940s and 1950s," master's thesis, School of the Art Institute of Chicago, 2010.

Böer 1978. Karl W. Böer and Gregory E. Franta, eds., *Proceedings of the 1978 Annual Meeting*, vol. 2.1 (Newark: American Section of the ISES, 1978).

Böer 1979. Karl W. Böer and Barbara H. Glenn, eds., *Sun II: Proceedings of the ISES*, vol. 2 (New York: Pergamon Press, 1979).

Butti and Perlin. Ken Butti and John Perlin, *A Golden Thread: 2500 Years of Solar Architecture and Technology* (New York: Van Nostrand Reinhold, 1980).

Carriere 1980. Dean Carriere, *Solar Houses for a Cold Climate* (New York: Scribner, 1980).

Cook 1950. Theodore N. Cook, "Solar Heat Shines In Winter Test," *CSM* (August 24, 1950): 1.

Daniels 1975. Farrington Daniels, *Direct Use of the Sun's Energy* (New Haven: Yale University Press, 1975).

Daniels and Duffie. Farrington Daniels and John A. Duffie, eds., *Solar Energy Research* (Madison: University of Wisconsin Press, 1955).

FLWA. Frank Lloyd Wright Archives, Frank Lloyd Wright Foundation, Scottsdale, Arizona.

Franta 1975. Gregory Franta, ed., *Solar Architecture: Proceedings of the ASC/AIA Forum '75* (Tempe: Arizona State University, 1975).

Franta 1980. Gregory E. Franta and Barbara H. Glenn, eds., *Proceedings of the 1980 Annual Meeting* (Newark: American Section of the ISES, 1980).

GBA. *Green Building Advisor: Musings of an Energy Nerd* (weblog), http://www.greenbuildingadvisor.com/blogs/dept/musings.

Gilmore 1974. C. P. Gilmore, "Can Sunshine Heat (and Cool) Your House?," *Popular Science* 204, no. 3 (March 1974): 78–81, 160.

Halacy. D. S. Halacy, *The Coming Age of Solar Energy* (New York: Harper & Row, 1963).

Hottel 1989. Hoyt C. Hottel, "Fifty Years of Solar Energy Research Supported by the Cabot Fund," *Solar Energy* 43, no. 2 (1989): 107–28.

Hottel Oral History. Hottel, interviewed by James J. Bohning, November–December 1985, Oral History Program, Chemical Heritage Foundation.

Hottel Papers. Hoyt C. Hottel Papers, MC 544, Massachusetts Institute of Technology, Institute Archives and Special Collections.

Jacobs and Jacobs. Herbert and Katherine Jacobs, *Building with Frank Lloyd Wright* (Carbondale: Southern Illinois University Press, 1978).

Jacobs Papers. Herbert Jacobs papers, Wisconsin Historical Society Archives, Madison.

Keck and Keck. Robert P. Boyce, *Keck and Keck: The Poetics of Comfort* (New York: Princeton Architectural Press, 1993), which derived from his "George Fred Keck, 1985–1980: Midwest Architect," Ph.D. dissertation, University of Wisconsin, Madison, 1986.

Keck Papers. George Fred and William Keck papers, Wisconsin Historical Society Archives, Madison.

Kidder 1977. Tracy Kidder, "Tinkering with Sunshine," *Atlantic* 240, no. 4 (October 1977), 70–83.

LWS. *Living with the Sun* (Phoenix: Association for Applied Solar Energy, 1958).

MIT 1950. Richard W. Hamilton, ed., *Space Heating with Solar Energy* (Cambridge, Mass.: Massachusetts Institute of Technology, 1954).

MIT OPR. Massachusetts Institute of Technology, Office of the President, Records of Karl Taylor Compton and James Rhyne Killian, AC 4, Massachusetts Institute of Technology, Institute Archives and Special Collections.

Olgyay Papers. Victor Olgyay collection, Special Collections, Architecture and Environmental Design Library, Arizona State University.

Peabody Papers. Amelia Peabody Papers, Massachusetts Historical Society.

Phoenix 1955. *Proceedings of the World Symposium on Applied Solar Energy* (Phoenix: Association for Applied Solar Energy, 1956).

Raymond Papers. Eleanor Raymond Collection, Special Collections, Frances Loeb Library, Graduate School of Design, Harvard University.

Sayigh 1977. A. A. M. Sayigh, ed., *Solar Energy Engineering* (New York; Academic Press, 1977).

Schweikher Oral History. "Oral History of Robert Paul Schweikher," interviewed by Betty J. Blum, *Chicago Architects Oral History Project*, rev ed. (1984; Chicago: The Art Institute of Chicago, 2000).

Shurcliff 1986. William A. Shurcliff, "Superinsulated Houses," *Annual Review of Energy* 11, no. 1 (November 1986): 1–24.

Shurcliff survey. William A. Shurcliff, *Solar Heated Buildings: A Brief Survey* (Cambridge: W. A. Shurcliff, n.d.).

Stonorov Papers. Oscar Stonorov papers, Collection 04375, American Heritage Center, University of Wyoming.

Tague Oral History. "Interview with Robert Bruce Tague," interviewed by Betty J. Blum, *Chicago Architects Oral History Project*, rev ed. (1995; Chicago: The Art Institute of Chicago, 2005).

Telkes Papers. Maria Telkes Papers, Accession #2007-04062. Arizona State University Libraries: Special Collections.

Tigerman Oral History. "Oral History of Stanley Tigerman," interviewed by Betty J. Blum, *Chicago Architects Oral History Project* (Chicago: The Art Institute of Chicago, 2003).

Tucson 1955. Transactions of the Conference on Use of Solar Energy—The Scientific Basis, 1955 (Tucson: University of Arizona Press, 1958).

UN 1961. Proceedings of the United Nations Conference on New Sources of Energy, 1961 (New York: United Nations, 1964).

William Keck foreword. William Keck, foreword in *The Hawkweed Passive Solar House Book* (Chicago: Rand McNally, 1980).

William Keck Oral History. "Oral History of William Keck," interviewed by Betty J. Blum, *Chicago Architects Oral History Project*, rev. ed. (1991; Chicago: The Art Institute of Chicago, 2001).

Yellott Papers AHC. John I. Yellott Collection, Collection 1064, American Heritage Center, University of Wyoming.

Yellott Papers ASU. John I. Yellott Papers, 2007-04075, Arizona State University Libraries, Special Collections.

YSH. Maron J. Simon, ed., *Your Solar House* (New York: Simon and Schuster, 1947).

Preface

1. Reyner Banham, *The Architecture of the Well-tempered Environment* (London: The Architectural Press, 1969), 12.

2. David Pearlmutter, "Architecture and Climate: The Environmental Continuum," *Geography Compass* 1, no. 4 (2007): 752–78.

3. Richard G. Stein, *Architecture and Energy* (Garden City, N.Y.: Anchor Press/ Doubleday, 1977), 23.

4. Xenophon's *Memorabilia* III, viii.

5. "Socrates and the Solar House," *Journal of the American Institute of Architects* 7, no. 3 (March 1947): 121–22; A. F. Dufton and H. E. Beckett, "The Heliodon: An Instrument for Demonstrating the Apparent Motion of the Sun," *Journal of Scientific Instruments* 9 (1932): 251–56; E. J. Burda, ed., *Applied Solar Energy Research: A Directory of World Activities and Bibliography of Significant Literature* (Stanford: Stanford Research Institute for AFASE, 1955), vii; Austin Whillier, "Principles of Solar House Design," *PA* 36 (May 1955): 122.

6. Rachel Snyder, "Passive Design: It's a Natural," SERI/SP-432-521 (Golden: Solar Energy Research Institute, 1980), 1.

7. On sanatorium architecture, see Paul Overy, *Light, Air and Openness: Modern Architecture Between the Wars* (London: Thames & Hudson, 2007). On housing, see Walter Gropius, "Flach-, Mittel- oder Hochbau?," in *Rationelle Bebauungsweisen* (Stuttgart: Julius Hoffman Verlag, 1931), 26–47; and Catherine Bauer, *Modern Housing* (Cambridge, Mass.: Riverside Press, 1934), 182ff. On Villa Girasole, see Chad Randl, *Revolving Architecture: A History of Buildings that Rotate, Swivel, and Pivot* (New York: Princeton Architectural Press, 2008), 76–87.

Chapter 1

1. Quoted in George Fred Keck, "Design and Construction of Solar Houses," *MIT 1950*, 89.

2. I generally credit George Fred (called Fred) with authorship of the work, and any reference to "Keck" refers to Fred. In March 1946, he included his younger brother, William, an architect, as a partner in his practice. Their official name was George Fred Keck, William Keck, Architects (not Keck & Keck). I do not mean to diminish William's contributions, but also do not wish to falsely inflate them.

3. Howard Sloan claimed credit for creating the "solar house" label in "Two Developments in Glenview, Illinois," *AF* 80 (March 1944): 86. Fred Keck attributed the phrase to the *Tribune*'s Al Chase in "Design and Construction of Solar Houses," *MIT 1950*, 87, and when interviewed by Thomas M. Slade, December 4, 1977, *Keck Papers*, M78-042.

4. Al Chase, "Sun Supplies Heat for New Type North Shore Suburb Home," *CT*, September 22, 1940, p. 20. The Sloan house was also described as a solar house in the *Winnetka Talk*, September 19, 1940 and the *Glenview View*, September 20, 1940, *Keck Papers*, M83-283, Box 1.

5. "Two Developments in Glenview, Illinois," 86.

6. Keck, "Design and Construction of Solar Houses," 87.

7. *Keck and Keck*, 75.

8. William studied a series of articles entitled "Figuring Solar Heat Gains of Buildings" by William Goodman, in *Heating, Piping, and Air Conditioning*, May through October 1938, and he corresponded with the editors to ask for additional information. *Keck Papers*, M86-464, Box 26.

9. The U.S. Weather Bureau would publish radiation data specifically for architects and engineers beginning in 1947. Irving F. Hand, "Solar Energy for House Heating," *Heating and Ventilating's Reference Section* (December 1947). The horizontal-to-vertical conversion was developed for the first time by the MIT team in 1946 but never published.

10. *Keck Papers*, M86-464, Box 26.

11. "'Solar House' Owner Starts Homes Project," *CT*, July 20, 1941, p. 14.

12. "Sun's Slanting Rays Save in Heating Glass-Wall Homes," *CSM* (November 26, 1941): 22.

13. "Two Developments in Glenview," 85.

14. "Does Modern Architecture Pay?" *AF* 76, no. 9 (September 1943): 69–76.

15. Keck's ventilating louvers were first published in Al Chase, "Show Postwar Home Building Possibilities," *CT*, November 22, 1942, p. 16, which pictured the 1941 Tenhune House in Meadowbrook Village.

16. *Bernick thesis*, 34–35.

17. "Complex Conditions Call For Expert Knowledge," *AR* 89, no. 3 (March 1941): 74–77. Architect John Yeon used custom-designed ventilating louvers even earlier; see "House in Portland, Oregon," *AF* 70, no. 4 (April 1939): 318–19. Earlier examples may exist.

18. *Schweikher Oral History*, 201.

19. "Co-op Houses," *AF* 84 (January 1946): 89–95.

20. Tigerman, "Introduction: A Salon des Refuseés," in Stuart Cohen, *Chicago Architects* (Chicago: Swallow Press, 1976), 8.

21. Marcus Whiffen, "A Conversation with Paul Schweikher," *Triglyph* 2 (Spring 1985): 9.

22. *Butti and Perlin*, 185.

23. *Keck and Keck*, 74.

24. *Schweikher Oral History*, 78, 147.

25. "Clay Units Save Metal For Radiant Heating," *Practical Builder* 7, no. 7 (July 1942): 9.

26. "Panel Heating with Clay Tule Ducts and Floor," undated manuscript, *Keck Papers*, M73-026, Box 2. There are many technical reports and a great deal of correspondence about the subject from the 1943–44 period in this collection.

27. Keck to Winslow Ames, April 12, 1944, *Keck Papers*, M86-464, Box 16. The summer cooling effect was also mentioned in "Prefabrication Progresses to a New Design Level," *AF* 83 (July 1945): 125–44.

28. R. S. Dill, W. C. Robinson, and H. E. Robinson, "Measurements of Heat Losses from Slab Floors," *Building Materials and Structures Report* 103 (U.S. Department of Commerce: National Bureau of Standards, 1945); and H. D. Bareither, A. N. Fleming, and B. E. Alberty, "Temperature and Heat Loss Characteristics of Concrete Floors Laid on the Ground," Technical Report PB 93920 (University of Illinois: Small Homes Council, 1948).

29. "Panel Heating with Clay Tile Ducts and Floor."

30. William Keck, "Potentialities in Solar Heating," undated manuscript (probably 1976), *Keck Papers*, M86-464, Box 26.

31. "Radiant Heating For Buildings," U.S. Patent 2,422,685, filed March 27, 1944, and issued June 24, 1947, and "Radiant Heating System," U.S. Patent 2,584,591, filed May 7, 1947, and issued February 5, 1952.

32. Sloan, "Insolation and House Design," *Pencil Points* 25 (February 1944): 77–82.

33. See *Bernick thesis*, 53, 64.

34. Keck to Rosamond Draper, July 20, 1943, *Keck Papers*, M86-464, Box 23.

35. Undated notes for Green's Ready-Built Homes, *Keck Papers*, M73-026, Box 27.

36. Peebles and Knopf, "Studies of Comfort Conditions and Thermal Properties of a House Employing Solar Auxiliary Heating," undated manuscript, probably June 1943, *Keck Papers*, M86-464, Box 23.

37. Keck to Dan Harvey (Kimberly-Clark Co.), March 11, 1941, *Keck Papers*, M73-026, Box 2.

38. Peebles, quoted in L. E. Grinter (vice president, Illinois Institute of Technology) to Keck, February 13, 1941, *Keck Papers*, M73-26, Box 5.

39. All quotes from Peebles and Knopf, "Studies of Comfort Conditions . . ." and Knopf to Earl Aiken, November 30, 1942, *Keck Papers*, M86-464, Box 23.

40. Ibid.

41. *Keck Papers*, M86-464, Box 23.

42. "Products and Practice: Solar Heating," *AF* 76, no. 8 (August 1943): 6–7, 114.

43. Keck, "Design and Construction of Solar Houses," 87.

44. Gordon, "The First of the Postwar Prefabricated Houses" *HB* 87, no. 11 (November 1945): 127–37.

45. Keck to Green, November 19, 1945, *Keck Papers*, M73-026, Box 27.

46. "Solar House Built Totally in Factory," *NYT*, April 19, 1945, 24; *Keck and Keck*, 86.

47. See Barry Bergdoll and Peter Christensen, *Home Delivery: Fabricating the Modern Dwelling* (New York: Museum of Modern Art, 2008), and Ryan E. Smith, *Prefab Architecture: A Guide to Modular Design and Construction* (Hoboken: Wiley, 2010).

48. Gordon, "The First of the Postwar Prefabricated Houses."

49. Another Keck-inspired project was "Prefabricated Solar House," *Arts and Architecture* 64, no. 12 (December 1947): 36.

50. "Wickes, Inc. . . . ," *AF* 86, no. 1 (January 1947): 98–100.

51. Elizabeth Gordon, "Summer Protector against Solar Heat is the Roof Overhang," *HB* 85, no. 9 (September 1943): 62–63. See also "William F. Deknatel, Architect: House For Walter J. Kohler," *AF* 71, no. 1 (July 1939): 50–53.

52. Carma R. Gorman, "Henry P. Glass and World War II," *Design Issues* 22, no. 4 (Autumn 2006): 4–26.

53. Classified ad, in *BG*, October 12, 1947, C36; "Harnessing the Sun," *BG*, February 9, 1947, 22A; Jedd S. Reimer, "You Can So Have a Solar House in a Cold Climate," *HB* 90, no. 6 (June 1948): 84–91.

54. *Keck and Keck*, 98.

55. *Keck Papers*, M73-026, Box 26.

56. Robert Woods Kennedy, *The House and the Art of Its Design* (New York: Reinhold, 1953), 478.

57. Keck to Ken Reid, February 7, 1944, *Keck Papers*, M86-464, Box 26.

58. *Tague Oral History*, 24.

59. Maxine Livingston, "Designed Especially for a Rigorous Climate," *Parents' Magazine* 23, no. 8 (August 1948): 59.

60. "Comfort of the Occupant is Vital," *Practical Builder* (November 1949): 56–58.

61. Al Chase, "Sun Will Help Heat 24 Homes in New Project," *CT*, June 1, 1952, A7.

62. *William Keck foreword*, 10.

Chapter 2

1. "Skill Is Needed in Planning Solar House, Spacing Glass," *CT*, October 10, 1948, n.p.

2. *Butti and Perlin*, 184.

3. The best secondary sources are Lisa Schrenk, *Building a Century of Progress: The Architecture of Chicago's 1933–34 World's Fair* (Minneapolis: University of Minnesota Press, 2007), and H. Ward Jandl, "The House of Tomorrow: America's First Glass House," in *Yesterday's Houses of Tomorrow: Innovative American Homes 1850–1950* (Washington, D.C.: Preservation Press, 1991), 127–39.

4. *House of Tomorrow* official pamphlet (1933), n.p.

5. Ibid.

6. Al Chase, "Sun Supplies Heat for New Type North Shore Suburb Home," *CT*, September 22, 1940, p. 20.

7. "'Solar House' Owner Starts Homes Project," *CT*, July 20, 1941, p. 14.

8. Keck, "Design and Construction of Solar Houses," *MIT 1950*, 87.

9. William received the award on behalf of both brothers in Kansas City, October 3, 1979. Keck and Keck, "The Development of Passive Solar Applications to Architecture in the Mid West," typescript, *Keck Papers*, M86-464, Box 23. The same quote is repeated verbatim in *William Keck foreword*, 9–10.

10. "Start Work on Glass 'House of Tomorrow'," *CT*, April 9, 1933, D14.

11. *Schweikher Oral History*, 67.

12. "A Chicago Housing Project," *AR* 73, no. 3 (March 1933): 159–63.

13. Judy Vick, "No Kicks About Their Keck Home," *Twin Cities* 5, no. 11 (November 1982): 72.

14. Erik Hendrickson, project engineer, National Park Service, in Anthony Denzer and Keith Hedges, "The Limitations of LEED: A Case Study," *Journal of Green Building* 6, no. 1 (Winter 2011): 25–33. Marsha Ackermann, "Yesterday's Futurism, Today's Environmentalism," *NYT*, August 31, 2002, A15.

15. Keck, "Crystal House," typescript, *Keck Papers*, M73-026, Box 2.

16. "Conversation between Mr. Barnes [Charles E. Barnes, realtor for Green's Ready-Built Homes] & Mr. Keck," typescript, January 12, 1943, *Keck Papers*, M73-026, Box 27.

17. Tague, *Keck on Architecture* (Colorado Springs: Taylor Museum of the Colorado Springs Fine Arts Center, 1947), 4.

18. *William Keck Oral History*, 70. Also, in the only thorough scholarly examination of the Crystal House, Thomas Slade noted: "The glass walls required total atmospheric control to make the house habitable." "The Crystal House of 1934," *Journal of the Society of Architectural Historians* 29, no. 4 (December 1970): 352.
19. Boyce, *Keck and Keck*, 59.
20. "Architect Stages 1-Man Design Job in Chicago House," *AR* 83, no. 2 (February 1938): 32–37.
21. Keck to Earl Aiken (Libbey-Owens-Ford), May 26, 1938, *Keck Papers*, M73-26, Box 5.
22. Boyce, *Keck and Keck*, 88.
23. "House for Mr. B. J. Cahn," *AF* 71, no. 1 (July 1939): 13.
24. Wright's was published in "Planned Sunshine," *House and Garden* 71, no. 1 (January 1937): 72. Keck's was not published until 1939 (ibid.) but was probably drawn as early as 1936. Le Corbusier drew his first two-dimensional shading diagram (for an Algiers office project) in 1938; see Kenneth Frampton, *Le Corbusier* (London: Thames & Hudson, 2001), 115.
25. Keck to Winslow Ames, October 19, 1945, *Keck Papers*, M86-464, Box 16.
26. Justin Estoque, "Heating and Cooling Robie House," *APT Bulletin* 19, no. 2 (1987): 38–51.
27. W. W. Ward, "Keep the Sun Off Your Windows and You'll Be Up to 20% Cooler," *HB* 90, no. 6 (June 1948): 92–95. Groff Conklin, "Sun Control Methods: Part 1," *PA* 31, no. 5 (May 1950): 95–99; and "Sun Control Methods: Part 2," *PA* 31, no. 6 (June 1950): 92–97. Conklin wrote: "Cloth shades . . . probably provide the least effective method of controlling solar heat in a room."
28. "Solar Orientation in Home Design," *University of Illinois SHC-BRC Council Notes* 2:2, Circular Series C3.2 42:25 (February 1945).
29. Nory Miller, "Fred Keck at 81, 'Hit of the Show' After 56 Years," *Inland Architect* 20, no. 5 (May 1976): 6–11.
30. "Architect Stages 1-Man Design Job in Chicago House."
31. "Water Cooled Roofs," *AF* 84 (June 1946): 165–69.
32. Leonard Bachman, "Rain on the Roof—Evaporative Spray Roof Cooling," *Proceedings of the Second Symposium on Improving Building Systems in Hot and Humid Climates* (1985).
33. F. C. Houghton, H. T. Olson, and Carl Gutberlet, "Summer Cooling Load as Affected by Heat Gain through Dry, Sprinkled and Water-Covered Roof," *ASHVE Transactions* 46 (1940): 231–42. *Life* magazine personnel reportedly conducted a test of their own, finding that a shallow roof pool produced a 25° interior temperature difference. This is mentioned in "Water Cooled Roofs," but has not been located in *Life*.
34. Kenneth Reid, "Houses for the People," *Pencil Points* 26 (September 1945): 59–66.
35. Mary Roche, "Museum Presents Small House Show" *NYT*, May 29, 1945, p. 18.
36. Elizabeth Mock, "Tomorrow's Small House: Models and Plans," *The Museum of Modern Art Bulletin* 12, no. 5 (1945).
37. Keck, "A House to Live In," *Coronet* 8, no. 5 (September 1940): 112.
38. Ibid., 113.
39. Keck, "Design and Construction of Solar Houses," 90–91.
40. Many of these issues are discussed in an unpublished book manuscript by Keck, written c. 1944, which included at least four chapters addressing solar issues. *Keck Papers*, M86-464, Box 26.
41. Pamela Gores, quoted in Christopher Mason, "Behind the Glass Wall," *NYT*, June 7, 2007, F1.
42. Michael Benedikt, "Class Notes," *Harvard Design Magazine* 11 (Summer 2000): 8.
43. Frank Lloyd Wright, *Modern Architecture: Being the Kahn Lectures for 1930* (Princeton: Princeton University Press, 2008), 65.
44. Elizabeth Gordon, "The Threat to the Next America," *HB* 95 (April 1953): 250.
45. James M. Fitch and Daniel P. Branch, "Primitive Architecture and Climate," *Scientific American* 203, no. 6 (December 1960): 134.
46. *Tague Oral History*, 14.
47. *Keck Papers*, M99-085, Box 1.
48. The excellent concept "thermal ghetto" is a recent one. See David Gissen, "Thermopolis: Conceptualizing Environmental Technologies in the Urban Sphere," *Journal of Architectural Education* 60, no. 1 (2006): 50–51.
49. *Tigerman Oral History*, 73–74.
50. Julian Whittlesley, "New Dimensions in Housing Design," *PA* 32 (April 1951): 65.
51. *Tigerman Oral History*, 73–74.
52. Paul Goldberger, "Energy Crisis May Doom Era of Glass Towers," *NYT*, December 6, 1973, p. 49.
53. Henrik Schoenefeldt, "The Crystal Palace, Environmentally Considered," *Architectural Research Quarterly* 12 (2008): 283–94.
54. Jeffrey Plank, *Crombie Taylor: Modern Architecture, Building Restoration and the Rediscovery of Louis Sullivan* (Richmond, Calif.: William Stout, 2010), 29.
55. Tague, *Keck on Architecture*, 17.
56. Plank, *Crombie Taylor*, 100–104.
57. Pickens to Keck, February 2, 1977, *Keck Papers*, M86-464, Box 16.

Chapter 3
1. John Sergeant, *Frank Lloyd Wright's Usonian Houses: The Case for Organic Architecture* (New York: Watson-Guptill, 1984), 83.
2. Jacobs, *We Chose the Country* (New York: Harper & Bros., 1948; Madison: Roger H. Hunt, 1981), 295.
3. Wright to Jacobs, February 8, 1944, reprinted in *Jacobs and Jacobs*, 82.
4. Elizabeth Gordon, "Did You Know that the Heat of the Sun Can Help Heat your House in Winter?," *HB* 85, no. 9 (September 1943): 61. None of the Jacobs II drawings in Wright's archive are dated, *FLWA*. Wright said he was "at work" on the hemicycle in December 1943, and he presented the idea to the Jacobses in February 1944.
5. Donald G. Kalec, "The Jacobs House II," in Paul E. Sprague, ed., *Frank Lloyd Wright and Madison: Eight Decades Of Artistic And Social Interaction* (Madison: Elvehjen Museum of Art, 1992), 129.
6. Thomas A. Heinz, "Frank Lloyd Wright's Jacobs II House," *Fine Homebuilding* 3 (June/July 1981): 20–27.
7. *Jacobs and Jacobs*, 83.
8. Kalec, "The Jacobs House II," 127.
9. See *Jacobs and Jacobs*, 121, and Kalec, "The Jacobs House II," 127.
10. Wright, *The Natural House* (New York: Horizon Press, 1954), 148.
11. Stu Campbell, *The Underground House Book* (Charlotte, Vt.: Garden Way Publishing, 1980), 14.
12. *Jacobs and Jacobs*, 89.
13. Keck to Professor Folke T. Kihlstedt (Franklin and Marshall College), May 28, 1980, *Keck Papers*, M86-464, Box 24.
14. Quoted by Betty Blum, *William Keck Oral History*, 165.
15. *ATB*, 9.
16. *Jacobs and Jacobs*, 121.
17. Chris Martell, "Mended Wright Classic Seeks New Owner," *Wisconsin State Journal*, February 22, 1987, sec. 7, p. 1.
18. Sergeant, *Frank Lloyd Wright's Usonian Houses*, 174 (n. 76).

19. Michael Utzinger, "Lessons From a Passive Solar Pioneer," *Wisconsin Architect* (August 1982): 12–13.
20. Martell, "Mended Wright Classic Seeks New Owner." Taylor's alterations are described in detail in Paul Sprague, National Register of Historic Places nomination, (July 21, 2001), National Register #74000074.
21. Donald W. Aitken, "The Solar-Hemicycle Revisited; It's Still Showing the Way," *Wisconsin Academy Review* 39 (Winter 1992–93): 33–37.
22. Ibid.
23. Herbert Austin Jacobs, "A Light Look at Frank Lloyd Wright," *Wisconsin Magazine of History* 44, no. 3 (Spring 1961): 163–76. See also "Our Wright Houses," *Historic Preservation* 28, no. 3 (July–September 1976): 9–13.
24. *Jacobs Papers*, M98-132, Box 1; Katherine Jacobs talk at Taliesin, July 20, 1989, *Jacobs Papers*, 1209A/2.
25. Wright, *The Natural House*, 177–78.
26. Koester, speaking at "Ecoliteracy in Architectural Education Roundtable," *Greenbuild International Conference and Expo*, Chicago (November 8, 2008).
27. "The Future of Solar Energy," *The Sun at Work* 4, no. 1 (March 1959): 18.
28. "Modern Homes on North Shore have Novelties," *CT*, November 8, 1936, B10.
29. "House for Mr. B.J. Cahn," *AF* 71, no. 1 (July 1939): 13.
30. The floor plan of the Cahn House measured about 5,100 square feet, while the Jacobs hemicycle had about 2,650 square feet of floor space on two levels.
31. Scott A. Johnston, "The Dynamic Pattern of Shading and Solar Heat Gains through Windows," *Vital Signs Curriculum Materials Project* (University of California, Berkeley), http://arch.ced.berkeley.edu/vitalsigns/res/downloads/rp/shading/shade.pdf.
32. Utzinger, "Lessons From a Passive Solar Pioneer."
33. *Keck and Keck*, 127–29.
34. At the Meyer House the glass wall was 32 feet from the center point; at Jacobs II it was 29 feet, 6 inches.
35. Laurent, interviewed by Gordon Boivey, October 4, 1995, *FLWA*.
36. Bruce Brooks Pfeiffer, *Frank Lloyd Wright Selected Houses* 7 (Tokyo: A.D.A. Edita Tokyo, 1991), 9.
37. Sergeant, *Frank Lloyd Wright's Usonian Houses*, 83.
38. Anne M. Nequette and R. Brooks Jeffery, *A Guide to Tucson Architecture* (Tucson: University of Arizona Press, 2002), 189.
39. *ATB*, 21.
40. Patricia Paylore, "From Cave to Cave," in Kenneth N. Clark and Patricia Paylore, eds., *Desert Housing* (Tucson: University of Arizona, 1980), ix.
41. Carolyn S. Murray, "For two busy people: A $16,225 House for a Difficult Climate," *HB* 104 (October 1962): 200–201, 206–8. See also Paul Spring, "The Architecture of Arthur Brown: Designs That Have Aged Well," *Fine Homebuilding* 11 (October/November 1982): 34–35.

Chapter 4
1. "Can an Old House be Remodeled for Solar Heating?," *HB* 87 (June 1945): 75.
2. *YSH*, 10.
3. Ibid.
4. Ickes, "We're Running Out of Oil!," *American* (December 1943): 37–43. See also L. M. Fanning, "A Case History of Oil-Shortage Scares," in *Our Oil Resources*, 2nd ed. (New York: McGraw-Hill, 1950), 306-406.
5. Julie V. Iovine, "Elizabeth Gordon, 94, Dies; Was House Beautiful Editor," *NYT*, September 17, 2000.

6. Gordon, "Did You Know that the Heat of the Sun Can Help Heat your House in Winter?," *HB* 85, no.9 (September 1943): 59.
7. *YSH*, 10.
8. *Solar Houses: An Architectural Lift in Living* (Toledo: Libbey-Owens-Ford, 1945).
9. *Ayres 1951*, 61.
10. *YSH*, 10.
11. This section is revised and expanded from Anthony Denzer, "The Solar House in 1947," in G. Broadbent and C. A. Brebbia, eds., *Eco-Architecture I: Second International Conference on Harmonisation between Architecture and Nature* (Southampton: WIT Press, 2008), 295–304.
12. C. Dean Lowry, "To: The 48-States Solar House Architects," November 19, 1945, *Stonorov Papers*, Box 27.
13. Lowry, "To: The 48-States Solar House Architects," January 4, 1946, *Stonorov Papers*, Box 27.
14. Lowry, "To: The 48-States Solar House Architects," January 30, 1946, *Stonorov Papers*, Box 27.
15. Robert Law Weed's Florida house included a solar water heater. Alfred Kastner's Washington, D.C., proposal followed Keck by including a layer of water on the roof "for summer cooling."
16. *YSH*, 97.
17. *YSH*, 7.
18. *Barber dissertation*, 95; Adam Rome, *The Bulldozer in the Countryside* (New York; Cambridge University Press, 2001), 55.
19. Andrew M. Shanken, "Architectural Competitions and Bureaucracy, 1934–1945," *Architectural Research Quarterly* 3, no. 1 (1999): 43–54.
20. "Solar Houses Win Approval Across Nation," *Washington Post*, October 17, 1948, R2.
21. Mary Roche, "New Ideas," *NYT*, November 2, 1947, SM44.
22. F. W. Preston, "How Not to Build a House—A Book Review," *The Glass Industry* (January 1948): 32.
23. Jane Sarah Katz and Victor W. Olgyay, "Your Solar House—Thirty Five Years Later," *Progress in Passive Solar Energy Systems* (Boulder: ASES, 1983), 641–46.
24. Nicholas Rajkovich and Gregory Thomson, "Unbuilt, Untested, Performance Unknown: Libbey-Owens-Ford and 'Your Solar House,'" *Proceedings of the Solar 2006 Conference* (Boulder: ASES, 2006), 608–13.
25. "Method and Apparatus for Use in Designing Solar Houses," U.S. Patent 2,452,417, filed December 13, 1946, and issued October 26, 1948.
26. Hutchinson, "The Solar House: A Full-Scale Experimental Study," *H&V* 42 (September 1945): 96–97.
27. Keck, "Design and Construction of Solar Houses," *MIT 1950*, 87.
28. Keck, "Apartment House Design Today," *Cleveland Engineering* (May 5, 1955): 35.
29. For example, "Purdue Experiments Show How Sun's Rays Can Help to Reduce Heating Cost in Home," *NYT*, December 1, 1946, R3; Hutchinson, "The Solar House: A Research Progress Report," *H&V* 43 (March 1946): 54–56.
30. Hutchinson, "The Solar House: A Second Research Progress Report," *H&V* 44 (March 1947): 55–59.
31. Hutchinson, "The Solar House: Analysis and Research," *PA* 28, no. 5 (May 1947): 90–94.
32. Telkes, "A Review of Solar House Heating," *H&V* 46 (September 1949): 68.
33. Frank N. Laird, "Constructing the Future: Advocating Energy Technologies in the Cold War," *Technology and Culture* 44, no. 1 (January 2003): 33.

34. Wright, "Site Planning and Sunlight," *American Architect and Architecture* 149 (August 1936): 19ff. This article includes a description of Henry N. Wright's heliodon. The name "heliodon" was coined in 1932 at the RIBA Building Research Station, though some similar devices were built as early as 1914 and given names such as "The Orientator" and "Sunshine Gauge." See A. F. Dufton and H. E. Beckett, "The Heliodon: An Instrument for Demonstrating the Apparent Motion of the Sun," *Journal of Scientific Instruments* 9 (1932): 251–56.

35. All quotes from "Products and Practice: Orientation for Sunshine," *AF* 68, no. 6 (June 1938): 18–22.

36. *Butti and Perlin*, 183.

37. "What a Big Difference a Little Re-Orienting Makes," *HB* 85, no. 9 (September 1943): 64.

38. "Facts I Wager You Don't Know About Solar Mechanics," *HB* 85, no. 9 (September 1943): 62. See also "Planned Sunshine," *House and Garden* 71, no. 1 (January 1937): 56–57, 72.

39. Hendrick P. Maas, "Short Cuts to Solar Angles," *AR* 99, no. 3 (March 1946): 125–33.

40. "Can an Old House be Remodeled for Solar Heating?," *HB* 87 (June 1945): 75. See also "Solar Weekend House," *AF* 81, no. 5 (November 1944): 136–41.

41. Nelson and Wright, *Tomorrow's House* (New York: Simon and Schuster, 1945), 179.

42. Kendig, "Ramirez Solar House: A Case Study of Early Solar Design," master's thesis, New Jersey Institute of Technology, 2001, 16–17 and 41–42.

43. Douglas C. McVarish, "The Ramirez Solar House: A Holistic Approach to a National Register Nomination," *Cultural Resources Magazine* 25, no. 3 (2002): 40–41; Thomas Solon, "Rehabilitation of Henry Wright's Ramirez Solar House," *AIA Architect* 15 (March 7, 2008), http://info.aia.org/aiarchitect/thisweek08/0307/0307s_solar.cfm.

44. Wright, "How to Put a Harness on the Sun," *HB* 91, no. 10 (October 1949): 158–61.

45. This section is revised and expanded from Anthony Denzer and Polina Novikova-Kinney, "Arthur T. Brown: Pioneer of Solar Architecture," in Rebecca Campbell-Howe, ed., *Proceedings of the Solar 2010 Conference* (Boulder: ASES, 2010).

46. Anne M. Nequette and R. Brooks Jeffery, *A Guide to Tucson Architecture* (Tucson: University of Arizona Press, 2002), 184.

47. "House, Tucson, Arizona," *PA* 28 (June 1947): 56.

48. *Butti and Perlin*, 216.

49. Ibid., 193.

50. "House, Tucson, Arizona."

51. Ibid.

52. Helen J. Kessler, "In the Solar Vanguard," *Fine Homebuilding* 11 (October/November 1982): 29–33.

53. Paul Berkowitz, *Arizona Solar Tours* (Phoenix: Arizona Solar Energy Commission, 1984), 7.

54. "House, Tucson, Arizona," *PA* 29 (October 1948): 70–72.

55. *ATB*, 8.

56. "They Heat Their House With Sunshine," *Better Homes and Gardens* 31 (February 1953): 174–75, 199.

57. *ATB*, 20.

58. *Butti and Perlin*, 216. See also "New Solar Heat Method Used For Tucson School," *Arizona Builder and Contractor* (December 1949): 28.

59. "Structural Components for School Buildings," *AR* 120, no. 2 (August 1956): 164–65.

Chapter 5

1. Hottel, "The Prospects for Solar Energy Utilization," typescript of speech to the National Industrial Conference Board, New York City, October 13, 1954, *Hottel Papers*, Box 19.

2. G. Pascal Zachary, *Endless Frontier: Vannevar Bush, Engineer of the American Century* (New York: Free Press), 1997.

3. Bush, "Power from the Sun," memorandum to Karl Compton, September 20, 1936, *MIT OPR*, Box 42.

4. Bush, "A Research Program on Direct Utilization of Solar Energy," September 25, 1937, *MIT OPR*, Box 42, 10.

5. Van Dresser, "Solar Construction in a Biotechnic Economy," in Costis Stambolis, ed., *Solar Technology for Building: Proceedings of the First International Conference on Solar Building Technology* (London: RIBA Publications, 1978), 109.

6. *Hottel Oral History*, 59.

7. "Harness for Apollo's Horses" was the title of "Research Reports" 5:4 (February 1940), unpublished typescript, *Hottel papers*, Box 61.

8. Hottel to Executive Committee of MIT, February 24, 1939, *MIT OPR*, Box 43.

9. *Kidder 1977*, 72.

10. Hottel, "The Sun as a Competitor of Fuels," typescript of lecture to Society of Arts, December 15, 1940, *Hottel Papers*, Box 62.

11. Contemporary descriptions of MIT I include: "Solar Radiation," *Science* 90 (November 17, 1939): 10; "To Heat and Air Condition House with Solar Energy Source," *Science News-Letter* 36, no. 21 (November 18, 1939): 332–33; and "Roof-top Heat Trap Stores Power from the Sun," *PopSci* 136, no. 2 (February 1940): 97.

12. Hottel, quoted in Ryan Allen Hackney, "Apollo's Elusive Harness: The Cabot Solar Energy Conversion Project and the Path of Practicality," bachelor's thesis, Harvard University, 1996, 22, from 1995 interviews with Hottel.

13. Hottel to Dean Edward L. Moreland, June 26, 1939, *MIT OPR*, Box 42.

14. Hottel to Horace Ford (MIT Treasurer), October 28, 1939, *Hottel Papers*, Box 18.

15. *Barber dissertation*, 125.

16. *Hottel 1989*, 112.

17. Sibley, "Harnessing the Sun."

18. E. A. Allcut and F. C. Hooper, "Solar Energy in Canada," (paper S/20) *UN 1961*, vol. 4, 304–9.

19. B. B. Woertz and I. F. Hand, "The Characteristics of the Eppley Pyrheliometer," *Monthly Weather Review* 69 (May 1941): 146–48. The episode is described wonderfully in *Hottel 1989*, 112–13.

20. Hottel and Woertz, "The Performance of Flat-Plate Solar-Heat Collectors," *Transactions of the American Society of Mechanical Engineers* 64 (February 1942): 91–104.

21. Hottel, "Residential Uses of Solar Energy," in *MIT 1950*, 107.

22. Quoted from Hottel, "Artificial Converters of Solar Energy," *Sigma Xi Quarterly* 29 (April 1941): 49–50, 60. Typescript, May 16, 1940, in *Hottel Papers*, Box 19.

23. *Hottel 1989*, 114.

24. "Pre-Fabricated Solar Home," *BG* (June 3, 1945), B1. Barbara Brooks, "Experts Say Solar Home Is Practical in New England," *BG*, June 10, 1945, C2.

25. Anderson's appointment is documented in James H. Killian, Jr. (Acting President), to Hottel, August 13, 1945, *MIT OPR*, Box 42. Hottel to Cabot, September 6, 1945, *MIT OPR*, Box 42.

26. Telkes, "Solar Heat Collection through South Windows and Flat Plate Collectors in Relation to the Heat Load in Cambridge," October 1945, *Hottel Papers*, Box 63,

and *Telkes Papers*, Box 71. Telkes's article "Solar House Heating—A Problem of Heat Storage," *H&V* 44 (May 1947): 68–75, is quite similar to this report, though the details are revised to provide storage for a longer period.

27. Hottel, Memo, November 19, 1945, *Hottel Papers*, Box 63.
28. Hottel to Dr. George R. Harrison (Dean of Science), April 29, 1953, *Hottel Papers*, Box 17.
29. Hottel, "Residential Uses of Solar Energy," 108.
30. W. Clifford Harvey, "M.I.T. Sets Trap for 'Old Sol,'" *CSM* (December 14, 1946): 1.
31. Ibid.
32. "Domestic Dwelling Project," memo, November 7, 1945, *Hottel Papers*, Box 17.
33. "Solar Energy Building," news release, December 5, 1946, *Hottel Papers*, Box 17.
34. K. S. Bartlett, "Using Sun for Furnace Man," *BG*, February 8, 1948, B6.
35. *Hottel Oral History*, 61.
36. Albert G. H. Dietz and Edmund L. Czapek, "Solar Heating of Houses by Vertical South Wall Storage Panels," *Heating, Piping, and Air Conditioning* 22, no. 3 (March 1950): 118–25.
37. *Butti and Perlin*, 208.
38. *Hottel 1989*, 114.
39. Bainbridge, *A Water Wall Solar Design Manual* (self-published), 1981, rev. 2005, 7.
40. Dietz and Czapek, "M.I.T. Solar House 2: South-Wall Collection, Storage, and Heating," in *Albuquerque 1976*, 171–82.
41. Cabot to Compton, July 16, 1947; Compton, Memo, August 15, 1947, *MIT OPR*, Box 42.
42. Hottel to Dean T. K. Sherwood, November 30, 1948, *MIT OPR*, Box 43.
43. Anderson, "A Solar House," typescript class assignment, October 22, 1947, *MIT OPR*, Box 42.
44. Haws, "A House Utilizing Solar Radiant Energy as a Heat Source by Means of South Facing Windows," bachelor's thesis, MIT, 1949.
45. *Barber dissertation*, 202.
46. John Kobler, "Like Living in Macy's Window," *Saturday Evening Post* (September 24, 1949): 42ff. See also "'Solar Heat' Versus Oil and Coal," *CSM* (February 14, 1949): 2.
47. News release, February 13, 1949, *MIT OPR*, Box 42. Also printed in "M.I.T. is Testing Use of Solar Heat," *NYT*, February 13, 1949, R1.
48. "M.I.T. Builds Solar-Heated House," *AR* 105, no. 4 (April 1949): 136.
49. Ibid., 135.
50. Whillier, "Performance of the Massachusetts Institute of Technology Solar House during the season of 1950-51," report H-18 (February 1952), *Hottel Papers*, Box 65, 19.
51. Czapek, "Performance of the Massachusetts Institute of Technology Solar Heated House during the Winter of 1949-50," report H-14 (July 1950), *Hottel Papers*, Box 63, 83.
52. *Anderson 1976*, 26.
53. "M.I.T. Builds Solar-Heated House," *AR* 105, no. 4 (April 1949): 138.
54. August L. Hesselschwerdt, Jr., "Performance of the M.I.T. Solar House," in *MIT 1950*, 99–106. Performance reported in *Cook 1950* appears to have been exaggerated.
55. Whillier, "Performance . . . 1950–51," 14.
56. Whillier, "Performance of the Massachusetts Institute of Technology Solar House during the season of 1951–52," report H-19 (March 1953), *Hottel Papers*, Box 65.

57. Hottel, "Residential Uses of Solar Energy," 108.
58. Hottel and Whillier, "Evaluation of Flat Plate Solar Collector Performance," *Tucson 1955*, 74–104.
59. Hottel, "Report on A Fire in the 3rd M.I.T. Solar House," typescript, December 23, 1955, *Hottel Papers*, Box 17.
60. Theodore N. Cook, "Present Outlook is Dim on Solar Heated Houses," *CSM* (August 21, 1950): 4; Kobler, "Like Living in Macy's Window," 162.
61. See, for example, classified ads in *BG*, December 19, 1948, C43.
62. Oral history interview with Lawrence Anderson, January 30–March 30, 1992, Archives of American Art, Smithsonian Institution, http://www.aaa.si.edu/collections/interviews/oral-history-interview-lawrence-anderson-12388.

Chapter 6

1. W. Clifford Harvey, "M.I.T. Sets Trap for 'Old Sol'," *CSM* (December 14, 1946): 1.
2. *Solar Houses: An Architectural Lift in Living* (Toledo: Libbey-Owens-Ford, 1945).
3. Hartley E. Howe, "Sun Furnace in Your Attic," *PopSci* 154, no. 3 (March 1949): 107–12.
4. Hottel, "Comments on Some 20 Papers Bound Together and Printed by M.I.T. in 1954 under the title, Space Heating with Solar Energy, Reprint Problems," undated typescript, 1976, *MIT OPR*, Box 57.
5. Among many examples, see Maria Telkes, "Space Heating with Solar Energy," *The Scientific Monthly* 69, no. 6 (December 1949): 394–97.
6. *Daniels and Duffie*, 32.
7. Giedion, *Space, Time and Architecture*, 5th ed. (Cambridge, Mass.: Harvard University Press, 1967), 211–17.
8. Paul Zucker, "The Role of Architecture in Future Civilization," *The Journal of Aesthetics and Art Criticism* 3, nos. 9/10 (1944): 37.
9. *Butti and Perlin*, 203.
10. Löf, "Solar House Heating—A Panel," *Phoenix 1955*, 134.
11. Carol Taylor, "Nation's First Solar-Heated Home was in Boulder," *Boulder Daily Camera*, August 8, 2008.
12. Löf, R. N. Hawley, and E. R. Irish, "Solar Energy Utilization for House Heating," report PB 25375 (U.S. Office of Production Research and Development), 1946, 72.
13. Löf and Thomas D. Nevens, "Heating of Air by Solar Energy," *Ohio Journal of Science* 53, no. 5 (September 1953): 279.
14. Löf, Hawley, and Irish, "Solar Energy Utilization for House Heating," 12.
15. Löf and Nevens, "Heating of Air by Solar Energy," 279. See also Löf, "House Heating and Cooling with Solar Energy," in *Daniels and Duffie*, 33–45.
16. Martin McPhillips, "An Interview with George O. G. Löf," *Solar Age* 1, no. 12 (December 1976): 28.
17. *Butti and Perlin*: 205.
18. Löf, "Solar House Heating—A Panel," 136–37.
19. Löf, Hawley, and Irish, "Solar Energy Utilization for House Heating," 87.
20. "Products and Practice: Solar House Heater . . . ," *AF* 86, no. 2 (February 1947): 121–26.
21. "Solar Heating Apparatus and Method," U.S. Patent 2,680,565, filed December 3, 1945, and issued June 8, 1954.
22. *Hottel Papers*, Box 17.
23. *Butti and Perlin*, 205.
24. *Application Engineering Manual* (Denver: Solaron Corporation, 1978), 100.1.
25. Taylor, "Nation's First Solar-Heated Home."

26. Löf, "Solar House Heating—A Panel," 136–37.
27. Telkes, "Solar House Heating—A Problem of Heat Storage," *H&V* 44 (May 1947): 68–75.
28. Doris Cole, *Eleanor Raymond, Architect* (London: Associated University Presses, 1981), 47.
29. Edgar J. Driscoll, Jr., "Amelia Peabody, Boston Sculptor, Arts Patron and Civic Leader; at 93," *BG*, May 31, 1984, p. 1.
30. Cole, *Eleanor Raymond, Architect*, 42.
31. Laura Haddock, "The Name Is Peab'dy," *CSM* (July 2, 1949): WM7.
32. *Behrman*, 89ff.
33. John Kobler, "Like Living in Macy's Window," *Saturday Evening Post* (September 24, 1949): 42ff.
34. *Raymond Papers*, Folder 4802.
35. Telkes, "A Review of Solar House Heating," *H&V* 46 (September 1949): 72.
36. Telkes and Raymond, "Storing Solar Heat in Chemicals—A Report on the Dover House," *H&V* 46 (November 1949): 83.
37. Raymond, "Architectural Problems in the Solar Heated House at Dover, Massachusetts," in *MIT 1950*, 97.
38. Ibid., 98.
39. Telkes, "The Story of the Dover House," undated typescript, probably 1949, *Telkes Papers*, Box 37.
40. Telkes, "A Low-Cost Solar Heated House," *H&V* 47 (August 1950): 72–74.
41. Cole, *Eleanor Raymond, Architect*, 43.
42. Telkes and Raymond, "Storing Solar Heat in Chemicals."
43. Gene Casey, "Rays of Sun Will Cool That Solar House," *BG*, June 2, 1949, p. 21.
44. Casey, "Cool in Summer, Warm in Winter," *BG*, July 24, 1949, C1.
45. "New Sun House," typescript, *Raymond Papers*, Folder 4802.
46. Nan Trent, "Award Winner Designs Houses Inside Out," *CSM* (October 31, 1961): 6.
47. *Cook 1950*.
48. Margaret Warren, "Former Budapest Society Girl Finds Homemaking Simple in Solar House," *CSM* (July 21, 1949): 10.
49. Telkes, "The Story of the Dover House."
50. See *Peabody Papers*, Scrapbooks vols. 5–6.
51. "World's First Sun-Heated Home," *Life* 26 (May 2, 1949): 90.
52. "Sun-Heated Homes," *Providence Bulletin*, September 17, 1948, n.p.
53. W. Clifford Harvey, "Home in the Sun," *CSM* (December 31, 1948): WM4; "World's First Sun-Heated Home," *Life* 26 (May 2, 1949): 90.
54. "Sunlight Heats this House," *Science Illustrated* 4 (1949): 28–31.
55. Harvey, "Home in the Sun."
56. *Barber dissertation*, 255.
57. "Test House Heated Only by Solar Heat," *AR* 105 (March 1949): 136.
58. Telkes and Raymond, "Storing Solar Heat in Chemicals."
59. Quoted in *Butti and Perlin*, 214.
60. Telkes, "Space Heating with Solar Energy," *The Scientific Monthly* 69, no. 6 (December 1949): 396.
61. Frank N. Laird, "Constructing the Future: Advocating Energy Technologies in the Cold War," *Technology and Culture* 44, vol. 1 (January 2003): 36.
62. Hottel, "Comments on Some 20 Papers." See also *Hottel 1989*, 117.
63. Hottel, "Report on M.I.T's Godfrey L. Cabot Solar Energy Research Program," typescript, May 8, 1964, *Hottel Papers*, Box 62, 6.
64. Telkes, "Home Heat by Stored Sunlight Described by M.I.T. Researcher" (transcripton of speech), *New York Herald Tribune*, March 7, 1949, p. 28. See also Telkes, "Future Uses of Solar Energy," *Bulletin of the Atomic Scientists* 7, nos. 7/8 (August 1951): 217–19.
65. Harvey, "Home in the Sun."
66. Telkes, "A Low-Cost Solar Heated House."
67. "Kendall Common Area," *Weston Historical Commission*, http://whc.wonk.com/?page_id=480.
68. Hartley E. Howe, 'New Sun Furnaces May Cool Houses, Too," *PopSci* 166, no. 6 (June 1955): 136ff.
69. *Shurcliff survey*, 13th ed., 1977, 120. See also *Carriere 1980*, 214–21.
70. David Fixler, "Hipsters in the Woods: The Midcentury-Modern Suburban Development," *Architecture Boston* 12, no. 1 (Spring 2009): 26–29. See also Paula M. Bodah, "Modern Love," *New England Home* (November/December 2010).
71. Gardenhire, "Solar Energy Heats New Mexico Home," *Sun at Work* 2, no. 1 (March 1957): 6.
72. "Letters to the Editor," *The Sun at Work* 2, no. 2 (June 1957): 2.
73. Richard Stepler, "Revolving Barrel Banks Solar Heat," *PopSci* 212, no. 5 (May 1978): 91.
74. Whillier, "Information Memorandum" to MIT Solar Energy Committee, August 27, 1954, *Hottel Papers*, Box 17.
75. Telkes and Richard P. Mozzer, "Thermal Storage in Salt-Hydrate Eutectics," in *Böer 1978*, 255–59.
76. *Behrman*, 107.
77. The symposium ran August 21–26, 1950. Activities included tours of MIT III, and the Peabody House in Dover. An interesting side note: participants were offered accommodations at the new Baker House dormitory by Alvar Aalto.
78. Theodore N. Cook, "Present Outlook is Dim on Solar Heated Houses," *CSM* (August 21, 1950): 4; "Debate Solar Heating," *NYT*, August 24, 1950, p. 54.
79. Whillier, "Solar Energy Collection and Its Utilization for House Heating," Ph.D. dissertation, MIT, 1953, 22.
80. "M.I.T. Experts Say Sun-Heated House Could Be Built for $10,000," *BG*, August 24, 1950, p. 2.
81. Anderson, "Architectural Problems," in *MIT 1950*, 108–16.
82. Anderson, Hottel, and Whillier, "Solar Heating Design Problems," in *Daniels and Duffie*, 47–56. See also Howe, "New Sun Furnaces May Cool Houses, Too."
83. Victor Olgyay, "The Temperate House," *AF* 94 (March 1951): 179–94; Victor and Aladar Olgyay, *Application of Climatic Data to House Design* (Washington, D.C.: Housing and Home Finance Agency, 1954).
84. R. E. Lacy, "Building and the Weather," *Nature* 201 (February 1, 1964): 436.
85. Hottel, "Introductory Lecture," in *MIT 1950*, 2.
86. Keck, "Design and Construction of Solar Houses," in *MIT 1950*, 87–91.
87. Löf, "General Significance and Summary of Course-Symposium," in *MIT 1950*, 153.

Chapter 7
1. Hunter, "The Architectural Problem of Solar Collectors—A Roundtable Discussion," *Phoenix 1955*, 205.
2. Whillier, "Principles of Solar House Design," *PA* 36 (May 1955): 122.
3. Hunter, "The Architectural Problem of Solar Collectors," 203–5.
4. Löf, "Solar House Heating—A Panel," *Phoenix 1955*, 138.
5. In addition to prior notes, see also *Cook 1950*; and "Debate Solar Heating," *NYT*, August 24, 1950, p. 54.

6. Hunter, "The Architectural Problem of Solar Collectors," 203–5.

7. "Denver Family Set for Winter in Solar-Heated Home," *NYT*, November 10, 1957, p. 313.

8. Roscoe Fleming, "Solar House In Colorado Cost $40,000," *CSM* (September 27, 1957): 15.

9. Wesley S. Griswold, "Will Your Next House Get its Heat from the Sun?" *PopSci* 172, no. 2 (February 1958): 110–13.

10. *Daniels 1975*, 159.

11. Löf, "Solar House Heating—A Panel," 145.

12. Löf, interview with author, Denver, Colorado, July 15, 2009; On Hunter's work in general, see "The Architect and His Community: James M. Hunter, Boulder Colorado," *PA* 34, vol. 12 (December 1953): 74–89.

13. Hunter, "The Architectural Problem of Solar Collectors."

14. Löf, "House Heating and Cooling with Solar Energy," in *Daniels and Duffie*, 33–45.

15. John L. Wilhelm, "Solar Energy, the Ultimate Powerhouse," *National Geographic* 149, vol. 3 (March 1976): 388.

16. Löf, M. M. El-Wakil, and J. P. Chiou, "Residential Heating with Solar Heated Air—The Colorado Solar House," *ASHRAE Transactions* 69 (January 1963): 417.

17. Whillier, discussion, in ibid., 416.

18. Löf, "Use of Solar Energy for Heating Purposes: Space Heating" (paper GR/14), *UN 1961*, vol. 5, 118.

19. R. B. Gillette, "Analysis of the Performance of a Solar Heated House," master's thesis, University of Wisconsin, 1959.

20. Löf, El-Wakil, and Chiou, "Residential Heating with Solar Heated Air," 406–17. See also Löf, El-Wakil, and Chiou, "Design and Performance of Domestic Heating System Employing Solar Heated Air—The Colorado Solar House" (paper S/114), *UN 1961*, vol. 5, 185–97.

21. "Solar Heating System and Operation Thereof," U.S. Patent 4,061,267, filed August 18, 1975, and issued December 6, 1977.

22. John C. Ward and Löf, "Long-Term (18 Years) Performance of a Residential Solar Heating System," *Solar Energy* 18 (1976): 301–8.

23. Wilhelm, "Solar Energy, the Ultimate Powerhouse."

24. *Hottel Oral History*, 62.

25. George R. Harrison, "Report on the Solar Energy Project under the Godfrey L. Cabot Fund," typescript, May 25, 1953, *MIT OPR*, Box 204.

26. *Hottel Oral History*, 62.

27. Whillier and Pelletier, "Notes of 1954 to Solar Committee" (July 1954), *Hottel Papers*, Box 65.

28. Earl Banner, "Tech Proves Sun Can Heat a New England House," *BG*, March 2, 1958, p. 43.

29. Whillier, "Solar House Heating—A Panel." See also: "Full-Size Solar-Heated House to Be Tested Here by M.I.T.," *BG*, November 4, 1955, p. 1; "A Place in the Sun," *BG*, November 6, 1955, A13E; and W. Clifford Harvey, "MIT Solar House in Metropolitan Boston to Trap 90% of Winter Heat," *CSM* (April 6, 1956): 16.

30. "Solar House," *Look* 24, no. 21 (October 11, 1960): 59.

31. *Hottel 1989*, 123.

32. Morgan Monroe, "Solar Energy to Heat, Cool Future Homes," *BG*, October 29, 1955, p. 6.

33. Telkes and Aladar Olgyay, "Solar Heating for Houses," *PA* 40, no. 3 (March 1959): 196.

34. Daniel D. Chiras, *The Solar House: Passive Heating and Cooling* (White River Junction, Vt.: Chelsea Green, 2002), 96.

35. Much additional technical detail can be found in Whillier, "Solar House Heating—A Panel"; C. D. Engebretson and N. G. Ashar, "Progress in Space Heating with Solar Energy," *ASME Paper 60-WA-88* (July 28, 1960); and C. D. Engebretson, "The Use of Solar Energy for Space Heating—M.I.T. Solar House IV," in *UN 1961*, vol. 5, 159–72.

36. *Butti and Perlin*, 216.

37. News release, March 2, 1958, *Hottel Papers*, Box 17.

38. Engebretson, "The Use of Solar Energy for Space Heating."

39. Banner, "Tech Proves Sun Can Heat a New England House"; "House M.I.T. Built Uses Solar Heat," *NYT*, March 2, 1958, p. 57.

40. Richard F. Dempewolff, "The House that Stores the Sun," *Popular Mechanics* 108, no. 4 (October 1957): 160.

41. *Butti and Perlin*, 216.

42. *Hottel Oral History*, 62.

43. The solar-assisted heat pump was proposed in 1952 by R. C. Jordan and J. L. Threlkeld and published in "Availability and Utilization of Solar Energy, Parts I, II, III," *ASH&VE Transactions* 60 (1954): 177–238. An earlier mention of the idea appears in *Ayres 1951*, 64.

44. C. P. Gilmore, "Higher Efficiency with Solar-Assisted Heat Pumps," *PopSci* 212, no. 5 (May 1978): 86–90.

45. Michael Amedeo, "First Solar-Powered Office Commemorated," *Albuquerque Journal*, September 21, 2006, A8.

46. "Solar Building," Bridgers and Paxton brochure, *Yellott Papers ASU*, Box 43.

47. The architectural design was credited to John Miller, about whom little else is known.

48. "Warm Winter Behind Glass," *Life* 41, vol. 25 (December 17, 1956): 71; "Solar-Heated Office Building Combines Good Architectural and Mechanical Design," *AR* 120, vol. 6 (December 1956): 202–3.

49. "Solar-Heated Office Building," *PA* 38, no. 3 (March 1957): 153–55.

50. Bridgers, Paxton, and R. W. Haines, "Performance of a Solar Heated Office Building," *ASHRAE Transactions* 64 (1958): 83–96. See also Bridgers, Paxton, and Haines, "Solar Heat for a Building," *Mechanical Engineering* 79 (1957): 536–38; and "Solar-Heated Offices Keep Occupants Warm," *Science News Letter* 72, no. 1 (July 6, 1957): 8.

51. Gilman, "Evaluation of the Solar Building, Albuquerque, New Mexico, Final Report" (DOE report COO-2704-22), 1979; Gilman and Douglas H. Sturz, "Solar Energy Assisted Heat Pumps Systems for Commercial Office Buildings," *ASHRAE Transactions* 80, no. 2 (1974): 374–81.

52. National Research Council, *Solar Heating and Cooling of Buildings: Activities of the Private Sector . . .* (Washington, D.C.: ERDA, 1976), 5. See also Bridgers, "Applying Solar Energy for Cooling and Heating Institutional Buildings," *ASHRAE Transactions* 80, no. 2 (1974): 365–73; and Bridgers, "Solar Heating and Cooling of Commercial and Institutional Buildings," in *Franta 1975*, 17.1–17.13.

53. Mary Davis and Lynn Bridgers, National Register of Historic Places (NRHP) nomination (July 14, 1989), National Register #89001589.

54. Bliss, "Solar House Heating—A Panel," *Phoenix 1955*, 151–58.

55. Bliss, "Design and Performance of the Nation's Only Fully Solar-Heated House," *Air Conditioning, H&V* 52 (October 1955): 92.

56. Hottel, "Residential Uses of Solar Energy, *Phoenix 1955*, 110.

57. Löf, "Memorandum of Discussion with Mr. Raymond Bliss, Jr.," June 24, 1954, *Hottel Papers*, Box 17.

58. C. D. Engebretson, memo, December 4, 1959, in "Minutes and Reports to Solar Energy Conversion Project Committee, May 1957 to December 1960," report H-31, *Hottel Papers*, Box 66.

59. Bliss, "The Performance of an Experimental System Using Solar Energy for Heating, and Night Radiation for Cooling a Building" (paper S/30), *UN 1961*, vol. 5, 148–57.

60. Bliss, "The Derivations of Several 'Plate-Efficiency Factors' Useful in the Design of Flat-Plate Solar Heat Collectors," *Solar Energy* 3, no. 4 (December 1959): 55–64.

61. Bliss, "Why Not Just Build the House Right in the First Place?," *Bulletin of the Atomic Scientists* 32, no. 3 (March 1976): 32–40.

Chapter 8

1. *Ayres 1951*, 65.
2. Daniels, "A Limitless Resource: Solar Energy," *NYT*, March 18, 1956, p. 218.
3. Richard N. Cooper, "Resource Needs Revisited," *Brookings Papers on Economic Activity*, 1975, no. 1 (1975): 238–45.
4. "U.S. Ends an Economic Era," *Life* 32, no. 26 (June 30, 1952): 18–19.
5. *Resources for Freedom: The Report of the President's Materials Policy Commission* (Washington, D.C.: Government Printing Office), 1952. See especially vol. 4, 213–20.
6. David Z. Beckler (Office of Defense Mobilization), "Memorandum on a World Solar Energy Project," unpublished typescript, June 18, 1954, *Hottel Papers*, Box 17.
7. Harvey Strum, "Eisenhower's Solar Energy Policy," *The Public Historian* 6, no. 2 (Spring 1984): 37–50.
8. Laird, "Constructing the Future: Advocating Energy Technologies in the Cold War," *Technology and Culture* 44, no. 1 (January 2003): 39.
9. Hubbert, "Nuclear Energy and the Fossil Fuels," *American Petroleum Institute Drilling and Production Practice* (1956): 7–25.
10. Franklyn M. Branley, *Solar Energy* (New York: Thomas Y. Crowell, 1957), 56.
11. Cook, "Two Solar Houses of the 1950s by Victor Olgyay," in M. J. Coleman, ed., *Proceedings of the 14th National Passive Solar Conference* (Boulder: ASES, 1989), 29–36.
12. *Halacy*, 60.
13. Daniels, "The Sun's Energy," *Phoenix 1955*, 20. Reprinted in *Scientific Monthly* 82, no. 5 (May 1956): 247–54.
14. Hobson, "The Economics of Solar Energy," in *Phoenix 1955*, 27–39.
15. Alexis Madrigal, *Powering the Dream: The History and Promise of Green Technology* (Cambridge, Mass.: Da Capo Press), 102.
16. Yellott, "Twenty-Five Years Later," in *Franta 1980*, 3–7.
17. Ibid.
18. John A. Duffie and Harry Z. Tabor, "The International Solar Energy Society: The First 25 Years, 1955 to 1980," in Karl W. Böer, ed., *The Fifty-Year History of the International Solar Energy Society and its National Sections* (Boulder: ASES, 2005), 12.
19. Frank N. Laird, "The Society Whose Time Had Come," *Solar Today* 19, no. 4 (July/August 2005): 36–39.
20. Harvey Strum, "The Association for Applied Solar Energy/Solar Energy Society, 1954–1970," *Technology and Culture* 26, no. 3 (July 1985): 571–78.
21. Residential energy use (per capita) in the U.S. rose from about 40 MBtu in 1950 to over 70 MBtu in 1973. See Rick Diamond and Mithra Moezzi, "Changing Trends: A Brief History of the US Household Consumption of Energy . . . ," Lawrence Berkeley National Laboratory, 2010, http://epb.lbl.gov/homepages/rick_diamond/LBNL55011-trends.pdf.

22. Adam Rome, *The Bulldozer in the Countryside* (New York: Cambridge University Press, 2001), 85.
23. Ibid., 72, 86.
24. Telkes, "Future Uses of Solar Energy," *Bulletin of the Atomic Scientists* 7, no. 7/8 (August 1951): 217–19.
25. Lewis L. Strauss, chairman of the United States Atomic Energy Commission, quoted in "Abundant Power From Atom Seen," *NYT*, September 17, 1954, p. 5.
26. *Kidder 1977*, 71.
27. *Halacy*, 74.
28. Pielke, "Book Review," *Policy Sciences* 35, no. 3 (September 2002): 313.
29. Curtiss-Wright news release, August 28, 1958, *Peabody Papers*, Scrapbook vol. 6. See also "Curtiss and N.Y.U. Join in Sun Study," *NYT*, August 28, 1958, p. 29.
30. Telkes to Peabody, August 28, 1958, *Peabody Papers*, Scrapbook vol. 6.
31. Telkes, untitled review, *The Scientific Monthly* 84, no. 6 (June 1957): 320–21.
32. Telkes, "Original program submitted to Curtiss-Wright in June, 1958" typescript, Telkes Papers, Box 71.
33. Telkes, "Solar Energy Program by Maria Telkes," typescript, August 20, 1958, *Telkes Papers*, Box 71.
34. See *Telkes Papers*, Box 14, and *Barber dissertation*, 321ff.
35. Aladar Olgyay, "Design Criteria of Solar Heated Houses" (paper S/93), *UN 1961*, vol. 5, 199–205.
36. Ibid., 204.
37. Telkes to Peabody, January 6, 1959, *Peabody Papers*, Scrapbook vol. 6.
38. *Barber dissertation*, 326.
39. Olgyay, "Design Criteria of Solar Heated Houses," 203.
40. Löf, "Use of Solar Energy for Heating Purposes: Space Heating" (paper GR/14), *UN 1961*, vol. 5, 119.
41. Telkes, "Solar Heated and Cooled House," typescript, July 7, 1959, *Telkes Papers*, Box 37.
42. Cook, "Two Solar Houses of the 1950s by Victor Olgyay."
43. Robert J. Pelletier, "Solar Energy: Present and Foreseeable Uses," *Agricultural Engineering* 40, no. 3 (March 1959): 144.
44. *Daniels 1975*, 150.

Chapter 9

1. E. J. Burda, ed., *Applied Solar Energy Research: A Directory of World Activities and Bibliography of Significant Literature* (Stanford: Stanford Research Institute for AFASE, 1955), vii.
2. *Halacy*, 63.
3. Jeffrey Cook, "John I. Yellott, Ambassador of the Sun," in Dennis A. Andrejko and John Hayes, eds., *Proceedings of the 12th Passive Solar Conference* (Boulder: ASES, 1987), 2–9. See also, "In Memoriam, Dr. John Yellott (1908–1986)," *Solar Energy* 38, no. 6 (1987): 387–88.
4. Yellott, "Solar Energy Hit of Salonika Trade Fair," *Sun at Work* 2, no. 3 (September 1957): 1.
5. "Simplified Solar House Displayed at Casablanca," *Sun at Work* 3, no. 2 (June 1958): 6.
6. "Solar Energy Featured at Tunis Trade Fair," typescript, undated, *Yellott Papers AHC*, Box 5.
7. This section is revised and expanded from Anthony Denzer, "The Solar House in 1957," in Rebecca Campbell-Howe, ed., *Solar 2009: Proceedings of the 38th ASES Annual Conference* (Boulder: ASES, 2009).

8. Jean Jensen, ed., "The Solar House," *Sun at Work* supplement 3, no. 1 (March 1958): ii.
9. "Solar House Opening Planned For April 13," *Phoenix Gazette* (undated), *Yellott Papers AHC*, Box 13.
10. *Living with the Sun* competition program, *Olgyay Papers*, Box 2, and summarized in *LWS*.
11. Daniel Barber, "Living with the Sun: Architecture and the Association for Applied Solar Energy, 1954–1958," *Fourth International Conference*, Association of Architecture Schools of Australasia, 2007.
12. Ibid. See also "Hundreds of Architects Vie in Global Solar-House Contest," CSM (July 26, 1957): 12.
13. Jensen, "The Solar House," i.
14. *LWS*, 41.
15. *Barber dissertation*, 417.
16. *LWS*, vii.
17. "Solar Energy Gives Warm or Cool Home," *NYT*, February 23, 1958, R1; Yellott, "Transfer of Heat from Sun to House Interior Explained," *Arizona Republic* (April 13, 1958): 5:2.
18. "Solar House Opening Planned For April 13."
19. "Solar House Faces Eclipse in Arizona," *CSM* (May 23, 1958): 3; Henry Fuller, "Solar House Sold To Ex-Iowa Pair For Advertised Price Of $49,500," *Arizona Republic*, September 4, 1958; *Yellott Papers AHC*, Box 13.
20. See various AFASE internal reports, *Yellott Papers AHC*, Box 12.
21. Yellott to Hottel, July 17, 1958, *Hottel Papers*, Box 20.
22. "Solar House Opening Planned For April 13."
23. *LWS*, vi.
24. Yanagimachi, "How to Combine: Solar Energy, Nocturnal Radiational Cooling, Radiant Panel System of Heating and Cooling, and Heat Pump to Make a Complete Year-Round Air-Conditioning System," *Tucson 1955*, 45.
25. Ibid., 37.
26. Yanagimachi, "Report on Two and a Half Years' Experimental Living in Yanagimachi Solar House II" (paper S/94), *UN 1961*, 244.
27. Yanagimachi, "How to Combine . . . ," 32–45.
28. See Yellott, "Japan Applies Solar Energy," *Mechanical Engineering* 82, no.3 (March 1960): 48–51; and "Japanese Sun House: Milestone in Use of Solar Energy," *Western Architect and Engineer* 219, no. 3 (March 1960): 22–25.
29. Ernest Douglas, "Japan Taps Solar Energy," *CSM* (December 16, 1959): 3. Most were discarded in the 1970s due to the increased availability of gas and kerosene. See Yellott, "Historical and International Perspective for Passive Solar Heating and Cooling," *3rd Passive Proceedings*, 510.
30. Yanagimachi, "Report on Two and a Half Years' Experimental Living," 246.
31. Ken-Ichi Kimura, "Solar Houses in Japan," in *Sayigh 1977*, 287–315.
32. "Improvements in Solar Heated Buildings," U.K. Patent 1,022,411, filed April 6, 1961, and issued March 16, 1966.
33. M. G. Davies, "The Contribution of Solar Gain to Space Heating," *Solar Energy* 18, no. 4 (1976): 361–67.
34. Ibid.
35. Joseph E. Perry, Jr., "The Wallasey School," *Proceedings of the Conference on Passive Solar Heating and Cooling*, report LA-UR-76-1561 (Los Alamos Scientific Laboratory, 1976), 223–37. See also Philip Steadman, *Energy, Environment and Building* (Cambridge: Cambridge University Press, 1975), 35–36, 160–62; Davies, "The Passive Solar Heated School in Wallasey, V," *International Journal of Energy Research* 11, no. 1 (March 1987): 1–20; Davies, "The Solar Technology of St. George's School, Wallasey, England," *Architectural Science Review* 22, no. 4 (1979): 89–93.
36. G. T. McKennan, "St. George's School Wallasey, the Visual Environment," *Building and Environment* 20, no. 1 (1985): 61–71.
37. Banham, *The Architecture of the Well-tempered Environment* (London: The Architectural Press, 1969), 280, 284–85.
38. Thomas Markus, "Solar Energy and Building Design, " *Architectural Review* 136, no. 809 (July 1964): 76.
39. Yellott, "Historical and International Perspective," 510. See also *Butti and Perlin*, 197–200.
40. *Behrman*, 60.
41. Johnathan C. Randal, "French Village Leads in Solar Heat," *Washington Post*, April 9, 1974, A8.
42. *Behrman*, 56.
43. Limited information is available in: J. D. Walton, Jr., "Space Heating with Solar Energy at the C.N.R.S. Laboratory, Odeillo, France," in *Allen 1973*, 127–39; and *Anderson 1976*, 31, 129.
44. Michel, "Introduction of Solar Energy in Architecture and Urbanism," in *2nd Passive Proceedings*, 20–22.
45. *Behrman*, 58.
46. *Shurcliff survey*, 13th ed., 1977, 279.
47. Trombe, et al., "Some Performance Characteristics of the CNRS Solar House Collectors," in *Albuquerque 1976*, 201–8. Reprinted as "Concrete Walls to Collect and Hold Heat," *Solar Age* 2, no. 8 (August 1977): 13–19, 35.
48. Trombe, et al., "Some Performance Characteristics of the CNRS Solar House Collectors."
49. Michel, "Introduction of Solar Energy in Architecture and Urbanism." See also Trombe and Michel, "Naturally Air-Conditioned Dwellings," U.S. Patent 3,832,992, filed June 26, 1972, and issued September 3, 1974.
50. Bruno Peuportier and Michel, "Comparative Analysis of Active and Passive Solar Heating Systems with Transparent Insulation," *Solar Energy* 54, no. 1 (January 1995): 13–18.
51. "The Trombe-Michel Solar Wall," *Architectural Design* 42 (October 1973): 652–53; Kelbaugh, "Kelbaugh House," in *Albuquerque 1976*, 119–28; Ania Savage, "The Passive Way," *NYT*, April 17, 1977, R6.
52. According to Douglas Balcomb (conversation with the author, May 20, 2010), Trombe said this in a 1978 lecture. I have not been able to locate the source.
53. Louis Gropp, *Solar Houses: 48 Designs* (New York: Pantheon, 1978), 24.
54. Kelbaugh, "Kelbaugh House."
55. Kelbaugh, correspondence with author, December 9, 2011.

Chapter 10
1. "The Plowboy Interview: Harold R. Hay," *Mother Earth News* 41 (September 1976): 16–17.
2. *Halacy*, 72.
3. *Behrman*, 13.
4. Hottel to Löf, July 27, 1964; Löf to Hottel, August 4, 1964, *Hottel Papers*, Box 19.
5. Van Dresser, "Energy-Conserving Folk Architecture in Rural New Mexico," in *Franta 1975*, 12.1–12.42.
6. "The Plowboy Interview: Peter Van Dresser," *Mother Earth News* 35 (September 1975): 13.

7. Van Dresser, "Solar Construction in a Biotechnic Economy," in Costis Stambolis, ed., *Solar Technology for Building: Proceedings of the First International Conference on Solar Building Technology* (London: RIBA Publications, 1978), 109.
8. *Halacy*, 72.
9. Van Dresser, "Sundwellings Presentation," in *Albuquerque 1976*, 272.
10. Van Dresser, *Homegrown Sundwellings* (Santa Fe: Lightning Tree, 1977), 128. See also Arthur Fisher, "Passive Solar—A Controlled Experiment in Home Heating," *PopSci* 212, no. 4 (April 1978): 76–79.
11. Van Dresser, "Solar Construction in a Biotechnic Economy," in Costis Stambolis, ed., *Solar Technology for Building: Proceedings of the First International Conference on Solar Building Technology* (London: RIBA Publications, 1978), 109.
12. Cook, "Foreword," in van Dresser, *Homegrown Sundwellings*, 10–11.
13. Norma Skurka and Jon Naar, *Design for a Limited Planet: Living with Natural Energy* (New York: Ballantine Books, 1976), 39.
14. "The Plowboy Interview: David Wright and His Passive Solar Homes," *Mother Earth News* 47 (September/October 1977), 20.
15. Yellott, ed., *Solar-Oriented Architecture* (Tempe: Arizona State University College of Architecture, 1975), 99.
16. "The Plowboy Interview: David Wright and His Passive Solar Homes," 18.
17. *Anderson 1976*, 108–9.
18. It was originally called "Unit One," the initial house in a planned environmental community called "First Village." Balcomb did not participate in its design. Wayne D. Nichols, "Unit 1, First Village," in *Albuquerque 1976*, 138.
19. Balcomb, "Passive Solar Space Heating," in *Franta 1980*, 699. See also Travis Price, "Low-Technology Solar Homes that Work with Nature," *PopSci* 209, no. 6 (December 1976): 95–98.
20. Balcomb, "State of the Art in Passive Solar Heating and Cooling," in *2nd Passive Proceedings*, 5–12. "Unit One: Solar Living in America's Southwest," *Mother Earth News* 59 (September/October 1979): 112–14. See also Sara Balcomb, "Living in a Passive Solar Home," *Energy and Buildings* 7 (1984): 309–14.
21. Balcomb, "Passive Solar Space Heating," 696.
22. "The Plowboy Interview: Steve and Holly Baer," *Mother Earth News* 22 (July 1973): 8.
23. *Shurcliff survey*, 8th ed., 1975, 67. See also Paul Davis, "To Air is Human: Some Humanistic Principles in the Design of Thermosiphon Air Heaters," in *Albuquerque 1976*, 40–45.
24. Baer, *Sunspots* (Albuquerque: Zomeworks Corporation, 1975), 66.
25. Baer, "Zome," in Lloyd Kahn, *Shelter* (New York : Random House, 1973), 135. See also "Structural System," U.S. Patent 3,722,153, filed May 4, 1970, and issued March 27, 1973.
26. Cook, "Introduction to Solar Architecture," in *Franta 1975*, 2.1–2.17.
27. *Kidder 1977*, 75.
28. *Anderson 1976*, 131; David A. Bainbridge, *A Water Wall Solar Design Manual* (self-published, 1981, rev. 2005), 7.
29. Baer, "Corrales Residence," in *Albuquerque 1976*, 200; "Zome," in *Shelter*, 135; Shurcliff, *Solar Heated Buildings*, 66.
30. Banham, "The Sage of Corrales," *New Society* 63 (1983): 431.
31. Richard Register, "Open up Your House and Let the Sun Shine in," *Los Angeles Times*, September 17, 1972, M10.
32. Thomason, "Economic Feasibility Reached in Solar Home," *Sun at Work* 5, no. 1 (First Quarter, 1960): 6–7.
33. *Kidder 1977*, 79.
34. Thomason, "Solar Space Heating and Air Conditioning in the Thomason Home," *Solar Energy* 4, no. 4 (October 1960): 13.
35. Yellott, "Solar Heating and Cooling of Homes," 378.
36. *Gilmore 1974*, 80. *Kidder 1977*, 80.
37. Thomason, "Experience with Solar Houses, *Solar Energy* 10, no. 1 (January–March 1966): 17–22.
38. Omer Henry, "The House that Has its Furnace in the Sky," *Popular Mechanics* 139, no. 6 (June 1973): 150–54.
39. Frederic Kelly, "Harry Thomason's Solar-Heated House," *Baltimore Sun* (June 3, 1973), SM36.
40. Thomason, "Economic Feasibility Reached in Solar Home."
41. Omer Henry, "Solar Homes," *Washington Post*, September 26, 1971, p. 332.
42. Thomason, "Solar Space Heating, Water Heating, Cooling in the Thomason Home" (paper S/3), *UN 1961*, vol. 5, 224–31. See also "No Chimney Used in 2nd Solar House," *Sun at Work* 6, no. 1 (First Quarter, 1961): 16.
43. Thomason and Harry Jack Lee Thomason, Jr., "Solar Houses/Heating and Cooling Progress Report," *Solar Energy* 15no. 1 (May 1973): 27–39. See also "Thomason Solar Homes," in *Allen 1973*, 180–84.
44. Shurcliff, *New Inventions in Low-Cost Solar Heating* (Andover, Mass.: Brick House Publishing Company, 1979), 104–5.
45. *Kidder 1977*, 80.
46. Thomason and Thomason, *Solar House Heating and Air-Coniditioning Systems: Comparisons and Limitations* (Barrington, N.J.: Edmund Scientific, 1974), 13.
47. *Behrman*, 113–14. See also Sandra Oddo, "The Flamboyant Success of Harry Thomason," *Solar Age* 4, no. 1 (January 1979): 7–10; and "The Plowboy Interview: Dr. Harry Thomason," *Mother Earth News* 60 (November/December 1979): 16–22.
48. "Solar Energy for Heating and Cooling," H.R. Rep. No. 93-13 (1973), 11.
49. Thomason and Thomason, *Solar House Heating and Air-Coniditioning Systems*, 42.
50. "Solar Energy for Heating and Cooling," 275.
51. Ibid., 170.
52. Kenneth Haggard, quoted in Elizabeth Douglass, "A Pioneer Refuses to Fade Away," *Los Angeles Times*, November 10, 2007, A1.
53. Hay, "Roof Mass and Comfort," in *2nd Passive Proceedings*, 23–27.
54. *Gilmore 1974*, 81.
55. Baer, *Sunspots*, 24.
56. John A. Jones, "Solar Power: More Than a Ray of Hope," *Los Angeles Times*, June 29, 1975, I1.
57. Hay, "John Yellott and Roofpond Development," *Passive Solar Journal* 4, no. 3 (1987): 244–45.
58. Skurka and Naar, *Design for a Limited Planet*, 39.
59. Baer, *Sunspots*, 24.
60. Hay and Yellott, "A Naturally Air-Conditioned Building," *Mechanical Engineering* 92, no. 1 (January 1970): 19–25.
61. Ibid.
62. Yellott, "Early Tests of the 'Skytherm' System," in *Albuquerque 1976*, 59.
63. John A. Duffie and William A. Beckman, "Solar Heating and Cooling," *Science* 191, no. 4223 (January 16, 1976): 143–49.
64. *Shurcliff 1986*, 1.
65. *Behrman*, 6.

66. Kenneth Haggard, "First Cost Economic Evaluation of the Atascadero Skytherm House," *Passive Solar Heating and Cooling Conference and Workshop Proceedings*, 250–51. See also Kenneth Haggard, "Prototype Evaluation and Roofpond Heating and Cooling," *Passive Solar Journal* 4, no. 3 (1987): 255–64.

67. Philip W. B. Niles, "Thermal Evaluation of a House Using a Movable-Insulation Heating and Cooling System," *Solar Energy* 18, no. 5 (1976): 413–19; Hay, "How to Stop Cooling Loads before they Start," in Francis de Winter, ed., *Solar Cooling for Buildings Workshop Proceedings* (Washington, D.C.: Government Printing Office, n.d.), 165.

68. Jones, "Solar Power: More Than a Ray of Hope."

69. "Harold Hay on Solar Energy" in Kahn, *Shelter*, 165. See also Hay, "Atascadero Residence," in *Albuquerque 1976*, 101–7.

70. A. Lincoln Pittinger, William R. White, and Yellott, "The Energy Roof: A New Approach to Solar Heating and Cooling," in *2nd Passive Proceedings*, 218–19.

71. Hay, "Thermopond Applicability to Climate and Structure," in *Böer 1979*, vol. 2, 1535–39; B. D Howard and H. Fraker, "Thermal Energy Storage in Building Interiors," in Bruce Anderson, ed., *Solar Building Architecture* (Cambridge, Mass.: MIT Press, 1990), 237.

72. Gene Clark, Fred Loxsom, and Philip Haves, "Performance of Roofpond Cooled Residences in U.S Climates," *Passive Solar Journal* 4, no. 3 (1987): 265–92.

73. Shurcliff, *Saunders Shrewsbury House* (Cambridge: W. A. Shurcliff, 1982), 1.03.

74. Saunders, "Weston Residence," in *Albuquerque 1976*, 94.

75. Ibid., 91.

76. Ibid., 97.

77. *Carriere 1980*, 187.

78. Saunders, "Weston Residence," 98.

79. Ibid., 100.

80. Jonathan Mandell, "What It's Like Living in a Solar Heated Home," *BG*, September 11, 1977, p. 61.

81. Saunders, "Weston Residence," 100.

82. *Carriere 1980*, 189.

83. Norah Deakin Davis and Linda Lindsey, *At Home in the Sun* (Charlotte, Vt.: Garden Way Publishing, 1979), 58.

84. Saunders, *Solar Heating Basics*, 45.

85. Saunders, "Weston Residence," 92.

86. Shurcliff, *Solar Heated Buildings of North America: 120 Outstanding Examples* (Harrisville, N.H.: Brick House Publishing, 1978), 129–30.

87. Robert Cooke and Jean Dietz, "Solar Pioneers Still Working out the Bugs," *BG*, April 24, 1978, p. 10; Saunders, "The Overall Solution to Solar Heating," *Proceedings of the Conference on Energy-Conserving, Solar-Heated Greenhouses* (Marlboro, Vt.: Marlboro College, 1977), 39–43.

88. Saunders, "Thermal Results of Certain Innovative Integrated Solar Heating Systems," in *2nd Passive Proceedings*, 66; "Heating, Lighting and Ventilation Systems," U.S. Patent 4,296,733, filed August 5, 1976, and issued October 27, 1981.

89. Saunders, *Solar Heating Basics*, 41.

90. Shurcliff, *Super-Solar Houses—Saunders's Low-Cost, 100% Solar Designs* (Andover, Mass.: Brick House Publishing, 1983), 23–87.

91. Shurcliff, *Saunders Shrewsbury House*, 1.06, 1.03.

92. Tybout and George Löf, "Solar House Heating," *Natural Resource Journal* 10, no. 2 (1970): 268–326; Löf and Tybout, "Cost of House Heating with Solar Energy," *Solar Energy* 14, no. 3 (February 1973): 253–78.

93. Shurcliff, *Saunders Shrewsbury House*, 1.04. Also Shurcliff, *Super-Solar Houses*, 3–4.

94. Hay, "John Yellott and Roofpond Development," 250. Douglass, "A Pioneer Refuses to Fade Away."

95. Daniels, "Utilization of Solar Energy—Progress Report," *Proceedings of the American Philosophical Society* 115, no. 6 (December 30, 1971): 493.

Chapter 11

1. "Solar Energy Remarks Announcing Administration Proposals," June 20, 1979, *The American Presidency Project*, http://www.presidency.ucsb.edu/ws/?pid=32500.

2. The 1970s oil crisis is chronicled thoroughly in Daniel Yergin, *The Prize: The Epic Quest for Oil, Money, and Power* (New York: Simon & Schuster, 1991), 606ff.

3. "Special Message to the Congress on Energy Resources," June 4, 1971, *The American Presidency Project*, http://www.presidency.ucsb.edu/ws/?pid=3038.

4. Rybczynski, "Sorry, Out of Gas," *Journal of the Society of Architectural Historians* 67, no. 3 (September 2008): 441–42.

5. *Shurcliff survey*, 13th ed., 1977, 6.

6. Thomas Hine, *The Great Funk: Styles of the Shaggy, Sexy, Shameless 1970s* (New York: Farrar, Straus, and Giroux, 2009), 56.

7. Cook, "Introduction to Solar Architecture," in *Franta 1975*, 2.1-2.17.

8. Shurcliff, "Active-type Solar Heating Systems for Houses: A Technology in Ferment," *Bulletin of the Atomic Scientists* 32, no. 2 (February 1976): 40.

9. See discussion in "Solar Soapbox," *Solar Age* 3, no. 9 (September 1978): 38.

10. See, for example, Vivian Loftness and Belinda Reeder, "Recent Work in Passive Solar Design," *AIA Journal* 67, no. 4 (April 1978): 52ff.

11. Yellott, "Passive Solar Heating and Cooling Systems," *ASHRAE Journal* 20, no. 1 (January 1978): 60.

12. "Steve and Holly Baer: Dome Home Enthusiasts," *Mother Earth News* 22 (July/August 1973): 9.

13. David A. Bainbridge, *The First Passive Solar Catalog* (Davis, Calif.: Passive Solar Institute, 1978), 2.

14. Balcomb, "Passive Solar Research and Practice," *Energy and Buildings* 7 (1984): 291.

15. *Shurcliff 1986*, 4.

16. Joel Swisher, "Passive Solar Performance: Summary of 1982–1983 Class B Results," SERI/SP-271-2362 (1984).

17. Löf, "A Problem with Passive," *Solar Age* 3, no. 9 (September 1978): 17–19. See also "Passive Solar Energy Programs and Plans," H.R. Rep. No. 95-111 (1978), 142–50.

18. Shurcliff, *New Inventions in Low-Cost Solar Heating* (Andover, Mass.: Brick House Publishing, 1979), 75.

19. Löf, et al., "Design, Construction, and Testing of a Residential Solar Heating and Cooling System," NSF/RANN/SE/GI-40457/PR/75/1 (June 1975).

20. Dan S. Ward and Löf, "Design and Construction of a Residential Solar Heating and Cooling System," *Solar Energy* 17, no. 1 (April 1975): 13.

21. Crowther, *Sun/Earth* (New York: Scribner, 1977), 182.

22. Ward, Thomas A. Weiss, and Löf, "Preliminary Performance of CSU Solar House I Heating and Cooling System," *Solar Energy* 18, no. 6 (1976): 541–48.

23. Ward, Löf, et al., "Design of a Solar Heating and Cooling System for CSU Solar House II," *Solar Energy* 19 (1977): 79–85.

24. Martin McPhillips, "An Interview with George O. G. Löf," *Solar Age* 1, no. 12 (December 1976): 29–30.

25. Löf, "Solar Space Heating with Air and Liquid Systems," *Philosophical Transactions of the Royal Society of London* 295, no. 1414 (February 7, 1980): 359.

26. Robert Hastings, "A Time Journey Through Solar Architecture: 1900 to the Future," *Proceedings of ISES World Congress 2007* (Berlin: Springer, 2009), 14.

27. Ward, W. S. Duff, J. C. Ward, and Löf, "Intergration of Evacuated Tubular Solar Collectors with Lithium Bromide Absorption Cooling Systems," *Solar Energy* 22, no. 4 (1979): 335–41.

28. Duff, T. M. Conway, Löf, D. S. Meredith, and R. B. Pratt, "Performance of Residential Solar Heating and Cooling System with Flat-Plate and Evacuated Tubular Collectors: CSU Solar House I," in Böer 1978, 390.

29. *Gilmore 1974*, 80.

30. *Behrman*, 94–95.

31. See "Oral History of Harry Weese," interviewed by Betty J. Blum, *Chicago Architects Oral History Project*, rev. ed. (1991; Chicago: Art Institute of Chicago, 2001).

32. Böer, "Solar Direct Energy Conversion System," in *1974 Annual Report: Conference of Electrical Insulation and Dielectric Phenomena* (Washington, D.C.: National Academy of Sciences, 1975), 188.

33. Richard Stepler, "Solar Salts—New Chemical Systems Store the Sun's Heat," *PopSci* 216, no. 3 (March 1980): 49–50.

34. M. A. S. Malik, "Solar One," in *Sayigh 1977*, 345–69.

35. Böer, "A Combined Solar Thermal and Electrical House System" (paper EH.108), *International Congress on the Sun in the Service of Mankind, Paris, 1973*; Telkes, "Storage of Solar Heating/Cooling," *ASHRAE Transactions* 80, no. 2 (1974): 382–87.

36. "Solar Energy for Heating and Cooling," 145. See also Böer, "The Solar House and its Portent," *Chemtech* (July 1973): 394–400.

37. Böer, "Payback of Solar Systems," *Solar Energy* 20, no. 3 (1978): 232.

38. Sean Wellesley-Miller, "Weather Responsive Building Skins: Concepts and Configurations," in *2nd Passive Proceedings*, 499.

39. Douglas Mahone, "Three Solutions for Persistent Passive Problems," *Solar Age* 3, no. 9 (September 1978): 20–23.

40. "M.I.T. Unveils 'Passive' Solar-Heated Building," news release, February 15, 1978, MIT Museum archives. See also Jean Dietz, "Solar Heat without Moving Parts," *BG*, February 23, 1978, p. 1.

41. *Hottel 1989*, 126.

42. Allan Frank, "Government Funding: Critical Choices," in Martin McPhillips, ed., *The Solar Age Resource Book* (New York: Everest House, 1979), 43.

43. Harvey Strum and Fred Strum, "American Solar Energy Policy, 1952–1982," *Environmental Review* 7, no. 2 (Summer 1983): 139-44.

44. Balcomb, "Passive Solar Research and Practice," 281.

45. Shurcliff, "Active-type Solar Heating Systems," 39.

46. Norah Deakin Davis and Linda Lindsey, *At Home in the Sun* (Charlotte, Vt.: Garden Way Publishing, 1979), 166. See also Richard Stepler, "Now You Can Buy Solar Heating Equipment for Your Home," *PopSci* 206, no. 3 (March 1975): 76; and Grace Lichtenstein, "Solar Heat's Future Now Here for Some," *NYT*, March 12, 1976, p. 46.

47. Shurcliff, "Active-type Solar Heating Systems," 40.

48. Martin Holladay, "Solar Versus Superinsulation: A 30-Year-Old Debate," *GBA*, October 8, 2010, http://www.greenbuildingadvisor.com/blogs/dept/musings/solar-versus-superinsulation-30-year-old-debate.

49. Daniel Richa and J. David Roessner, "Tax Credits and US Solar Commercialization Policy," *Energy Policy* 18, no. 2 (March 1990): 186–98.

50. "Golden, Colorado Remarks at the Solar Energy Research Institute on South Table Mountain," May 3, 1978, *The American Presidency Project*, http://www.presidency.ucsb.edu/ws/?pid=30746.

51. Fredrick H. Morse, "The Growth Years: 1977–1980," in Donald A. Beattie, ed., *History and Overview of Solar Heat Technologies* (Cambridge, Mass.: MIT Press, 1997), 136–37.

52. "Solar Energy Remarks Announcing Administration Proposals."

53. Richard Halloran, "Solar Lobby—Striking While the Iron Is Still Hot," *NYT*, April 29, 1979, E20.

54. Moore, "Educators Roundtable," *Journal of Architectural Education* 30, no. 3 (February 1977): 2.

55. Forrest Coile and Associates and Charles W. Moore Associates, "NASA Project Tech Technology Utilization House Study Report," NASA CR-144896 (December 1975), 2.

56. "The House that NASA Built" (unknown, 1977), http://crgis.ndc.nasa.gov/crgis/images/c/c0/1977-01_The_House_that_NASA_Built.pdf.

57. Irvin L. Hamlet, "Summary Results from The NASA Tech House One Year Live-in," *AIAA Conference on Terrestrial Energy Systems* (June 1979): 8; http://crgis.ndc.nasa.gov/crgis/images/7/7e/AIAA-TP-79-0987.pdf.

58. Richard S. Levine, "Integrative Design: The Raven Run Solar House," *2nd Passive Proceedings*, 142.

59. Paul Goldberger, "Assessing Solar House Architecture," *NYT*, October 15, 1981, C1.

60. Löf, interview with author, Denver, Colorado, July 15, 2009.

61. Thomas L. Friedman, *Hot, Flat, and Crowded* (New York: Farrar, Straus, and Giroux, 2008), 13.

62. *Shurcliff 1986*, 5.

63. Holladay, "Solar Versus Superinsulation: A 30-Year-Old Debate."

64. Robert S. Dumont, "Experiences from Low Energy Houses in Canada," *Proceedings from the Symposium on Energy-efficient Building* (Copenhagen: Technical University of Denmark, 2005), 24.

65. Wayne L. Schick, Richard A. Jones, and Michael T. McCulley, "Illinois Lo-Cal House," *University of Illinois SHC-BRC Council Notes* 5, no. 2 (Fall 1981, originally 1976). See also John Lawrence Nicol, "Evaluation of Energy Conservation Components in a Lo-Cal House," master's thesis, University of Illinois at Urbana-Champaign, 1985.

66. "Solar Orientation," *University of Illinois SHC-BRC Council Notes* 2, no. 2 (Fall 1977).

67. Michele Gaspar, "'Lo-Cal' House?," *CT*, February 13, 1977, W-B2A. See also "'Lo-Cal House' Puts Energy on Diet," *CT*, July 24, 1982, N-A4.

68. Joseph W. Lstiburek, "Building America," *ASHRAE Journal* 50, no. 12 (December 2008): 60–61.

69. R. W. Besant, R. S. Dumont, and G. J. Schoenau, "The Passive Performance of the Saskatchewan Conservation House," in *3rd Passive Proceedings*, 713–19; "The Saskatchewan Conservation House: Some Preliminary Performance Results," *Energy and Buildings* 2, no. 2 (April 1979): 163–74; "The Saskatchewan Conservation House: A Year of Performance Data," in *Böer 1979*, 907–11; "Saskatchewan House: 100 Percent Solar in a Severe Climate," *Solar Age* 4, no. 5 (May 1979): 18–23.

70. "The No-Frills, No-Furnace House that Gene Built," in *Approaching Free Energy* (Emmaus, Pa.: Rodale Press, 1982), 90. See also Leger, "Superinsulated Homes," *Environmental Science & Technology* 22, no. 12 (1988): 1399–1400.

71. Holladay, "Forgotten Pioneers of Energy Efficiency," *GBA*, April 17, 2009, http://www.greenbuildingadvisor.com/blogs/dept/musings/forgotten-pioneers-energy-efficiency.

72. Shurcliff, "Arrival of a Fifth Kind of Solar Heating System for a House" (press release, June 29, 1979), reprinted in J. D. Ned Nisson and Gautam Dutt, *The Superinsulated Home Book* (New York : Wiley, 1985), 9. See also Shurcliff, *Superinsulated Houses and Double-Envelope Houses: A Preliminary Survey of Principles and Practice* (Cambridge: W. A. Shurcliff, 1980).

73. Ibid.

74. Paul Ingrassia, "Lo-Cal House Design Slashes Energy Bills Without Costly Gear," *Wall Street Journal*, February 7, 1980, pp. 8–9.

75. "The No-Frills, No-Furnace House that Gene Built," 89.

76. Lstiburek, "Building America," 61.

77. Holladay, "Forgotten Pioneers of Energy Efficiency"; Lstiburek, "Building America."

78. Ibid.

79. Feist, et al., "Re-Inventing Air Heating: Convenient and Comfortable within the Frame of the Passive House Concept," *Energy and Buildings* 37, no. 11 (November 2005): 1187. See also "An Interview with Wolfgang Feist," *Energy Design Update* 28, no. 1 (January 2008): 1–6; and Hattie Hartman, "Lessons from Abroad," *The Architects' Journal* 227, no. 8 (February 2008): 58–59.

80. Holladay, "Are Passivhaus Requirements Logical or Arbitrary?," *GBA*, April 1, 2011, http://www.greenbuildingadvisor.com/blogs/dept/musings/are-passivhaus-requirements-logical-or-arbitrary.

81. Feist, "Re-Inventing Air Heating."

82. See "Passive House Database," http://www.passivhausprojekte.de.

83. W. Stahl, K. Voss, and A. Goetzberger, "The Self-Sufficient Solar House in Freiburg," *Solar Energy* 52, no. 1 (January 1994): 111–25; Voss, et al., "The Self-Sufficient Solar House in Freiburg—Results of 3 Years of Operation," *Solar Energy* 58, nos. 1–3 (July–September 1996): 17–23.

84. "Rolf Disch SolarArchitektur," http://www.rolfdisch.de.

85. Andy Walker, et al., "Advances in Solar Buildings," *ASME Journal of Solar Energy Engineering* 125 (August 2003): 243.

86. Mark Eastment, et al., "Solar Decathlon 2002: The Event In Review," DOE/GO-102004-1845 (2003), 45.

87. See, for example, W. Eric Showalter, "Lessons Learned From the Solar Decathlon," *Proceedings of the 2003 ASEE Midwest Section Meeting.*

88. Amanda Griscom, "Collegians Compete to Let the Sun Shine In," *NYT*, October 3, 2002, F7.

89. "Winning Teams and Innovative Technologies from the 2005 Solar Decathlon," H. R. Rep. No. 109-30 (2005), 23.

90. John Reynolds, "Revisiting the Solar Decathlon," *Solar Today* 23, no. 7 (September/October 2009): 74–76.

91. "Winning Teams and Innovative Technologies from the 2005 Solar Decathlon," 32.

92. Susan Moon, et al., "Solar Decathlon 2005: The Event In Review," DOE/GO-102006-2328 (2006), 6.

93. Cecile Warner, et al., "Solar Decathlon: Collegiate Challenge to Build the Future," NREL/CP-520-32215 (May 2002), 1.

94. See, for example, Donald D. Liou, "Engineering a Sustainable House for Solar Decathlon 2002," *International Conference on Sustainable Engineering and Science*, 2004, http://www.thesustainabilitysociety.org.nz/conference/2004/Session5/25%20Loiu.pdf.

95. Eastment, "Solar Decathlon 2002," 44.

96. Timothy L. Hemsath, et al., "Zero Net Energy Test House," *Journal of Green Building* 6, no. 2 (Spring 2011): 38.

97. Warner, et al., "Solar Decathlon."

98. Quale, "Foreword," in Michael Zaretsky, *Precedents in Zero-Energy Design* (New York: Routledge, 2010), ix–x. See also Quale, *Trojan Goat: A Self-Sufficient House* (Charlottesville: University of Virginia School of Architecture, 2005).

99. Robert Dunay, Joseph Wheeler, and Robert Schubert, "No Compromise: The Integration of Technology and Aesthetics," *Journal of Architectural Education* 60, no. 2 (2006): 8–17.

100. "History," http://web.mit.edu/solardecathlon/history.html.

101. Ted Shelton, "Frugality and Robustness: Negotiating Economy and Ecology in Architecture," *Journal of Green Building* 2, no. 1 (Winter 2007): 109.

102. Griscom, "Collegians Compete to Let the Sun Shine In."

103. Quale, "Foreword."

104. "Solar Decathlon 2005," DOE/GO-102005-2184 (October 2005), 18.

105. "CHIP 2011," http://www.chip2011.com.; "Team Purdue INhome," http://www.purdue.edu/inhome.

Acknowledgments

This book is the result of five years of scholarly research, and I was helped by librarians and archivists too numerous to mention. Also, a number of students helped me in various ways: Alex Jording, Bailey Brown, Polina Novikova-Kinney, Gretchen Heberling, and Richard Cisneros. And my friend Jim Laukes, formerly of the National Center for Appropriate Technology, offered some excellent research assistance, discussion, and feedback on the manuscript.

About the Author

Anthony Denzer is Associate Professor of Architectural Engineering at the University of Wyoming, and a founding board member of the U.S. Green Building Council, Wyoming Chapter. He earned a Ph.D. in Architecture (history/theory) from UCLA, an M.Arch. from the University of Kansas, and a B.A. in journalism from the University of California, Berkeley. He is the author of *Gregory Ain: The Modern Home as Social Commentary*, published by Rizzoli in 2008.

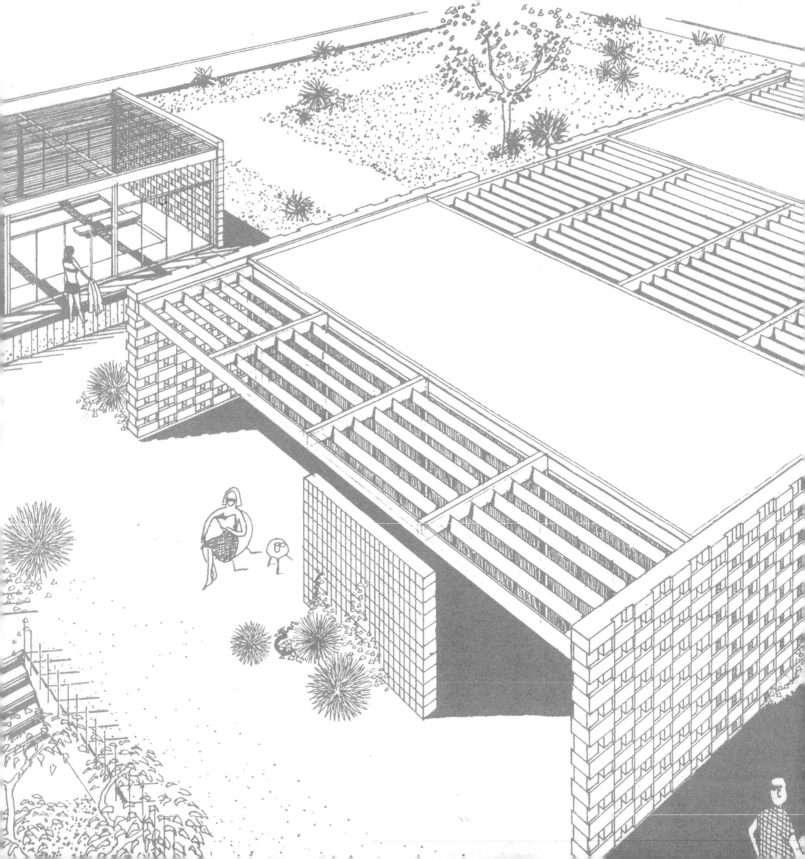